Confessions of an Original Sinner

JOHN LUKACS

Confessions of an Original Sinner

Ticknor & Fields

New York · 1990

CIP data is available.

ISBN: 0-89919-956-9

Printed in the United States of America

DOH 10 9 8 7 6 5 4 3 2 1

Book design by Ronnie Ann Herman

DILECTISSIMÆ STEPHANIÆ

This book, published in 1990, was written between 1983 and 1988, interrupted by other work, including the writing of *Budapest 1900*, for about three years. A portion of chapter 2 was published in *Harper's* (November 1988). A version of chapter 3 was part of my *1945: Year Zero* (1978).

Contents

An Introduction

THIS BOOK IS NOT a history of my life. It is a history of some of my thoughts and beliefs. To some of these, American readers may be unaccustomed. Yet they are neither original nor individual. There is no such thing as an original idea, or even a wholly original thought. Neither is there such a thing as an individual wholly separate from the rest of the world. In any event, this is not a history of "myself" but of a participant: a personal participant in this world, in some of its places and at a certain historical time. The Hungarian poet János Pilinszky wrote: "There are the personal and the nonpersonal and the collective areas of life. One cannot reach the nonpersonal except from what is personal; the collective never. Something must become personal first; after that one may go forward to what is no longer personal." He also wrote that he might one day attempt an autobiography. (He died too early for that, alas.) "It would not be my autobiography but the autobiography of my attention. I cannot draw a line where I end and where my attention begins, that attention of which I am subject and object at the same time. If I were to write a regular autobiography, the most important matters might be left out. It is not merely events that have made me but what I have noticed, what I have recognized during my life."

It is an interesting fact that autobiography hardly existed before the Modern Age. Its appearance was inseparable from the cult of self, beginning with the Renaissance, and eventually with the development of historical consciousness. During the last four hundred years the variations of autobiography defy categorization of course. I know that I am very far away from Benvenuto Cellini, that first modern autobiographer, who took what at that time was a new kind of pleasure in writing about his own material experiences. I am convinced that the most important matter in this world, and perhaps especially in our times, is what people think and believe; and that the material conditions of their lives (and the very material structure of their world) are but consequences of that. Thus this book is in accord with the practice I followed in my other, very different books, its principal content being the history of my thoughts and beliefs.

This is easier said than done, whence the difficulties in writing it. Before this book I thought that this kind of writing would be much easier than that of my other books. There would be none of the burdensome duties of research. None of the endlessly growing lists of books and articles and documents to hunt up, no nervous flipping through hundreds of yellowing cards in the library catalogues, no dilemma whether to run off for two or three days to a special library where I might or might not find something valuable, no sinking feeling in my stomach before the cascading march of green letters and numbers on a computer screen, no boxes of cards, no disorderly heap of disordered notes of all kinds, no hesitation to hound the librarian for yet another arcane request of an Interlibrary Loan, no alarmingly bulging folder of xeroxed pages, etc., etc. Still the most important problem remains the same: what to include? what to exclude? In one important way research *is* easier. It has limitations that autobiographical writing has not. There is no limit to what one might tell. Of course one leaves out many things, but not only because of the wish to leave certain matters untold (or unremembered). I have now learned that it is not easy or even pleasant to write about myself. There is, too, the not uncomfortable recognition with the coming of age, the knowledge that one is not really very interesting. "If you want to bore the reader," Voltaire once wrote, "tell him everything." Voltaire was wrong about many things, but not about that. So often during this writing I have been thinking of how different this book could have been. How many things I should have been able to tell! Pleasant things; funny things. Landscapes; cityscapes. Great contemporaries; small contemporaries. Remarkable men; attractive women. Friendships. Travels. And with plenty of color, for I am a writer of sorts. And without boring the reader with "everything."

Instead I have kept to my last: I am cobbling together words about thoughts and beliefs. Do thoughts exist apart from the words with which we can associate them? That is a difficult question. I am inclined to think that they do not: but this introduction is not the place for an exposition of an epistemological philosophy. It is, however, the place for a brief explanation of something that I owe to my American readers. They are the titles of the first and of the last chapters of this book (and also of its title): "Confessions of a reactionary," and "of an original sinner." Believe me that these are not words I have chosen to shock people, *pour épater les bourgeois.* To the contrary: what I want to do is to remind people, *rappeler les bourgeois;* and also to explain, no matter how briefly, how these two words of *sinner* and *reactionary* connect in my mind.

I think that the belief in the existence of sin, and in the sinful nature of humankind, is not a dark and muddy and fear-ridden article but a healthy and realistic and enlightening perception, available to us not only through religious revelation but through the evidences of historical experience—that is, of our self-knowledge. We are born with the proclivity to sin. That very word, *sin,* is truly not cruel. Its very existence suggests the moral range of human nature. That range is what makes us unique. Other living beings do not sin, because they cannot. Human beings sin, because of the existence of their spirit. There is no such thing as a sin of the flesh alone. Every kind of sin involves the spirit to some extent, and when the sins of the spirit predominate they are worse than those of the flesh. This has been so from the beginning of mankind. Sin is something else than a taboo; and it is not an idea or a category dependent on changing social conditions. It was not invented by Abraham or Moses or Calvin; and its existence, from within our very consciousness, will not be expunged by Darwin or Marx or Freud. We know that we sin when we sin. (One may actually enjoy sinning.) This does not necessarily involve a sense of guilt. What it involves, sooner or later, is remorse and repentance and a sense of responsibility—and responsibility is something quite different from the, often self-indulgent, feeling of guilt.

I ask my readers to consider that in this paragraph I said nothing about the traditional Catholic teaching about sin, in which I happen to believe. This is a book by a historian, not a theologian. It is also because I am a historian that I know how, while all human conditions change, human nature does not really change. This may be called a reactionary view. It is at this point that I must defend the word *reactionary*. Much more than a *conservative*—which is a very malleable word—a reactionary knows, and believes, in the existence of sin and in the immutable essence of human nature. He does not always oppose change, and he does not altogether deny progress. What he denies is the immutable idea of immutable progress: the idea that we are capable not only of improving our material conditions but our very nature, including our mental and spiritual nature. We must never deny the potentiality of possible improvements of the human condition. But we must be aware—especially at this time, near the end of the twentieth century—of the need to think about what progress means. We must rethink the meaning of progress, its still widely current meaning that has become corroded and useless. Near the end of an age there occurs a heavy accumulation of accepted ideas and of institutionalized ways of thinking, against which thinking men and women must *react*. In 1930 the Dean of the Divinity School of the University of Chicago said that "the doctrine of Original Sin was a theory of human behavior adequate to the scientific knowledge of Saint Augustine's time, but overthrown by more recent research." In 1989 every intelligent reader will recognize what is the laughable pomposity in this statement by a Progressive Churchman: not his reference to Original Sin but to "scientific knowledge," and his dogmatic assertion of the validity of "more recent research." It is high time to reassess the sense of certain words—that, for example, *progressive* is not necessarily good, and *reactionary* not necessarily bad.

I will begin this book with a more mundane attempt to distinguish *reactionary* from *conservative* by telling how, at an early age, the adjective *reactionary* first attracted my attention and soon thereafter my respect. This happened in a world that was very different, and at a time that is very remote, from today. I was born in Hungary in 1924 and grew up there for twenty-two or twenty-three years, which were my most impressionable years, including those of the Second World War. I have lived in the United States for nearly two-thirds of my entire life, a condition that is also reflected in the proportions of this book: of its nine chapters, three involve my youth in Hungary and six my life in America. But I hope that my readers' reactions to the first chapters will not merely reflect the condition that these pages deal with a faraway place and time, exotic enough to evoke the interest of American readers with the implicit understanding that my conclusions of those experiences are not really applicable to them. The very opposite is true. I am convinced that the reactionary ideas of this original sinner have become, at least potentially, as meaningful to Americans in 1989 as they were to a young man in Hungary forty-five years ago—perhaps even more so. The main purpose of this book is a reminder: not a reminiscence about myself but a reminder for my readers. I wish to remind them of certain things that they, too, know.

Confessions of an Original Sinner

CHAPTER 1

Confessions of a Reactionary

A REACTIONARY IS MADE, not born. It is wrong to believe that the progeny of royalty or of aristocracy, whether hereditary or financial, are natural reactionaries. There exist remnants of reactionary manners (kissing a Mother Superior's hand or telling a doctor's secretary that your name is not Joe but Mr. Brown), but reactionary types ceased to exist long ago. A reactionary, in the twentieth century, is the result of becoming, not being; like Stendhal's idea of love, the result is one of crystallization; unlike Stendhal's *amour*, the crystallization is not sudden and its results are not transitory. Men and women at the top of their societies have always tried their best (and sometimes their worst) to incarnate ideas that are current and respectable, often at the cost of their independence of mind. Thus two hundred years ago the Whig magnates in England distrusted Burke who, in Fox's words, was "too wise too soon"; thus during the 1930s some of their moneyed successors distrusted Churchill who, unlike Chamberlain, was "not steady." A conservative will profess a preference for and a trust in Ronald Reagan; a reactionary will not, and not because Reagan was a Hollywood actor but because he never stopped being one.

A reactionary considers character but distrusts publicity; he is a patriot but not a nationalist; he favors conservation rather than conservatism; he defends the ancient blessings of the land and is dubious about the results of technology; he believes in history, not in Evolution. To be a reactionary in the second half of the twentieth century has every possible professional and social disadvantage. Yet it has a few advantages that are divine gifts during this dreary decline of Western civilization. A reactionary will recognize how, contrary to Victor Hugo's hoary nineteenth-century cliché, An Idea Whose Time Has Come may not be any good. This kind of skepticism is, of course, a reaction to the largely mechanical propagation of ideas in the twentieth century, to their management and their marketing through the crude machinery of publicity.

There is more to this. Near the end of a great epoch many of its accepted ideas become senseless (as, too, many of its institutions become sclerotic). Their superficial reformulations (leading to the endless churning out of more and more answers to increasingly senseless questions) will not amount to anything that is inspiring or even useful. The main example of this is the still present idea of "Progress," the meaning and the odious applications of which we must begin to rethink. Such a rethinking necessarily begins with a conscious reaction: a reaction against such inanities as Human Rights Amendments and "Star Wars"; Sex Education and the Intelligence Community (whatever *that* is); World Government and Making the World Safe for Democracy; Abstract Art and the Gross National Product; Nuclear Power and Genetic Engineering; Quarks and Black Holes; Ecumenicism and The Science of Economics; Cybernetics and National Security; Computer Intelligence and Opinion Research; Psychohistory and Quantification, and so on, and so on. Note that the reactionary distrust of such things transcends the now increasingly outdated and even senseless categories of "conservative" and "liberal."

It marks, rather, a commonsense way of thinking against the abstract projections of progressive nonthinking. Another advantage, related to the above, is that a few expressions of common sense may nowadays give the impression that one is a profound thinker. In this we are about fifty years ahead of Ortega y Gasset. Ortega, circa 1941: "I have the disturbing conviction that, at least in our time, there are no intelligent men other than intellectuals. And since the majority of intellectuals are not intelligent either . . ." More than the majority, alas.

The third, and least important, advantage is that you can be a reactionary without being a snob, since the top layers of society have become so uninteresting that there remain few attractions, including practical and esthetic ones, for associating with them. The most lavish parties, restaurants, hotels, resorts and houses are not only full of people who are not very appealing, but unlike not so long ago (historian as I am, I estimate the change came around 1955) these are no longer the best parties and restaurants and hotels and resorts and houses with the best food, the best setting, the best decor, the best comfort, the best talk. Evidence, accumulating agreeably before the eyes of this fairly impecunious and unfairly aging scholar, suggests that this recognition has not the recognizable flavor of sour grapes. To the contrary, it has (at times) the winey taste of sweet grapes, advancing to their destiny, which, I hope, is not the age of raisin.

All my life I have been interested in how people think. This kind of interest may not be reactionary, but it is surely different from the psychoanalytic "why?"—the latter being but a premier version of the most pestilential intellectual habit of the twentieth century, which is the attribution of motives. I know something (not much) about my motives; about the motives of others I know much less. But purposes are a different story: not where a person's thoughts come from but where they are going. There were three top soccer clubs in my native Hungary: Ferencváros, Hungária, Ujpest; their respective colors green-and-white, blue-and-white, violet-and-white. When I was ten I met a boy who said that he was a fan of the blue-and-whites. There was nothing wrong in this, except for one thing: this boy was not interested in soccer. Yet he said that he was a blue-and-white partisan, which was obviously what he thought he ought to think. This kind of mental adjustment has put me in rages through a long and fairly wearisome life.

I think I know why I liked the green-and-whites. Still, this book is not an autobiography; it is not a memoir of my doings and sayings, but a conscious attempt at Confessionalism, eschewing many things material and immaterial, excluding everything relating to the subconscious, in whose existence I am strongly inclined to disbelieve.

"When writing of oneself, one should show no mercy," wrote Georges Bernanos. I was a disagreeable and unprepossessing adolescent, my only excuse for this being that my late childhood and adolescence were not happy. My parents were divorced when I was eight years old. Thereafter I lived with my mother and my stepfather, who was a good-natured man but who did not like me very much. My mother was very beautiful, intelligent, impulsive and chic. I think that I was the only child of divorced parents in a class of fifty or more students, many of whom were middle class to the core. This contributed to my relative loneliness among the other boys in my school. The conformism of their parents was repeated by their children. I allowed myself to be affected by the kind of split-mindedness that comes naturally to the young. On the one hand, I envied the respectability of some of my fellow students, including their school performance. On the other hand, I relished— or, perhaps, I took refuge in—the knowledge that my parents and I were more sophisticated than my fellow students and their parents were. I wanted to assert that I was different; at the same time I was desperately desirous of acceptance and recognition.

The official nationalism of that time in Hungary was extreme. In the first grade of elementary school we were taught that a Hungarian child must love his country even more than he must love his parents. Sometime later I heard that my father had objected to the principal about this. One day I overheard my stepfather saying something to the effect that my father was a radical. I admired (and feared) my father, whom I saw once each week. I did not say to my father (I doubt whether he would have appreciated it) that I was a "Socialist"; but I began to say it to others, especially to my classmates. This was the usual syndrome: the professing of a kind of radicalism as a form—an easy one—of rebellion, a rhetorical surrogate for a bruised soul and a wanting pride. I did not know this then;

I know it now. How many examples of this have I seen since that time of this kind of rebelliousness, of the avowal of radicalism serving as a refuge of weirdness, of a kind of selfishness that is but the festering result of self-hatred: the public display of a persona whose construction, in reality, rests on very shaky foundations; and the consequent wish to profit from the reforming of the world without a single thought of reforming oneself.

What your ideas are is less important than *how* you entertain them. My declarations of my "Socialism" had little to do with socialism. There was in them, I think, an element of empathy for poor people; there was in them an element of internationalism (my parents were cosmopolitan, and there was a world beyond Hungary, a world as beautiful as Hungary and about which I knew something). Yet these inclinations were inseparable from my desire to proclaim that I was different from the bourgeoisie. Again, how often since that time have I seen the same syndrome, when people would choose an idea or a party because these seemed to represent the opposite of what they disliked in the world around them (often including what they disliked in themselves).

I was not yet twelve when Mussolini invaded Abyssinia, and not yet thirteen when the Spanish civil war broke out. Most of Hungary was *bien-pensant:* in favor of Mussolini (who was the only European statesman sympathetic to Hungarian aspirations) and of Franco (because of Hungary's disastrous experience with a wretched Communist episode less than twenty years before). I said that I was rooting for the Abyssinians and for the Spanish Republicans. The inclinations for such opinions were perhaps not altogether shallow, but what I know, too, is that I voiced such opinions merely to demonstrate my individuality. These were but early examples of the condition that I have since then recognized so often: that we think what we choose to think, which may be excusable, but only as long as we ourselves know *why* we want to think this or that. But that "why" is not the psychoanalytic one. It is that other "why," referring not to categories of the "past" but to inclinations toward the future: to purposes, not to motives.

* * *

I was born and I grew up in interesting times, which is a dubious blessing. I was born on January 31, 1924, seven days after Lenin died and two days before Wilson died. I have a weakness for coincidences (Chesterton called them "spiritual puns"), especially for chronological ones, a weakness sometimes unworthy of a serious historian. That Mussolini was born in the year Marx died, that Hitler became Chancellor of Germany on Roosevelt's birthday are coincidences that occasionally I cannot let go without mentioning. When I read that Mussolini received Ezra Pound on January 30, 1933—the starriest of days in Pound's career, since he kept the invitation framed on his wall during the rest of his life, and also the day Hitler became Chancellor of Germany (Pound's biographers knew the first of these facts but not the second)—my mind responds with a little *frisson.* At times the reading of a date will charge my mind with such a pulsation, a weakness perhaps not unworthy of a historian. On my father's hundredth birthday I stood at his grave in Budapest. Engraved in the stone were his dates: 1883–1956. I gazed at these two numbers from which, more than from anything else at the moment, my deepest thoughts welled up. Their essence was a rich mixture—mixture, not merely compound—of history and emotion, a mixture that is sometimes the product of the mysterious alchemy of human memory. How much, how deeply, how completely my father belonged within that parenthesis of time, within those tragic seventy-two years of the history of his city and country. *1883. 1956.* He was born in the year Marx and Wagner died, and in the year Mussolini was born; he died a few months before the Hungarian Revolution. He survived Lenin and Wilson and Mussolini and Hitler and Stalin; but at what cost . . . His mind was formed during the end of the nineteenth century, mine during the second quarter of the twentieth. I grew up in the age of Mussolini and Hitler. By the 1930s Lenin and Wilson were mummified remnants.

I ceased to be a "Socialist" around the age of sixteen. My mother sent me to school in England in 1938 and 1939. One of the masters, a Mr. Harrington, was a Socialist. When I told him that I was one, he greeted this with an un-English exclamation of pleasure; obviously he was glad to see a young comrade from the Continent. But my talks with him, as well as my reading of some of the English Socialist literature, soon revealed that there was something wrong with the English Socialist view of the world. Mr. Harrington was a decent man, an English idealist, full of illusions that had but a frail relationship to reality. We both rooted for the Left (they were called Loyalists then) in the Spanish civil war; but this pragmatic Englishman kept telling me (and himself) that they were winning when they were evidently losing. He seemed much more interested in the Spanish civil war (which, in retrospect, was but a sideshow, only marginally related to the enormous development in the center of the Continent) than in Germany and Hitler. He thought that Hitler, like Mussolini or Franco, was a Fascist and therefore a reactionary, and the enemy of the German working class. Being an Englishman, he did not particularly like Germans, but being a Socialist, he also disbelieved (or at least professed to disbelieve) in the existence of national characteristics. Disarmament, Collective Security, National Self-Determination, the injustices of the Versailles Treaty—in 1938 he still professed to believe in them. He wouldn't believe that the German masses were solidly behind Hitler; nor did he realize that Hitler was the main beneficiary of Wilson's disastrous proposition of national self-determination, in virtue of which tens of thousands of Austrians and Sudeten Germans pelted him with flowers as he drove slowly through their streets.

But in Hungary, too, there was something antiquated—at best, so antiquated as to be positively decent—about the Social Democratic Party. Its newspaper breathed a musty smell of something that evoked a grayness—gray prose, gray images, gray paper—of decades before. And during the 1930s the Social Democratic Party was abandoned by tens of thousands of the very people whose cause it tried to espouse: by the proletariat, by the masses. The young and ambitious of the lower classes were moving in a different direction. That opposite direction was not capitalism. They were still socialists, but national and not international socialists. They also admired the new Germany that was modern, motorized, successful and powerful. Shortly before enrolling in the university, I spent a few months among the working class. My grandfather, moved by old-fashioned ideas of training the whole man, knowing my interest in books and printing, suggested that I have some experience with manual work; he had me engaged as a part-time apprentice in the printing shop of a large publishing concern. There I found that the Marxist ideas about the working class were illusions. There was hardly any difference between the aspirations of the workers and of the so-called bourgeoisie. Together with an endless preoccupation with the female body or, more precisely, with every potential variant of its sexual functioning, the aspirations of my fellow workers were not a whit different from those of other people: they were directed to position and property, to personal security and vanity, in sum, to the satisfactions of respectability. Except for a vague dislike of the rich (and, in some cases, of Jews), I found not a trace of proletarian pride among them. Their class consciousness was negative, not positive. This is not a criticism: on the whole, these forty or fifty workers in the printing shop were not a bit worse than my fifty classmates in the Gymnasium or any fifty people gathered from the streets of Budapest at random.

One of the two workers to whom I was closest during those months was the most decent man in the shop, an elderly printer, less profane than the others, infinitely patient, with a slightly bent back. In 1941 he expressed his dislike of the Germans: he was the only one who said that he was still a Socialist—there was something appealingly old-fashioned about him. The other was one of the youngest and surely the most dynamic of the men in the shop, a muscular short-legged athlete, a good sportsman, a tad better dressed than the rest, proud of his expensive camera, something that no other workman possessed. One day he admitted to me that he was a member of the local Nazi party, the Arrow Cross. We argued for a long time; he believed that England was finished, that Germany was bound to win the war. I have no bad memories of this man; he had none of the marks of the Nazi brutalitarians. He believed in the Germans because they were dynamic, powerful and *modern:* the wave of the future. I understood this then, but it was many years later that I read a sentence by Proudhon which illuminated the superior quality of Proudhon's understanding of human nature over that of Marx, Proudhon saying that people react not to ideas about social contracts but to realities of power.

But I am running ahead of time. From my early teens I was a voracious and precocious reader. At the age of sixteen, having claimed for four or more years that I was a Socialist, I thought that I ought to read Marx. I found Marx hopelessly dull and outdated. This is not a frivolous statement. Whatever he wrote had hardly any relationship to the realities of the twentieth century. For one thing, he paid no attention to nationality or to the nation, which he confused with the state. In the beginning I was impressed with the rich learnedness of his prose, but that learnedness was often heavy and less and less stimulating as I chewed forward; he was redolent (and the odor was not always pleasant) of many things in the nineteenth century. This, alas, was not true of Hitler. It was around that time that I read *Mein Kampf.* I was appalled by the brutal cruelty of it. But—and perhaps this will shock my readers—Hitler was cleverer than Marx: for a powerful mind that is moved by hate is bound to express itself more clearly than a theorist moved by resentments. Reading *Mein Kampf* I found that I was in the presence of a genius of evil; reading *Das Kapital* I was in the presence of a ponderous and sometimes powerful lecturer whose genius was constricted by his proclivity to theorize. The very structure of *Mein Kampf* made an impression on me. The first portion of it was an autobiography of sorts: Hitler's description (in which, as I suspected then and found out later, he had twisted some things about his personal past) of *how* his ideas had crystallized, this self-made history of his mind until 1918 when, near the age of thirty, "I decided to become a politician" (this last sentence ending the first part of *Mein Kampf*). Compared to this, Marx's "scientific objectivity" was, again, outdated and abstract. And here and there, in the midst of that diabolical German stew of verbose speculation and rancorous rhetoric, were stumpy chunks of sentences that struck my mind with the shock of recognition, as when Hitler wrote: "I was a nationalist. I was not a patriot"—a crucial distinction that would have wholly eluded Marx.

In 1938 and 1939 there came to me another recognition, one that has governed my mind ever since then, a recognition even more important than that national consciousness is deeper and more powerful than class consciousness and that nations are more solid and enduring realities than classes, the recognition that made first Mussolini and then Hitler truly post-Marxist thinkers. This other recognition came from my early experience with the insubstantial nature of economics—indeed, of the materialistic interpretation of history and human nature. People who wished Hitler ill took every kind of comfort from economics. Hitler, they said, ran the German economy into the ground. The German mark was not worth anything: it was mere paper. The steel of the German army was paper-thin; and butter in Germany was not to be had at all. The Kaiser had had a large colonial empire and all kinds of raw material; this Third Reich now had little or none. It was not equipped to fight a war. Against it were arrayed the British and the French world empires, with their abundant materials and goods, and their five hundred million people. These things were propounded by the most reputable economists. Articles and books to this effect were published in Britain, France, the United States. In one instance, a brave Hungarian scholar published a pamphlet questioning Germany's economic potential for war. It was a political and intellectual best-seller of sorts in 1939 (and its author was to suffer for it). And then Germany beat the richest world empires; it produced both guns and butter, the first surely of first-rate quality. The Chamberlain government rested its entire war strategy on economic calculations: that Germany was bound to run out of essentials—of oil, steel, rubber, chromium, vanadium, titanium, whatnot. "No government action could overcome economic laws, and any interference with those laws must end in disaster," said the President of the Board of Trade in the House of Commons in London at the beginning of World War I. This was Walter Runciman, a prototypical English Liberal figure, whom Chamberlain then sent to Czechoslovakia in 1938 in order to find a solution to the Sudeten crisis and the threatening war. In 1938 the Runciman mission seemed to represent the best in the English tradition of pragmatism, compromise, fairness. In reality, it represented the feeble ideas of tired old men. In 1939 and well into 1940 the British government believed that Germany would be defeated by Economic Warfare, by an economic blockade, that certain Economic Laws were insuperable, and that Hitler would be incapable of overcoming them. But the Chamberlain government was not alone in believing this. This kind of economic determinism was a dogma of the socialist Left, even more than of the capitalist Right.

The war was a reality; the Economic Laws were not. We know (or we ought to know) that these were lamentable miscalculations. But there was more to them than miscalculation. They derived not only from wishful thinking or from a narrow view of history but also from an insubstantial, though widespread, view of human nature itself. Among the few people who recognized this then were poets and mystics such as Georges Bernanos and Simone Weil, not economists. Nearly forty years after those events and a few years ago, I ran across something Simone Weil wrote in an unpublished essay, in 1942. "If Hitler despises economy, it is probably not simply because he understands nothing about it. It is because he *knows* (it is one of the notions of simple common sense that he clearly possesses and that can be called inspired since such ideas are so little understood) that economy is not an independent reality and as a result does not really have laws, since in economy as in all other spheres human affairs are ruled by force. . . . It seems to me difficult to deny that Hitler conceives, and conceives clearly . . . a kind of physics of human matter . . . He possesses an exact notion of the range of the power of force. . . . Nothing could be less primitive than Hitler, who would be inconceivable without modern technique and the existence of millions of *uprooted men.* "* When Simone Weil wrote this in England, I was a callow youth in Hungary; still this was exactly what I saw and thought. But this was also part of a larger recognition: of the intrusion of mind into matter, to the

---

*Quoted by Simone Petrément, *Simone Weil: A Life* (1976), pp. 510–11.

description and the explanation of which I would devote much of my work, twenty, thirty years later. I saw, early in my life, that Economic Man is a myth; that economics plays a much lesser part in the lives of people—including my family and people I knew—than it seems and, indeed, than they themselves are wont to think; that vanity is so much more powerful, and so much more widespread, than greed; that when people think (and not only say) that they can afford something they will afford it, and when they say that they cannot afford something they perhaps don't really want to afford it; that economic statistics and figures and transactions are fictions, in the proper and original sense of that word, because what happens is inseparable from what people think happens and that therefore the worth or the price of anything, even of the crudest piece of matter, is what people think it is. It took me a quarter of a century to formulate this: that the very opposite of not only what Karl Marx but also of what Adam Smith had said is true—that the essential matter, whether in the history of persons or in that of nations, is what they think and believe, while the material organization of society and of their lives is the superstructure of *that*.

One of the great books that remain to be written is the history of Anglomania. Since such a book, if properly conceived and composed, would call for a great talent capable of collecting, surveying and understanding all kinds of evidences of certain human aspirations and sensitivities through two centuries, from every corner of the world, it will probably never be written. This is a pity because something is happening now that I had not thought would happen in my lifetime: Anglomania is fading; there are fewer and fewer Anglomaniacs. This is not happening only because of the end of the British Empire and the decline of British might; it is happening, alas, because of the weakening of British prestige. Yet for two hundred years the prestige of an Englishman was a phenomenon almost unequaled in the history of mankind, because it was social and civilizational even more than political. Sometime during the eighteenth century the admiration for England and for things English began to affect the French, and a few people in Italy and

Germany. After 1800 this admiration spread athwart Europe and to many other places of the globe. Oddly, Anglomania was the avocation of many men and women who did not know English, unlike Francophilia, whereof knowledge of the French language was the essential component. This was curious, because by 1900 the principal element in Anglomania was no longer the admiration for British liberty and for British parliamentary government; it was the admiration for the British male ideal of a gentleman, for his clothes, manners, sports, his cool and dauntless spirit. In the 1930s, during the rise of Hitler's Third Reich, this Anglomania revived. People who previously did not know much about England (including those Europeans who for a century or more were looking to Paris for inspiration) were now looking at England, at the British lion incarnating the opposition of Might and Justice against Hitler. A division arose within the nations of the world, a division that lasted through the Second World War and beyond, a division that existed in Bulgaria as well as in the Argentine: the upper middle classes were generally Anglophile, while the lower middle classes were generally Germanophile.* This had something to do with the liberal democracy then represented by England and with the total state incarnated by Germany, but not much. It had more to do with the images of England and Germany as cultural and civilizational prototypes. There were people whose social and cultural aspirations were naturally and expectably Germanophile. Toward the end of the Thirties this division in Hungary became acute and recognizable. The Anglophilia of those who disliked the Germans and the Nazis was not an ephemeral avocation; it was a respect and a yearning for ideals and standards that represented the best of what still continued to exist in the civilization of the world.

In my life the Anglomania of my mother was decisive. She knew English, she read English, she had me taught English and sent me to school in England at the ages of fifteen and sixteen. In this, too,

---

*Or, Anglophobe. This was true of certain national groups in the United States, too; their Anglophobia (sometimes the result of their distrust and dislike of what at that time was still the Anglo-Saxon element at the top of American society) was the source of their "isolationism," not the reverse.

I differed from my classmates, among whom the sons of middle-class families would learn some French in addition to the customary German; I may have been the only one who knew English then. In the summer of 1938 my mother took me to an English school. Passing through Paris, we crossed the Channel from St. Malo on the overnight boat. We landed at Southampton on a cool and sunny morning.

I enjoyed myself in England, especially during the second of my two terms. What contributed to my enjoyment were certain amatory experiences; I got along with English girls even better than with my English schoolmates, who were, well, less worldly than I was. I was impressed with the traffic in London, with the Tube, with the large newspapers, with Salisbury Cathedral, with the Tidworth Tattoo, with the warships in the Solent that we visited, with the prim greenness of an English summer day, with the pinkness of English girls, with the easygoing common sense of some of the people, and with the great gulps of English history and English literature that I swallowed. Yet I returned from England with views that were somewhat different from those held by my mother and by the determined minority of Anglophiles in Hungary. I took my Cambridge entrance examination on the day of the German-Soviet Pact and arrived back in Hungary a few days before the Second World War began. I respected and even admired the English. That I wished them to win the war goes without saying. But I also knew that they would be maddeningly slow. They were not braver and quicker and smarter than the Germans in every respect. I kept saying this to the friends of my parents, sometimes to the extent of unnerving and irritating them.

I had an experience during that second term in England that sticks in my mind even now. My school in England was in summer session, with a sprinkling of foreign boys such as myself. For some unexplained and unexplainable reason, tennis was no longer played after the previous term, and the lawn court was in some disrepair. We wanted to put the court into shape and mount a small tournament, with a refreshment tent to which we would invite girls. I went with a delegation to the Headmaster, who agreed to this on the condition that the court be mowed, the lines painted and the net put up by the handymen. The tournament and the party were to start at four on a Saturday afternoon. That morning—there were no classes on that Saturday—we found that the court was untended, there were tufts of grass, no net, no lines. We put out the tables and the refreshments. At eleven o'clock I took upon myself the task of seeing the Headmaster. He was obviously irritated, suggesting to me, in so many words, that this kind of nervy insistence and impatience was fairly distasteful to an Englishman who knew what had to be done and when. I slunk out of his office with my tail between my legs, sadly convinced that the Headmaster was, of course, right. So far as manners go, he may or may not have been right; so far as practicality went, he wasn't. At two o'clock it began to rain. In half an hour the rain stopped, but the grass was too wet to mow or paint the lines. The handymen took a look at it and left. Our guests arrived at four, sipping lemonade, with their backs turned to the netless court, including a very pretty girl with a straw hat who presently disappeared. Twenty minutes later the Headmaster came himself, with his pipe in his mouth, in a cheerful ha-ha-ing mood, carrying the heavy net and urging us to get the court ready. We could have done all of it in the morning. Now it took us two hours, with the planned order of the tournament hopelessly out of whack.

Later, during the war, I sometimes thought, and my mother often speculated, what would have happened if I had stayed in England in September 1939. Especially in 1944, when the horrors of the war finally overwhelmed Hungary and my family, she would often say that had I remained in England I would have been spared all of that: I knew that she imagined me in a natty British uniform, perhaps even as a young subaltern of the charmed RAF. I thought of that, too, but came to the later conclusion that, with all of the suffering and the dread and the German and the Russian conquests of Hungary, my staying in Hungary was a blessing in disguise. Some blessing! Some disguise! Yet a blessing, nonetheless. What I learned in Hungary during the war, not out of books but about people, including Nazis, Communists, Germans, Russians and, more important, about good and evil in multitudinous shapes incarnadine was, in the long run, an inestimable asset to my education. I doubt whether I would have learned all that in England, in an England where I would have remained an alien, a refugee, mucking about in some Pioneer Corps at best, deeply anxious about my family in Hungary. Frustrated by English snobbery whereof I would have been inevitably a victim (I had few connections and no money), ending up as one of the many refugees in London, going from circle to circle, loyal to England but sodden in the pelting rain. Had I remained in England it is at least possible that I might have remained a Socialist, befitting the role of a Central European refugee intellectual. It was my life in the midst of wartime Europe that led to my reactionary convictions.

I had an ambivalent feeling, in 1939 and ever since, about the curious lack of imagination that was so prevalent among the English, perhaps even more among Englishmen than Englishwomen. In many ways, this was an asset: it often contributed to the strength of English common sense and of the English character (is there a proverb more English than "we'll cross that bridge when we come to it"?*; but as we have seen, they are also often unprepared for the crossing when, or even after, they come to it). During most of the Modern Age, from the sixteenth century onward at least, the English national tendencies of pragmatism, Protestantism, practicality, non-intellectuality, common sense, loyalty, racial pride, fairness, sportsmanship, respect for the law, perseverance, social discipline, gentlemanly snobbery, etc. consisted of virtues (as well as of certain vices) that worked in their favor, since they were particularly suitable for their endeavors during the Modern Age. But sometime after 1900 their unthinking but deeply rooted beliefs in the virtues of these characteristics were weakening. Moreover, some of these characteristics ceased to be assets in the late modern, or post-modern, world. Among them was the ancient British virtue of complete indifference to the opinions of non-British people—a virtue that

---

*On the other hand, "A watched pot never boils." Ah! I agree. Yet, at their best, the English sense of this proverb is different from mine. I am impatient with the pot; they say to themselves: stop watching it.

could easily degenerate into the vice of being uneasy with and unresponsive to the affections that other people had for them. Unlike Francophilia, Germanophilia, Russophilia and, of course, Americanophilia, the result of Anglophilia is unrequited love to the extent that the British would often repulse the very people who admired them to the point of imitation—a British reaction of racial and insular pride that is, however, not unmixed with uncertainty.*

And when we consider that, unlike the French or the Germans, the British often improve when seen at close range, their indifference to the affection of foreigners has done them immeasurable harm. As late as 1945 they could have assumed the leadership of Western Europe for a song. But they were unaccustomed to music, to that kind of music. And I understood when I read, decades later, the bitter experiences and frustrations of those who truly loved and admired the British—not through illusions and not because of their own sense of racial inferiority but because of their deep knowledge of and respect for British virtues. So, for example, the superbly intelligent V. S. Naipaul, whose bitterest thoughts have been directed to those super-modern Englishmen and perhaps especially Englishwomen who allowed themselves to seek profit and pleasure from incarnating the very opposites of traditionally English ideas and behavior, or who sought carnal congress with Africans or Indians. In any event, something happened during the twentieth century to Anglo-Saxon males, a fatal weakening of convictions and of

---

*Is the proverbial and widespread English characteristic of shyness a virtue or a vice? Surely it is the former; indeed it is one of the most charming of English characteristics—as long as you are not up against it. Deeply felt pride and modest shyness: what an attractive combination! Yet their relationship ought to be examined a bit further. The source of pride is certainty, the source of shyness is good manners; yet the latter is not unmixed with uncertainty. Both English pride and English shyness include a certain unwillingness to think. This is even true of English intellectuals who would rather be boring than vulgar, which is why so many of them have naturally gravitated to the Left. But this has now begun to change: there are now manifestations of British vulgarity that are not preferable to German or American vulgarity. Were—are—the Beatles shy? Are Kingsley Amis and Anthony Burgess shy?

imagination of which Englishwomen were often instinctively aware (the probable reason that Englishwomen are attracted to foreign men more often than are Englishmen to foreign women).

For some time I continued to be attracted by things and ideas and people that were "modern." But around the age of fifteen I noticed something interesting about the political usage of the words *reaction* and *reactionary.* The democratic statesmen of the West were all satisfactorily anti-dictatorial, progressive, opposed to Hitlerism, etc., but somehow something was missing. Chamberlain, Daladier, Blum, Attlee, Hoover, Hull: Conservatives, Radicals, Socialists, Republicans, Democrats: I thought even then that their reactions to the Hitler phenomenon, expressed by their rhetoric, were somehow unconvincing and unsatisfactory; that they did not really understand what was going on in the middle of Europe and in the minds of millions; that their eventual (and often conditional) willingness to stand up to Hitler was unduly compromised not only because of their own political calculations and the circumscriptions of their situations but also because of their views of the world and perhaps of human nature itself. There was an exception to them: Churchill. He was still a political outsider in 1939, but somehow his voice was being heard, even though so many people in his own country refused to hear it. When I read some of his statements and phrases and excerpts from his speeches in England I found them exhilarating, and not merely because of his rolling Augustan rhetoric; I thought that I was in the presence of a true realist. Some people— not only his enemies but many of his later allies—saw him as a reactionary. I did not yet see him that way, but I am sure that I saw then that Churchill had Hitler exactly right, seeing in Hitler the incarnation of something evil that was very ancient as well as very modern. A little later I was gladdened to see that Churchill was not alone, that there was a group of English Tories who stood on his side and not on Chamberlain's. What impressed me was how their Tory patriotism differed from that of most other Conservatives who were, in reality (like many American Republicans or French Radicals of that period), surviving representatives of a nineteenth-century materialist liberalism. Unlike the Chamberlainites, these Churchillite Tories did not believe in national self-determination; unlike the Liberals, they did not believe in the League of Nations; unlike the Labourites, they did not believe in disarmament; but their dislike for Communism or their indifference to the League of Nations did not compromise their determination to stand up to Hitler, no matter with what allies. They had a sense of honor but no ideology; they were patriots and not nationalists. In this these men and women of the Right were the very opposites of Hitler and of his allies. And when, around that time, I first read the words of the Nazis' fighting and marching anthem, the Horst Wessel Song: *"Kameraden, die Rotfront and Reaktion erschossen"*—"Our Comrades, Killed by the Reds and by Reactionaries!"—that cold word *reaction* began to glow in my mind.

Back in Hungary, too, the words *reaction* and *reactionary* began to acquire an increasing charm for me. That the history of politics (indeed, that the history of human thought) is the history of words I did not then know. But I was sufficiently sensitive to political rhetoric to understand something to the effect that a political and ideological revolution had taken place, which was manifest, too, in a revolution in political terminology, in the accepted meaning of words that had come down from the nineteenth century. For example, the words *people, popular, populist,* which had been monopolies or near-monopolies of the Left for one hundred and fifty years at least (in Hungary "people" had been a Leftist and "nation" a Rightist term), now became adopted by a new radical "Right." This development had begun in Germany a few decades earlier (assisted by the peculiarly tribal and mystic German word *Volk*). It was taken up by Mussolini in 1914 when he called his radical nationalist new newspaper *Il Popolo d'Italia.* Twenty-five years later, when the Second World War began in Europe, *folkish* and *populaire* became the favorable designations of Fascist and Nazi sympathizers throughout the Continent. These, as indeed the newfangled nationalist populists in Hungary, began to attack those men in the establishment and government who were "old-fashioned" (that word, in Hungary as well as in the United States, had a definitely pejorative

connotation at that time), "reactionaries," that is, ossified representatives of an antiquated order. (In 1945 and thereafter the Communists and their allies would use the same word in the same way.)

My interest and respect for some of these "reactionaries" began
to grow. I saw in some of these men—politicians, publicists, historians, Sándor Pethő and Gyula Szekfü, for example—something akin
to the Churchillite Tory patriots in England, but in a deeply rooted
Hungarian version. Like other conservatives, they had been anti-
Communists and even anti-liberals; yet they had become patriots
and not nationalists, acutely aware of the German menace and of
the vulgar populism of the Hungarian National Socialists, not only
because of their temporary reactions to the political situation of
their day but because of their old-fashioned convictions and, yes,
because of their sense of honor.* Their very style was inspiring.
Their very use of the language reflected a patriotism that had risen
above ideology, as in the case of Szekfü, who had become famous
around 1920 because of his great anti-liberal and at times even anti-
Jewish history *(Három nemzedék)* in which he described what he
saw as the degeneration of the nineteenth-century liberal dog-
matology through three generations. Now, less than twenty years
later, he saw that the great danger came from elsewhere, from the
Third Reich and its vulgar and brutal Hungarian followers. Now
he took up the cause of defending the older Hungarian freedoms,
the cause of patriotic democracy, opposing, among other matters,
the humiliation and the persecution of Hungarian Jews when this
cause and when such an opposition were both unpolitic and unpopular: a kind of patriotic evolution that had its rare examples
elsewhere in Europe, too, exemplified by such men as Georges
Bernanos, certain shining examples (soon to become martyrs) of the
old Prussian aristocracy and, in many ways, Churchill.

These examples contributed to my conversion to the Right, from
an avowal of Socialism to an increasing respect for conservatives—

---

*It was at that time that the increasingly outdated nature of the designations
Right and Left began to occur to me. Was a Nazi to the Left of the conservatives
or to the Right of them? Were men such as Horthy or Franco to the Left or
to the Right of Hitler? Much of this made less and less sense.

or, rather, of *certain* conservatives. For the late 1930s and the first years of the Second World War demonstrated—or they ought to have demonstrated—both the failure of the Left and the split of the so-called Right. The favorites of the Left, the Spanish Republicans, Beneš of Czechoslovakia, the French Socialists, etc., etc. (not to speak of Stalin, Hitler's acquired and devoted partner in 1939) surrendered to Hitler and Mussolini or thought it best to get along with them; authoritarian dictators such as Metaxas in Greece and Salazar in Portugal did not. The democratic Czechs gave up without even a semblance of a fight; the patriotic and "Rightist" Poles fought with a bravery unequaled in the war. This did not mean, however, that the Right was everywhere more courageous and principled than the Left. If the German Marxist mass melted away in the Hitler heat, so did the principles of the German Konservatives, people such as Papen or Neurath (and, alas, of many of the churchmen of Germany). The Konservative Papen—a staunch Catholic politician and principal member of the *Herrenklub*—would go on, serving Hitler; the reactionary Count Stauffenberg would sacrifice his life in the conspiracy against Hitler. If there were plenty of former Socialists or Communists who found an ideological haven in the Nazi camp, there were plenty of conservatives and anti-Communists in that camp, too.* But not reactionaries; not by a long shot.

We are now in the hot, dazzling days of June 1940 in Hungary. I was sixteen then. I had a short but painful sprint of love with an older girl with honeyed hair: painful, because she had taken up my courtship and flirtation for about a fortnight, which made me plunge into a sentimental pond of romantic illusions, after which she made it obvious that I was too young for her, spurning my requests for rendezvous, preferring the solidly established thirty-year-old bachelors who responded to her attractions. Besides being

---

*In America, too, where in 1940—and also later—conservative Republicans such as Taft and Hoover (and, at that time, the parvenu Kennedy family) thought and said that standing by Churchill against Hitler was wrong, while an old-fashioned Boston gentleman such as Henry Stimson or a Virginia gentleman such as General Marshall did not.

stupid with hope I was also stupid with vanity. I remember a day in that brilliant and tragic second week of June when Mussolini, too, had declared war on the West, when Paris had fallen to the Germans, and when one of my classmates saw me walking home from the tennis club on Margaret Island with the aforementioned girl and another older girl, her friend, both arm in arm with me, the impression of which gave me a great deal of pleasure. In our town apartment, with the cool linen slipcovers on the chairs and sofas, the shutters tightly closed against the relentless summer sun, my mother was listening to the BBC. It was the day of one of Churchill's great speeches. I cannot honestly say whether I heard that speech then or whether I heard it weeks later (it still lifts my spirit when I read it). What I remember was the news (four days before, when the Germans had entered Paris, my mother cried out: "and they, in their big boots, are now in that Guerlain shop on the rue St. Honoré!"—this may sound flat now, but it was then a fragrant phrase) that the wind that stood from France was not all foul, that a French general by the name of De Gaulle had spoken from London for French resistance. It was the first time that I heard the word *resistance*—a word that, when you think of it, is a reactionary word, not a progressive one.

A few days later I indulged in my first reactionary act. The university students (especially those in the Polytechnical University, prospective engineers who were the most pro-German ones) were marching down the quays of the city, cheering the collapse of the Versailles order and the victory of Germany over France. I had a small enameled French flag, the kind of marker that one kept sticking into maps; I stuck it on my lapel and so walked the summery streets of Budapest that day of the French surrender. The flag was small and also unexpected; few people noticed it. I sweated in the sun and fought the temptation to shed my jacket (it was difficult to keep that flag pinned to my shirt); when I met an acquaintance or two I had to show them what I was sporting and why. I am not particularly pleased with the memory of myself *aetatis* sixteen. I was melancholy about the defeat of France, and I was more than melancholy with the loss of that girl, that wondrous brief apparition in my life; the wearing of that small flag somehow alleviated my spirits, but not much. Still I write about it, since this was perhaps the first time that the consciousness of being a reactionary may have surfaced in my mind. For on the way downtown that morning, wearing my linen jacket and that minuscule enamel rectangle of that tricolor flag so self-consciously, I passed a newsstand and saw the latest edition of the *Illustrierter Völkischer Beobachter,* the principal German Nazi newspaper, with a cartoon on its cover. It was a vulgar and hateful drawing, a symbolic caricature of a defeated France—or, more accurately, what France represented to the Nazi. The group of people in that cartoon consisted of an idiotic brute of an African soldier in French uniform, obviously representing Race-Mixing; a horrid caricature of an ugly Jew clutching his moneybags, obviously representing Corrupt Capitalism; there were other figures, too, that I cannot now remember, except for a skeletal, aristocratic French cavalry officer, with his nose up in the air, obviously representing Reaction. I have his picture still before my mental eye, and I remember exactly what I thought then, which was that there ought to have been more of his kind.

In 1940 I was not yet a reactionary. But I appreciated the reactionary element in what was best in the resistance to Hitler, in men such as Churchill and De Gaulle. Thirty-three years later I was finishing the writing of a book about the history of those years, 1939–41 (with the title *The Last European War*). "For one thing," I wrote, "Hitler's enormous successes during these years were the results, less of the organization of German material power than of his conviction of German superiority, a conviction that he succeeded in imparting to the minds of millions. Conviction, too, made Churchill and De Gaulle his principal opponents. Lamenting the state of civilization of the West between the wars, Yeats wrote his famous lines that 'the best lack all conviction / while the worst / are full of passionate intensity.' When Yeats died in that bleakest of Januaries, in 1939, it seemed so. And yet it wasn't so. In 1940 the best did not lack all conviction, even when the worst may have been full of passionate intensity. And this is the lesson—perhaps the only inspiring lesson—of the Last European War." A few months after I wrote this paragraph near the end of a long book that was at least partly inspired, of course, by my reminiscences of 1940, and less than a year after this book was published, I read the reminiscences of a contemporary in New York in *The New York Times Magazine.* This was Irving Kristol, the principal neo-conservative political philosopher in the United States. His nostalgic article bore the title "Memoirs of a Trotskyist."* There was the unbridgeable abyss between my past and that of the New York intelligentsia. In September 1940 my generation in Europe was divided between devotees of Hitler and devotees of Churchill, or between partisans of Pétain and partisans of De Gaulle. These New York intellectuals were divided between devotees of Stalin and devotees of Trotsky. Even thirty-six years later Kristol wrote that "the elite was us—'the happy few.' " "What I now recollect most vividly is [our] incredible vivacity. . . . Our presentations were intellectually rigorous. I have never since seen or heard their equal. . . . It *was* [his italics] an authentic educational milieu," this areopagus in the cafeteria of the City College of New York, divided, as Kristol recounted, between Alcove 1 (the Trotskyists) and Alcove 2 (the Stalinist) Left. "It was between these two alcoves that the war of the worlds was being fought." I would have thought that in 1940 the war of the worlds was being fought in the sky over England; but then these are the confessions of a reactionary, *tout court.*

All of the foregoing has nothing—or, at least, very little—to do with ideology. A Rightist is not necessarily a better person than a Leftist, a Trotskyist is not necessarily a better person than a Stalinist, just as a Christian is not necessarily a better man than an atheist, although he ought to be. My soporific reading of Marx and my wide-eyed recognition of the nonsense of Economic Man contributed to my crystallization of a view of the world which could be called idealist, as being the very opposite of materialism; but it took me some time to recognize that a categorical idealism (especially the German type) was as wrong as, and could be even more disastrous

**The New York Times Magazine,* January 23, 1977.

than, a categorical materialism; that ideas do not exist in the abstract, that mind is not only anterior to matter but that matter is inseparable from mind, intimately entangled with it, as indeed the idea is with the person.

All of this goes against the grain of not only Freudian but of Dostoevskian thinking: against the first, because the functions of the conscious mind are knowable, more important and also more interesting than the functions of the subconscious; against the second, because what ideas do to men is much less important and also less interesting than what men do with ideas. During the war my interest was attracted not merely by ideas but by their movements: by the process with which people were choosing, renting, buying, adopting, wearing and eventually replacing them. I became interested, and at times fascinated, by two related matters in the movement of ideas: by the phenomenon of momentum, and by that of opportunism. The first involved the slowness of public opinion. In this, too, Marx was wrong: for much more consequential than the accumulation of capital is the accumulation of opinion. It is because of the accumulation of opinion that An Idea Whose Time Has Come is usually no good; that people and politicians and governments will often fail to pay sufficient attention to really important matters until it is already too late. It is therefore, too, that people will espouse ideas not so much because of their attractiveness but because of their current accumulation. This is how the inflation of money, too, is but a consequence of the inflation of ideas—that is, of phrases and words (just as the pollution of matter, e.g., the throwing around of trash, is a consequence of the pollution of minds).

Opportunism is something for which intellectuals have especial talents because of their aptitude for managing vocabulary at the expense of thought; but opportunism is widely practiced by "simple" people, too. I write "simple" in inverted commas, because I found that the "simple" people, surely in this century, are not really simple; their mental operations are often very complex indeed. In 1945 I read about a shoemaker who finally inscribed himself in the local Nazi party during the siege of Budapest when the Russian armies were literally *ante portas,* a mile or so away and approaching fast. He joined that party not because of fanaticism or a last-ditch heroism, but because he could no longer withstand the pressures of some of his relatives, Arrow Cross Party members, in the close quarters where they had lived. This is what he said at his postwar trial, and I believe that this was largely true. Was he, therefore, the very opposite of an opportunist? No: his timing was wrong. He was the last one to climb on that bandwagon, a moment or so before that bandwagon fell apart; but he was unwilling to think much ahead, and the bandwagon was . . . well, a bandwagon.

What people choose to think has less to do with *why* than with *how* they think; and that *how* is intimately involved with *when.* I saw innumerable examples of this during the war. To certain people this kind of adjustment came so naturally that they sought and found no rhyme or reason to explain this to others, since they found no need to explain it to themselves: they hardly knew what they were doing because they didn't want to. Others found it necessary to rationalize their behavior, at least to themselves. Such varieties of opportunism are, of course, endless. There were the Italians, whose realistic and unsentimental cynicism (a variant of hypocrisy) was human, not brutal: in public they would say one thing one day and another thing another day because this was how the world was, they had to protect their own lives, their appetites were normal human ones, eschewing the prospects of martyrdom. There was the Carpatho-Ukrainian corporal of my unit who in October 1944—the day after the out-and-out local Nazis were installed by the SS to rule Hungary—announced that he was a convinced Germanophile and Nazi; when I ran into him six months later he announced that he was a convinced Slavophile and Communist. I was impressed how this brute, who knew that I knew what he had said and how he had behaved six months earlier, did not make the slightest effort to justify or explain his conversion; indeed, I felt that had I asked him about that, in no matter how friendly a tone, he would have been perplexed rather than disturbed. To him, it was the most natural thing in the world, like kicking someone who is down. In adjusting one's mind (and not only one's conduct) to conditions—first of all, to conditions of power, without a thought to the contrary and without a thought to justification—perhaps here lies the difference between opportunism and hypocrisy, but also between the savagery of barbarism and the relativity of a, no matter how corruptible, civilization.

Sometime around the age of nineteen, I began to see that some of the men and women whom I admired the most were not the smartest people and not even the cleverest ones, but the opposites of opportunists. This did not mean that they would not change their minds; the unwillingness, rather than the inability—at bottom, a moral, rather than an intellectual shortcoming—to change one's mind does not amount to probity of character. What I saw were a few men and women who adhered to certain conventions and convictions, rather than to political or even national preferences or ideologies; and these conventions and convictions were almost always representative of old-fashioned virtues. Such men and women were of all kinds, truly individual without being individualists. Years later I read Chesterton, who said that it is "a great mistake to suppose that love unites and unifies men. Love diversifies them, because love is directed towards individuality. The thing that really unites men and makes them like each other is hatred." I certainly saw enough of the latter. Eventually I began to detect that in most of the cases (though not in all) the principled behavior of these reactionaries rested on religion, in Hungary often on the Catholic religion. This made an impression on me, even though I was not a fervent believer or more than a desultory practicant. Apart from my Socialist past and from my modern and cosmopolitan inclinations, I was for a long time bored and vexed by the condition that in the Hungary of my youth (as also in other Central and Eastern European nations) the "Christian" adjective meant something that was nationalist, ideological and therefore negative: "Christian," in popular and political usage, meant non-Jewish, non-Marxist, non-liberal, non-cosmopolitan. Nationalism and Christianity were too

closely identified for my taste, then indeed as now. I also remember
how early my first realization of the difference between an older and
a younger, between a more traditional and a more democratic and
populist Christianity occurred, around the age of fifteen. As I wrote
before, nationalism and Christianity were closely allied and propagated by the regime. Religious instruction in the school was manda-
tory, and so was Mass-going, which was monitored almost as
strictly as was class attendance. Our religion teacher and chaplain
at the Gymnasium was an old, doddery, fusty priest, droning
through the Mass and his sermons, spending an inordinately long
time on the faculty toilet, at whose expense we mounted endless
tricks, trying to make his life at least as miserable as those of other
professors. In 1938 or thereabout he was replaced by a younger priest
who attempted to be popular. He spoke a more demotic lingo; he
would, on occasion, joke with the students and insist that he was
a soccer player. His lectures and sermons, his very diction and
language were populist. He made only a few political remarks (the
old priest had made none), but it was evident that he represented
a younger and more dynamic clergy, nationalist with a touch of
anti-Semitism, a "people's church" in a new Europe. Occasionally
he would introduce a Hungarian text after the Latin canon; on
other occasions he would make jocular references to the standings
of the national soccer league. Being then of an anti-clerical dispensa-
tion, I paid no particular attention to him until in a religion class
one of my classmates asked him something about the Germans. He
declared that he would not go into politics, whereafter followed a
ten-minute disquisition on the need to fight the greatest evil in the
world, which was Communism. Then and there I knew the difference between him and his old predecessor, who surely feared and
hated Communism, too, but the way in which this youngish, callow, melon-headed and crew-cut priest talked disconcerted me even
more than what he said.

A few days later (this, too, was compulsory at that time) I went
to confession in his booth. Of the Catholic sacraments, I found
confession one of the most meaningful, even then: I thought, as I
do now, that a good confession and a good confessor surely preempt

the need for any psychiatrist or analyst. (Unfortunately this is easier said than done. During my lifetime the practice and the meaning of the sacrament of confession declined lamentably, and a good confessor is hard to find.) There was, again, something very different in the ways in which the older priest and this new chaplain listened to my sincere babbling. I could hear the wheezing and the occasional eructations of the old fat priest behind the grillwork of the confessional. I knew he was tired and sleepy, forcing himself to spend his time in that narrow stuffy box, listening to the unpleasant tales of unattractive schoolboys; but I also sensed that, beneath all of that tiredness, he was listening to me. What he said before my absolution was admonitory, in a serious way. His successor was not necessarily inattentive; I felt that he was ready to pounce on this or that serious transgression of mine; I also had the sense that he knew who I was; yet, after having questioned me about this or that, his advice and absolution were perfunctory; he was a modern confessor, a spiritual scoutmaster, a regular fellow.

Neither of my parents was particularly religious, though my mother was more so than my father. She, too, went to church very seldom, a few times each year. During my adolescence my memories of churches were merely esthetic: good occasional organ music or the beauty of a wintry midnight Mass—entering or leaving a church across an alley of rime-laced streets as the last tunes of the organ were dying away. Otherwise I found the Mass—even High Mass at Easter—often interminable and boring. I heard the sermons in a mood that varied from indifference to disdain. There were, however, exceptions to this aridity of soul. I think that I always believed in God, even in my "Socialist" period, when I was tempted on occasion, *pour épater les bourgeois,* to say that I was an atheist. I believed in God not out of fear but because of a sense that has accompanied me through my life, the sense that had not much to do with the catechism, the sense that there is another world than this, but that the sublime order of that world somehow involves this imperfect and human one, because it is from that world that intimations of truth and of infinite goodness are coming to us in ways that are not given to us to know, though at times we are allowed to

understand them.* Another—minor—element was the respect that
my parents helped to instill in me for the beauty of religious art, of
the great churches, monuments, sculptures and paintings of the past
which, on occasion (I remember my awe at the horizontal Man-
tegna Christ in Milan that I saw at the age of fourteen), impressed
me deeply, as had some church music (César Franck more than
Mozart) and, again on occasion, the religion latent in fine poetry
and great literature. Still, the most important in my development
was the example of a few religious people. This is not a spiritual
autobiography, and I am not inclined to describe—in part because
such a description would be necessarily inadequate, skirting the
limits of involuntary falsity—the evolution of my religious progress, if progress it was (and is). I could, and would, crack a low joke
at a priest; I could never joke at the sight of an old woman mum-
bling her rosary (or at an old Jewish woman reading her Hebrew
prayer book). But it was not until around the age of twenty that I
began to realize gradually how true Christians were . . . well,
something else: that their convictions rested on something that was
both more ancient and deep than the convictions of people otherwise committed, including people with convictions that I may have
liked or even shared.

My respect for religion was not the result of a sudden revelation;
as a matter of fact, it was intellectual—at times excessively so—
rather than the response to an emotional need or even to a kind of
spiritual thirst. It came from reading and not from sermons; from

---

*Many years later I read the prison meditations of the tragic German Pastor
Bonhoeffer when he had been stripped of all hope and of all illusion about the
contemporary spiritual succor of the churches: *"Nicht von der Welt zu Gott,
sondern von Gott zur Welt geht der Weg Jesu Christi. . . . "* The way of Christ goes
not from this world to God but from God to this world. Now compare this
to (1) Cardinal Bertram of Breslau, who said in 1939: "I told the children: Heil
Hitler—that is valid for this world; Praised be Jesus Christ—that is the tie
between earth and heaven." No neater formula could be imagined, except
perhaps that of (2) Albert Einstein: "I believe in Spinoza's God who reveals
himself in the orderly harmony of what exists, not in a God who concerns
himself with the destiny and actions of human beings." (So much for Einstein
the humanist.)

literature and not from theology; from my contemplation of this world more than from my contemplation of Heaven (or Hell). It was not only that the behavior of men and women with religious convictions inspired me with respect; it was not only, after everything was said, that the Catholic Church was, at least in principle, supra-national and not national, that it was less bound to the kind of, at worst provincial, at best cultural, nationalism from which Protestants in Hungary could seldom liberate themselves, and from which the Orthodox churches farther to the east would not even attempt to liberate themselves. What mattered even more in my mind was the fact that the Roman Catholic concept—doctrine as well as view—of human nature corresponded with what I was seeing and experiencing, especially during the last years of the war, when its sufferings and horrors struck my native country in a condensed version within a twelvemonth. The teaching of free will—that men and women are responsible for what they do and say and even think, because they are free to do so—and of original sin—that the moral range of a human being is infinitely greater and different from that of any other living being, since being naturally inclined to both evil and good, we are both beasts and angels—made a great deal of sense to me. In any event a Hungarian (or perhaps a European Catholic), especially in the twentieth century, did not require Dostoevsky to describe the plausibility of this coexistence of good and evil within a single soul. He experienced this in his very flesh, or at least saw it with his own eyes.

There was another discovery that began to crystallize in my mind around the age of twenty—when I did not yet know, because I did not consider myself, a reactionary. What follows may again jolt the accustomed categories in the minds of my readers: it was the gradual discovery that to be reactionary may be compatible with being a bourgeois. This requires explanation. I did not like the word *bourgeois:* as a matter of fact, *bourgeois* was one of those terms that stuck in my mind after having read Marx, and that I kept using irresponsibly during my "Socialist" period. It was a good curse word, especially appealing to a young mind. Even as I grew away from Socialism, the pejorative sense of the word remained: *bourgeois* meant narrow, petty, selfish, fussy, fusty, stuffy, hopelessly middle-class. Yet around the same time I began to appreciate certain bourgeois virtues: solidity, reliability, probity, decency, modesty (perhaps even, as I wrote earlier, hypocrisy)—and, most of all, the cult of privacy, of interiority, indeed, of the family. My paternal grandparents died when I was very young. My mother's parents lived to be eighty-six and ninety. They had lived more than half of their lives under the Dual Monarchy of the Habsburgs; during the second half of their lives (by 1914 both of them were forty-two) they lived through the First World War, a revolution, a short-lived Communist regime (wherefrom they fled to Vienna), a counter-revolution, the Second World War, Hitler, the German occupation of Hungary, the deportation and the extermination of Jews, the destruction of Budapest, the Russian conquest, the Soviet dictator-ship and the Revolution of 1956. They were the most admirable people I have ever known. Until I was fifteen I saw them as good grandparents. Then my affection for them assumed a more con-scious form. At that time I saw them almost daily because they lived close to my school; conveniently (we had just moved) I had my midday dinner, after school, with them. They were well-to-do, modest, Jewish and thoroughly bourgeois. My grandfather could have afforded an automobile with a chauffeur; he had none, whereas my stepfather had one. Their apartment, with its old, indifferent furniture, was comfortable, without a single touch of luxury. It was not elegant, but it was not an overstuffed middle-class apartment, either. Its very smell—freshly dusted rugs, furniture polish, the slight clean-scorched odor of linen ironed, cold wintry sunlight and fresh air, with perhaps a faint undertone of milky coffee—is in my nostrils still. What mattered was my recognition that they repre-sented something to which I had been either indifferent or even hostile earlier. Their older standards, their character, their self-discipline, their modesty were less brittle than the standards of their daughters and of their in-laws, even though my mother, my aunt, my father and my stepfather had many admirable characteristics of their own. My grandparents were not only wise; they were utterly reliable: they said what they meant and they meant what they said.

Perhaps this affection for my grandparents was the natural reaction of someone whose parents were divorced. But there was another element, too: the fact that, even more than the Marxists, the Nazis and the extreme nationalists hated everyone and everything that was bourgeois, *bürgerlich.* This, then, became involved with my deepening and widening interest in history, which, in turn, included a nostalgia not so much for the aristocratic eras and the Middle Ages (I was no Miniver Cheevy) as for the relatively recent bourgeois period of European and Hungarian history, a mental development to which I shall come in a moment. I admired many members of the Magyar aristocracy for their style, handsomeness, elegance and manners: indeed, of all the social classes during the terrible crucible of the then present and the previous fifty years the old nobility had a better record than any other class. Between the ages of seventeen and twenty-one I passed through the snobbish period of my life, which fortunately caused me little harm. I was still a fairly insufferable youth. My self-confidence had begun to rise, but only because of a few early social and amatory successes. At that time my aspirations were not at all bourgeois: they were aristocratic. (That is typical of certain conservatives: in the early 1980s I met a rich young man from Michigan who professed his admiration for Barbey d'Aurevilly and Ronald Reagan.) I could have ended up as a snob save for two salutary conditions: I didn't have enough money and sufficient energy to be one, and in Hungary at that time being a snob was a full-time job, requiring not only an assiduous single-mindedness but concentrated work. The other salutary condition was my great curiosity and rising appetite for history—particularly for the near-contemporary history of the nineteenth and early twentieth centuries, in which I could still imagine myself having lived; it was hopelessly gone, far away, and yet within a touching and sensing distance. I may have been a conservative before I became a reactionary, but that is neither here nor there. What I can see in retrospect is that the reactionary virtues I admired were more patrician and bourgeois than they were aristocratic and nobilitarian: the cult of the family, for example, or of personal dignity, privacy, the cult of an authentic interior life.

This is not a sociological distinction. The aristocratic virtues of a more distant past were traditionalist rather than historical, and not humanist. (See, in this respect, Ortega's neo-aristocratic essays in praise of the nobility of the hunt, and of the toreador.) But what happened during the last one hundred years was the adoption of the older bourgeois and humanist virtues by many aristocrats themselves, in part because their often unthinking traditionalism was becoming replaced by a more conscious historicism; and also because of their dislike for those vulgarities and excesses of the kind of populism that has become an inevitable ingredient of all extremist (and anti-bourgeois) ideologies and parties.

I recall an odd thought, or wish, that kept recurring in my mind during my adolescence. It went like this: how wonderful it would be to find two numbers that do not add up right; if, say, 123456 added to 654321 would not produce the same result as the same calculation performed in reverse.* The reason behind this kind of wish was not an impulse for destructive anarchy, out of a hatred for mathematics. It was, I think, a wish to discover some evidence of a new kind of truth, to the effect that numbers are not the ultimate reality, that a leak in arithmetic may reveal that mathematical logic is far from being absolute truth. This is not a retrospective explication of the above-mentioned childish wish: I remember that I respected mathematics and mathematicians, but that of all the subjects that were imposed on us in the Gymnasium, the one I truly loathed was the philosophy course of Logic which, to me, was nothing but verbal mathematics, a senseless and nearly oxymoronic contradiction in terms.

In sum, I disliked systems well before I fully realized that every system leaks *because* it is man-made. To call this preference of mine

---

*It was not until twenty or more years later that, reading Heisenberg, I learned that in quantum physics such a possibility does indeed exist, that on occasion a times b may differ from b times a, dependent on the order in which these calculations are being performed—information that gave me considerable pleasure.

humanism is probably too simple; but it was involved in my early, and fast developing, interest in history. That interest, too, was preceded—or, rather, it grew gradually out of—my interest in literature. Around the age of thirteen I became an avid reader of novels—of all kinds of novels, not only historical ones; as a matter of fact, I was not especially interested in historical novels except in certain instances. This direction of my interests must have developed very early. What I relished in certain novels was every kind of historical detail. These things attracted my mind as had the history courses at the Gymnasium and the university. I think that I had at least the uncrystallized sense of the understanding that history and literature were not leakproof and entirely separate categories. And so this relationship began to interest me long before I realized that history is more than an academic discipline, that it is a form of thought.

Then I read Huizinga and Macaulay and even Spengler; and some of the great Hungarian historians. Yet few writers impressed me as did the extraordinary Hungarian writer Gyula Krúdy. He is still, for me, the most magical, if not the greatest, of all prose writers of the last one hundred years. I read him with an avid appetite, not only because of the magical resonances of his own, often archaic language; not only because of his deeply Hungarian and impressionist style, but because of the rich fullness of historical details of every kind, including his magisterial throwaway descriptions of houses, towns, scenes and places: of how people looked, dressed, ate, drank, aspired and desired in a Hungary not so long ago, yet in a way long ago. In addition, Krúdy's subdued, cello-like evocations of a then sunken, yet still visibly and palpably imaginable world corresponded with the kind of nostalgia that I wrote about a few pages earlier. For among other dualities in his character, Krúdy, that otherwise bohemian figure, was suffused with a beautiful nostalgia for the older Magyar patrician ways of life, for the Hungarian Biedermeier, of the historical period for which I have an aching longing even now, in Hungary as well as elsewhere: for the houses and the gardens, the people, the interiors and the landscapes after 1810, breathing, I wrote thirty years later, "a kind of comfort to which we instantly respond because, to some extent, they are still familiar and comprehensible for us. How curious this is!"

At the end of the Modern Age millions of people become attracted to bourgeois things. Certain bourgeois scenes have now become idyllic to our minds. This would have surprised the Romantics: they would have revolted against the very notion of it. And yet it was they, the Romantics, who, having made a breakthrough in the direction of consciousness, provided for the development of this rich and still interiority, all of their aristocratic and neo-medieval [and often reactionary] pretensions notwithstanding. The bourgeois were once the deadly enemies of the Romantics. Or, rather, they only seemed to be. Now we know that the Romantics were bourgeois, and that the bourgeois were Romantics, to a considerable extent, far more than we (and, of course, than they themselves) were accustomed to think. These are not abstract or literary speculations: we can understand them historically. The zenith of Romanticism was the period around 1820. That was the beginning of the bourgeois Zenith, of the Modern Age, too, before the enormous smoky swelling of cities, before the revolutions of 1848, before even in eastern America Jacksonian democracy set in. Characteristic of the architecture and of the furniture before the 1830s was a kind of patrician, rather than aristocratic, elegance, something that evokes in us a real nostalgia: for we could live in those rooms ourselves, unlike in the glittering, coldly magnificent rooms of the eighteenth century. . . . The idyllic component is real, not merely Arcadian. Perhaps this interior stillness reflected a momentary state of high equilibrium, the peak achievement of an age. The spirit, even more than the style, of bourgeois interiority suffused the landscape, and it penetrated the minds of millions even in countries and places where a bourgeois class hardly existed at all.*

The Passing of the Modern Age (1970), p. 202.

It was thus that, at the age of twenty, while engaged in certain history courses at the university, I began to realize the direction of my vocation. I read the Goncourts' diaries with as much interest as I read Aulard or Michelet, and Fontane or *Buddenbrooks* with as much interest as Friedjung or Srbik. By then I knew not only how history and life consisted of continuity and change, and not only how Budapest in 1943 was different from Budapest in 1938; I also understood and knew at least a fair amount of how the Budapest of 1910 differed from the Budapest of 1905. During the siege of the city in December 1944 I lived in a cellar, huddled, hungry and fearful, a soldier absent without leave, a fugitive from instant sentences of death. Thoughtful memoirists of prisons and concentration camps have described how mental appetites do not fade even in extreme conditions, how the life of the mind wants nourishment as well as the life of the body. I remember how my mind was attracted to the past even more than to the prospects of a future at that time. I remember how amidst that misery it was exhilarating to ruminate and even talk about some things of the past, how my mental appetite was drawn to what Burckhardt once described as the essence of historical understanding: a high qualitative sense or feeling, *ein hohes Qualitätsgefühl.* Or, as my other great master, Huizinga, wrote: the kind of sensation that may be inspired by some historical detail (or a print, a pamphlet, an old legal document) is not necessarily or purely esthetic. "A feeling of immediate contact with the past is a sensation as deep as the purest enjoyment of art; it is an almost ecstatic sensation of no longer being myself, of overflowing into the world around me, of touching the essence of things, of through history experiencing the truth." Or: "There is in our historical consciousness an element of great importance that is best defined by the term historical sensation. One might also call it historical contact. . . . This contact with the past, a contact which it is impossible to determine or analyze completely, is like going into another sphere; it is one of the many ways given to man to reach beyond himself, to experience truth. The object of this feeling is not people as individuals nor human life or human thoughts. It is hardly an image which our mind forms. . . . If it takes on a form at all this remains composite and vague: a sense [an *Ahnung*] of streets, houses, fields as well as sounds, colors or people moving. . . . There is in this manner of contact with the past the absolute conviction of reality and truth. . . . The historic sensation is not the sensation of living the past again but of understanding the world [perhaps] as one does when listening to music . . ."*

We did not engage in profound philosophical discussions in that cellar. But I recall when an older friend of my family, hiding with us in that sublunary gloom, asked me what I planned to do after the siege was over, after the war would be over, I said that I didn't really know; yet, as our talk went on, I said something about my interest in history; and, more and more intoxicated by the talk, I said that I wanted to write history, and a history of a new kind, the kind of history when the writer knows, in the marrow of his bones, not only that France in 1789 became different from France in 1788, but how, say, Paris in 1905 differed from Paris in 1902; a new kind of history that would be a combination, indeed, that would transcend a combination of Balzac and Michelet, of Flaubert and Fustel, of Mann and Friedjung, of Krúdy and Szekfü.

Someone once wrote that a novel has to have shape but life doesn't have any. Perhaps not. But history does. As a matter of fact, all we see are its big, rough shapes. And to fill out those shapes . . . to draw attention to those shapes . . . and to redraw and repaint the terrible beauties of those shapes . . . I began to see that as my task.

---

*And Professor E. H. Kossmann, the editor of the paper of the Huizinga Conference at Groningen (at the centenary of his birth, in 1972), then says: "I find it difficult to understand what exactly Huizinga was trying to describe in these passages." I don't. But I must give Kossmann credit when, a few lines later, he writes "that [Huizinga's] description of the historical sensation never takes the form of an apology for subjectivity. Huizinga dreaded and despised subjectivism as one of the most dangerous elements in cultural decline. For him the historical sensation represented a fundamental quality of the human mind, enabling it to surpass its own subjectivity and to reach a level of understanding where subject and object are undivided." Much of my life work has been devoted to an exposition of this fundamental quality, particularly in my *Historical Consciousness*.

"Genius," Ortega y Gasset once wrote, "is the ability to invent one's own occupation." I have recognized that occupation, without being able to invent it (save for a few scattered examples, here and there).

I have not departed from this aspiration during my life, even though I have not achieved it and I doubt whether I ever will. But my conviction that this is where the future of history and perhaps of *all* literature now lies became stronger and more definite every passing year—the recognition that history is more than the recorded past; that Clio has become the Muse of other Muses; that history has yet to produce its Dante, its Shakespeare; that the future is the past; and that this is something different, more truthful and forward-looking than nostalgia.

"The beginning and the end of all literary activity," Goethe said, "is the reproduction of the world that surrounds me by means of the world that is in me." That is certainly true. We experience the world from the inside out as well as from the outside in; and there is more to seeing than what meets the eye. But Goethe wrote "literary activity." The writing of history is surely a literary activity; but Goethe's statement (and he did *not* yet know that in his time) applies to the study and to the consciousness of history as well. That consciousness has made me a historian and not a novelist; and my conviction of the increasing presence of that consciousness (a presence of which still very few people are consciously aware, including those who are actually driven by it in their writing) led me decades ago not only to the exposition of it in *Historical Consciousness* but to a search for a few new ways of writing history. But it was not long ago that I ran across a very relevant passage in a book that I had read before, Antal Szerb's *Magyar irodalomtörtenet* (*History of Magyar Literature*). In his Introduction, in 1934, Szerb wrote, among other things: ". . . The new science of psychology is still in its infancy, so much so that for an auxiliary science it is nearly useless. In that field the writer of literary history remains alone, bereft of assistance; what he may try could be, at best, an attempt toward a new kind of science that would consist of the study of the historical developments of spiritual and mental structures; perhaps one day that will be called spiritual history—that is, once it appears."

That is—perhaps—what I have tried to do, here and there, many years before I ran across Szerb's startling and wonderful passage. In any event, this is different from the current, and faintly fashionable, historical study of *mentalités*. In their professional elaborations of a scientific historical methodology, French historians have often been wrong in this century. Yet, as so often happens, it is an anonymous aphorism, expressed in their incomparable language, that sums up my convictions: *Ce qu'il y a de plus vivant dans le présent, c'est le passé*—What is most alive in the present is the past. A very different writer, James Baldwin, said the same thing: "I think that the past is all that makes the present coherent."

CHAPTER 2

Love and War

HERE IS A SKETCH of a place in the middle of the Second World War in the middle of Europe and myself in the middle of it. The place is a lakeside resort in Hungary, the time August 1943, the subject this writer as a young dog. Love at first sight has just occurred. He has dared (after some trepidation) to ask a beautiful woman, sitting at a table across a terrace with her duenna-like mother, to dance. She agreed. Then they danced again. He did not get her name right at first; but then she gave him her telephone number in the city, 364-005, which he cannot forget. Even now.

There is a dry, gold-dusted quality to the color of Hungarian August afternoons. The vineyards and the lake were shimmering around us. At six in the afternoon the sun was still high in the sky, but that *thé dansant* was shaded and cool under the awnings of that garden restaurant. There were the sounds of those awnings peaceably flapping in the breeze from the lake, the occasional tinkle of tableware and glass, the soft crunch of walking feet on the gravel outside and the dance music of the trio inside, many American tunes, of the "Begin the Beguine" kind. When I left that terrace with my head and heart aflame, the gypsy musicians were ambling in, setting up their stringed instruments for the dinner music; from the restaurant kitchen came the clanging of dishes and a faint smell of consommé.

Such was the customary sequence of summertime, in a summer

place, in Hungary, in times of peace. But this was a time of war. Two hundred, three hundred miles away entire portions of German cities, entire Russian villages, Balkan forests, Sicilian groves, crematoria in Poland were burning. A decimated Hungarian army was retreating across the Ukraine. Yet we in the middle of Hungary lived as if on an odd island of relative peace. We had our share of war-related hopes. Mussolini had just abdicated. Sometime soon the war would be over. Whether its fires would reach us we did not know. We did not think much about it; not I, on my magically successful summer afternoon.

During the two years that followed—from the surrender of Italy to the surrender of Germany—came the German occupation of Hungary, the bombing of Budapest, a short-lived but at that time interminable terror of a regime of Nazified criminals, the deportation and the extermination of most Hungarian Jews, the destruction of my native city during a long and horrible siege, the barbarian flood of Russian armies and the hopeless end of the war. During those two years I progressed from being a spoiled stripling of a university student to a proscribed member of a forced labor batallion and then a soldier and then a hunted renegade and then an underground escapee and then an undernourished reactionary; from a life on sunny terraces and houses to a dark, cold cellar and then to an apartment in ruins without light and heat. During these two years my love flamed and died. Like the war.

So in August 1943, at the age of nineteen, I had fallen in love, perhaps for the third or fourth time in my young life. I know that "falling in love" is almost outdated now. The phrase harks back to the sentimentalities of the eighteenth century, when love was seen as a sudden event coming from the outside, a delicious illness, an affliction, the heart being wounded by the arrow of an Amor or a Cupid. It was then that the président Des Brosses, traveling in Italy, was charmed when, calling on a lady in Rome, his card was returned by her maid, who told him regretfully that milady could not receive him: "*la Signora è inamorata,*" she was ailing from having fallen in love. Less than a century later Stendhal found the metaphor of "crystallization," a reactive process in a lover's mind. Another century and a half later I feel compelled to write that, yes, I fell in love because I involved myself in it, and consciously so. (Like materialism, the obsession with the subconscious should have made sense in the eighteenth, not in the twentieth century; but that is another story.)

The correspondent in this involvement, the object of my passionate desire, was a married woman, twelve years older than I, with two children, living with her decent and fairly unhappy Hungarian husband (I suspect unhappy because unknowing, rather than the reverse) and her German mother, who knew when to keep her eyes and ears closed. K. was half-Prussian, incredibly beautiful, with the only physical flaw of slightly imperfect legs and baby-like hands. This love affair was the high graduate seminar of my sentimental education, compared to which Flaubert's story of Frédéric's love for Madame Arnaud in *Sentimental Education* was purely elementary. It was then I found that not only love but sexuality, too, is an abstraction when considered independent of the historical and social situation of the lovers. Their idea of finding themselves on an island that is entirely theirs while the waves of the world are lapping outside is an absolute illusion. That "situation" of the outside world is connected with the essence of their minds; and the flora and the fauna of their imaginary island are not only threatened by the wind and sea, they are sodden with their waters. Because perspective is an inevitable component of reality, the historical condition of lovers is an inevitable component of their passion—"inevitable" in the human sense, meaning that it may be transcended but only by their conscious knowing of it.

I write of my passionate desire for this woman, but perhaps desirable passion would be more accurate. In *De l'Amour* Stendhal wrote brilliantly about vanity-love and passion-love; I am inclined to believe that these two variants are seldom separable. I was desirous of a grand passion throughout my youth. That women are interested in men even more than in sex contains a great deal of truth, which sometimes applies to men, too; and what could be more desirable than a passionate romantic love accepted and shared by a beautiful and worldly woman of thirty-one? Had that same beautiful face and body belonged to a peasant girl or to the erring wife of a bus driver my carnal desires would have been aroused the same, but there would have been no such passion, no such love. The commingling of my vanity-love and passion-love for her included not only my callow pride in having such an affair with such a woman (I talked about her shamelessly to my friends), but my appreciation of her scents, her furs, her fashions, her aspirations, her intellectual and physical preferences and her voice—matters that were not always attractive. Perhaps the condition that she was Prussian-German falls into that category, too: had she been French or Norwegian or English my vanity-passion would have been more ideal. She was not a Nazi but German enough, which, as also the tinny timbre of her voice, her odd amorality and her sentimentalities, provided the ground for occasional misunderstandings, at times reductive and at other times additive to the heat of my passion. But all of this occurred on the level of my conscious and not unconscious mind. My passion was created out of my consciousness. I was pulled by the purpose of my aspirations, by my desire for a love affair, and not pushed by some dumb subterranean biological force or psychological motive. The entire affair belongs not to my psychoanalysis but to my personal history, including—yes, *including*, in a miraculous way that transcends the "laws" of space— the history of the outside world that was enveloping both of us. My desire was a period piece; it belongs to the history of a period.

To understand this is easier than to know it, and to know it is easier than to write about it. It is easier to write a first-rate novel than a first-rate history, but it is easier to write a mediocre history than a mediocre novel. This love affair had episodes whose inclusion would be too much for a decent novel. Here are three of them.

In early June 1944 I was a prisoner: not in jail but in a barrack guarded by soldiers on the outskirts of Budapest: a member of a forced labor battalion of undesirables—subversives, resistants, half-Jews, suspicious people. When we were marched out of the compound, collectively or individually, we had to go between armed guards. But this was my native city, and an exceptional country. My father, who had been a highly decorated officer in the First World War, had his military connections. I was suffering from a bad rash, a kind of allergy from the dirty, dusty straw on which we slept. He had arranged for me to present myself at a military hospital once a week for treatment. I was taken there by an elderly corporal who carried a bayoneted rifle. Having deposited me in the waiting room he went off on his own for the day. After my calcium injection I, too, walked out through a side door to the nearest trolley stop and went home, to spend a few splendid hours with my family, with their friends, in the tub and in clean linens and at the dinner table, until five in the afternoon, when I had to return to that military hospital to meet up with my escort, having put on my dirty tunic and the hated white armband. These weekly excursions from squalor to luxury were wonderful, but I was in love, too. On the third occasion of my absence-without-leave I dressed in my best summer suit and told my mother that I wouldn't be staying home that day. She was not happy; she knew where I was going—to that woman. I had telephoned K. She was alone. I took a taxi. It was an incredible day. At ten in the morning the city glistened under a glorious sun; the bridges and the bend of the Danube were bathed in a pearly halo. Along the avenues of Buda the almond trees were in full bloom. The garden of their house was heavy with the smell of apricots. She opened the door. She wore a black negligée; she was barefoot, with her toenails freshly painted. "You heard the news?" she said. "They landed in France this morning." It was D-Day.

Four weeks later I was in the anteroom of death. It was the second of July, a Sunday. The Fifteenth United States Air Force gave us a heavy bombing. The bombers laid down "carpets"—that is, aiming for a target, they would plaster an entire rectangle with bombs. One of these was railyards, not far from our barrack. The bombers were not accurate: the edge of the "carpet" moved over us. We were shaking and trembling in a cellar while the buildings shook and trembled above us; our noses were full with the awful dust and smell of pulverized brick. Suddenly we were ordered out. An officer shouted: "Go and dig out your friends!" A bomb had exploded in a house, perhaps half a mile away, where the remaining British and American citizens in Hungary, about a hundred and fifty, were interned. There was nothing left of the house. From a mound of stone and cement and brick we dug. Perhaps ten of the hundred and fifty were pulled out alive. I tugged on a leg of a woman, silk-stockinged and still warm; she was dead. It was beastly hot; the brilliant blue sky over Budapest was besmirched by huge black clouds; the bombers had hit oil tanks and water mains; there was no water. Once I had steadied my right arm on a piece of brick a piece of human brain stuck to my palm. In the early evening we were marched back to the compound, filthy and shaken. One of my friends was shot by a sadistic guard: he had taken a rest, he had not worked fast enough. By nine in the evening most of us were asleep in the reek of dust and dirt. Suddenly the corporal who had been the silent accomplice of my weekly vacations called my name. His voice was unusually harsh. He pushed me through a door. I was half asleep but now half awake with anxiety. The door closed behind me. I was out in the open, under the night sky, three yards or so from an ancient paling about four feet high. On the other side of that fence stood my love. She had heard that this part of the city was bombed. She had taken a taxi, drove here across the town and bribed a guard. She was dressed in black because of the family custom of mourning, one of her husband's uncles having died the week before. Her blond hair shone in the moonlight; she was scented with the perfume I had given her some time ago, "Shalimar." We had five minutes under the stars, across the fence; we could only hold each other's heads while we kissed.

The third episode: the morning of Christmas Day, 1944. The siege of Budapest had begun. I was a deserter (so were perhaps thirty thousand others) from the Hungarian army, living in a cellar with my family, waiting for the Russians. On the night before Christmas their army moved into the Buda hills, somewhere around the district where K. lived. All electricity was gone and, worse, water too. I tried the telephone, and to my surprise and joy it still worked. For many months now, telephoning had been a gamble: more often than not one could not get a dial tone; even more often there was nothing but a faint diabolical hum after the dialing. I dialed; and my heart jumped. It rang once; and she answered. She said that the Russians had been there since the early morning. How do they *look?* I asked. She started to tell me, then she decided that she'd better hang up. The German and the Hungarian military evidently forgot to cut the telephone lines off. So one could still telephone across a world war, across the front where the two greatest armies of the world were fighting down each street, sometimes shooting it out from building to building, floor to floor. By noon the telephone was dead.

It was two months before I saw her again. Another three months and the war was over, at least in Europe. During that war I made what I still think is an important discovery: that the relations of nations repeat, in many ways, the relations of people. Something like this discovery had been made, of course, by Hegel, who wrote that the State is indeed Man writ large: "macroanthropos." I had not read Hegel then, but Hegel (and Marx) did not really comprehend the difference between states and nations. *Mutatis mutandis,* Hitler and Goebbels believed, too, that the world war they had begun in 1939 merely repeated, on a larger scale, the struggle they had fought and won in Germany before 1933. Then one National Socialist had been worth two Communists or three Social Democrats in the streets and beer halls; and now one German soldier was worth at least two Russian soldiers or three French ones. This was a half-truth powerful enough to bring Hitler close to victory, but no further. Years later I ran across a fragment by Proust, written during the First World War, that was more than a half-truth, and I wrote it down with an eager hand. "The life of a nation," Proust wrote, "merely repeats, on a larger scale, the lives of their component cells; and he who is incapable of understanding the mystery, the reactions, the laws that determine the movements of the individual, can never hope to say anything worth listening to about the struggles of nations." That was exactly what I saw during the war and from my reading of history thereafter: that essence of the relations between nations which, in any event, is utterly different from the fraudulent "discipline" pompously and imprecisely named International Relations.

In early April 1944 American and British planes bombed Budapest for the first time. There was before an unwritten and unspoken agreement between the Hungarian regime and the Western Allies to the effect that Hungary, even though en route to southeastern German and Austrian targets from the Allied airfields in southern Italy, would not be attacked. But on March 19, 1944, a dreadful Sunday morning, the Germans suddenly occupied Budapest. They had information about the attempts of the Prime Minister to extricate Hungary somehow from its German alliance. Now Hitler forced the Regent to install a thoroughly pro-German and even pro-Nazi administration, after which the full force of the war broke over Hungary in an increasingly furious, condensed way. That Allied bombing was the first taste of this, with hundreds of dead in the industrial suburbs. Yet the headline of one of the pro-Nazi newspapers next day shouted: WE WERE BOMBED!, trumpeting this joyously, together with the expectably indignant maledictions of the "Anglo-American-Jewish war criminals." There was an evident element of relief, and even a touch of delectable joy, in that headline and in the tone of these editors and writers to the effect that their nation had, finally, become a worthy ally of Hitler's Germany, bloodied by the Anglo-Saxons. For these people, to be bombed was evidently preferable to not being bombed at all.

What attracts certain people to each other is the essence of human relationships, including that of nations. That essence is deeper than sex, but there is a sexual element within it.* (This is probably why

---

*Here is a crude example of something that happened nearly forty years later, in the Falkland war. That war had nothing to do with economics, or even with strategy—nothing. (It had everything to do with national pride.) The British outfought the Argentinians, for all kinds of reasons, in which we must include the fact that the Argentinians lied shamelessly, deceiving their people and deceiving themselves, throughout the war. The superiority of the British was latent in the better quality of their rhetoric from the beginning, but this was not merely a stylistic or esthetic difference; it was a reflection of different kinds of self-discipline and, therefore, of *morale.* Besides the repellent Argentinian habit to blame others for their defeat (in this case, the United States), there was

friendship between men and women is precious because it is rare, being seldom altogether asexual; while sexual relations, unlike friendship, often have at least a small tinge of enmity within them— but then, alas, this is part of their attraction and sometimes even of their charm.) Had I not been involved in my sentimental education I think I would have understood less about the relations of nations. I write sentimental, rather than sexual education, since my relation with the woman I loved involved, in essence, our minds; what we did with each other's bodies was consequent to what was going on in our minds. Love, as Pascal said, is not really blind. Our carnal relations were deeply satisfactory, in spite—or, perhaps, because— of the condition (condition, not fact) that my lover was frigid, or nearly so; but that relative frigidity, too, was both less and more than a biological malfunction; it was involved with other matters within her personality, sentimentally moral and cruelly amoral on occasion. Around that time I read a sentence by Esmé Wingfield-Stratford about Disraeli that echoed in my mind: "He loved England! though not quite in the English way." Well, K. may have been frigid or half-frigid, in the German way. In any case, this curious and profound relationship of nationality and sexuality, of culture and biology, of mind and matter is something that few writers (and no historians) have attempted to describe or even to probe, though a few years ago I ran across a passage by Jean Rhys in *Good Morning, Midnight,* touching on it. A gigolo, talking to her in Paris, was setting out for England, expecting conquest after conquest of untouched and unsatisfied Englishwomen, "just gasping for it, oh boy!" "That's his big idea. But he'll find out that he will be up against racial, not sexual characteristics"—something that (of course) neither Marx nor Freud, nor perhaps even Henry James

---

another factor. Watching the television news in the early days of the war I saw a young beefy *porteño* buck for a moment, talking into the microphone put before him by an American newsman who had asked him why Argentinians wanted the Falklands. "Are nice big gerls there," he said. "Arhentine men, British gerls, we make good breeding." It was as good an explanation of the Argentine national passion as any; but it takes two to tango, and for Mrs. Thatcher breeding as well as tangoing with them was unthinkable.

or Evelyn Waugh had properly understood: a matter whereof a profound and moving description must remain the task of a genius in the future.

War is less predictable than love, but they have essentials in common. Napoleon must have recognized this when he said, in a cruel quip, that war and prostitution are the only professions in which amateurs are sometimes better than professionals. The behavior of a soldier in battle depends on two entangled matters: on his will to carry on, and on his will to live, matters whereof the progress and the resolution are not necessarily parallel. Napoleon said that an army marches on its stomach, but he also said that the morale of an army matters about thrice as much as its equipment; and the second statement sounds truer than the first.

In 1813 Stendhal watched the battle of Bautzen from a hill: "From noon until three o'clock we had an excellent view of all that can be seen of a battle—that is, nothing at all." (His description of the battle of Waterloo in *The Charterhouse of Parma* is much better than Victor Hugo's because it is more realistic: one long chapter of confusion.) One hundred and thirty years later I watched the Second World War, not from a hill but from the middle of Europe and with the aid not of field glasses but of a radio equipped with a shortwave band. This war, Hitler's war, was different from Napoleon's. For millions of people in Europe the mental earthquake was greater than the physical one. They had to adjust their minds to circumstances, which was true of fewer people in Napoleon's time. In 1812 there were millions of people, including large masses of Russian peasants and even some French peasants in the depths of France, who had never heard the name of Napoleon. In 1943 everyone knew the name of Hitler. During this war I saw protean evidences of what I am wont to call the mental intrusion into the structure of events—in other words, the inseparability of what happens from what people think happens. Among other things, I saw this in the few instances when I was close to actual battle, before and during the siege of Budapest. That was a fifty-day siege of a city without walls. Military historians write of "hand-to-hand fighting" till this day. Yet in reality even the frontline infantryman seldom saw enemy soldiers. This was due to the technical improvement of weapons in the twentieth century—together with other wonders of applied science whereby, for example, the extermination of millions of Jews was made possible with very few Germans (including even the SS guards) actually seeing what was going on in the gas chambers, even though it took hundreds of policemen, engine drivers, trainmen, etc., to expedite the process. Had Napoleon given orders to a French regiment to kill all the men, women, children and old people in a conquered town, his officers and soldiers would not have believed it. They would have resisted for all kinds of reasons, one of them being that to execute such an order would have been physically impossible: after an hour of muzzle-loading and firing rifles and bayoneting people the regiment would have been dog-tired, demanding rest. During the 1950s in the United States I met a Hungarian refugee scientist who told me proudly what an important military job he had had during the war. Where? I asked. In Washington, he said, where he had served as Target Selector for the operations of the Army Air Forces involving Hungary. He must have grease-penciled the map of Budapest between two trips to the Pentagon cafeteria or to the water cooler. That this meant destruction and the death of thousands did not seem to have preoccupied his mind. I did not much blame him for this: in order to win the war against Hitler, the cities of Hitler's allies had to be bombed. What disgusted me was that this man had chosen to become a pronounced professional anti-Communist and a proponent of nuclear weapons, conveniently forgetful of the fact that less than ten years earlier his job was meant not only to facilitate the defeat of Hitler but the conquest of Hungary by the Red Army.

The war was a war of minds, in all kinds of ways. This does not mean that the propaganda of the war was decisive; often the contrary was true. It did not mean that the war was decided by ideology, that ultimately the ideas of Democracy and Communism triumphed over the ideologies of Nazism and Fascism. As Jean Dutourd once wrote, the pen *is* mightier than the sword; but philosophy will *not* stop a bullet. The popularity of Fascism disappeared with Mussolini; the popular appeal of Nazism died with Hitler. Had Hitler conquered Russia in 1941 there would be few Communists in the world today. The war was a war of minds because people—all kinds of people—were thinking about what was happening around them and in the world at large: they adjusted their ideas to circumstances, which is much easier than adjusting circumstances to one's ideas. The brave and individual exceptions notwithstanding, resistance did not really begin to be effective in Western Europe until more and more people were convinced that the Germans were losing the war. Instinctive opportunism was even more evident in Eastern Europe and Russia, where partisan warfare against the Germans began to spread after Stalingrad, when many a German grenadier was picked off by the same Cossack or Ukrainian sniper who had helped the Germans in rounding up Jews a year or two before. In May 1940, when Mussolini was getting up to war, while the British and the French were reeling in defeat, many Italians were not altogether happy about this. Some told their remaining English and French acquaintances in Rome: come on, bring us just *one* little victory, *una piccola vittoria,* it might do the trick. *Una vittoria:* Hitler was aware of that. He knew in December 1944 that, even if successful, his last desperate offensive in the Ardennes would not drive the Anglo-Americans out of Europe. What he hoped was that a hard defeat and painful losses of the American armies might weaken the resolution of the American people: they would think twice whether to support Roosevelt in order to carry on the war for more years, all the way to Berlin. When toward the end Goebbels and Ribbentrop implored Hitler to try to get into contact with Stalin, he said that this would be useless unless the German armies scored one decisive victory in the field. Compared to the movements of the armies, propaganda was not very effective. I found the comparison of the military communiqués of the warring nations instructive. The Germans exaggerated more than the British, the Russians more than the Germans, and the Japanese war communiqués were the furthest removed from reality—perhaps because of different ethics of rhetoric, including the diminishing habit of the public admission of unpleasant things as one moves from West to

East. Of all the radio news programs the BBC's were the most respected because of their relative truthfulness.

There was an amazing coexistence of continuity and change, even during some of the most extraordinary conditions, a coexistence evident not only in certain material situations but in the minds of people. On the one hand, people would adjust their minds to changing conditions with great subtlety and speed; on the other hand, habit and momentum and lassitude prevailed, often amazingly so. One example of this was the effect of bombing on large populations. Before 1939 all kinds of books, military as well as popular, described the decisive and swift results of air bombardment in the coming war. The opposite happened. "Strategic" bombing— that is, the massive bombardment of the industries of the enemy— was largely ineffective; and when the exasperated strategists gradually changed over to area bombing, to the destruction of cities in order to break the spirit of their populations, that was largely ineffective, too. The ability to restore the functioning of industries and municipal services asserted itself: for the modern capacity of destruction will be equaled by the capacity of reconstruction, as long as the mental impetus for such a reconstruction exists. The massive bombing of the cities did not break the spirit of the people. Neither did it make them rebellious; rather the contrary. Unlike slabs of meat, the pounding of people often made them tougher and not more tender. They went on with their daily lives, doggedly and often unthinkingly: they had enough immediate problems to occupy them.

When I insist upon the human capacity of adjusting one's mind to circumstances I do not refer only to opportunists. During the war I was often startled to see how people went on with their daily lives and self-imposed tasks a few hours after their accustomed conditions had been turned upside down. A relative of ours, an old woman, always dressed in rusty black, walking her dog every day in the park, sitting and ruminating in her stuffy small apartment amidst her lace runners and bibelots; at a sunny two o'clock her apartment was destroyed by a bomb. That evening came another air raid; again she had to descend to the cellar. Her dress, her bearing, her facial expression were unchanged. I do not want to give the impression that here was a rare heroine of cool bravery; instead, a kind of female fatalism seems to have settled on her, like the mist of masonry dust on a city after its bombardment. She had some canned food in her pantry. "I'll have to go upstairs and find those conserves," she said in that cellar, thinking how after the All-Clear she would have to wend her way among those ruins, in the same voice and, I think, with the same kind of tired resolution as if she had been sitting in her armchair in her room, thinking that she ought to get up and walk to the pantry in order to cope with a change of her plans for dinner.

To all kinds of people endowed with moderate intelligence a great advantage accrues in a world of censorship and dictatorship and war: the honing of their mental ability to distinguish between what is significant and what is important. "Significant" and "important": the first suggesting quality, the second quantity—the difference between the Pascalian and the Cartesian views of the world. On a big surface a small crack may be unimportant, but it can be significant. Significance suggests the potentiality that is inherent in every actuality, perhaps especially in human actuality; it is a tendency, not a category: the evidence of something that may eventually become important. Because of this, people acquired the ability of reading between the lines of newspapers, without anyone teaching or showing them how this is done. As the great historian Jakob Burckhardt told his students in Basel more than a century ago, there is perhaps only one thing that the student of history must do: *bisogna saper leggere*, he must know *how* to read. Thus the appearance of a favorable review of a book by a politically unfashionable belletrist (or the reverse), the casting of an actress of noted liberal persuasions (or with a Jewish husband) in one of the national theatres, publicity given to a civil lawsuit against a notorious Germanophile publicist, a subtle change of the phraseology in the reporting of a routine appointment or event were matters that many readers would detect immediately. Sometimes they were printed in certain newspapers with that purpose in mind. Of course this was not very different from what happens under whatever despotism, as when the Kremlinologist commentators watch and draw conclusions (often wrong ones) from what Politburo member appears when and where on the parade stand or on Soviet posters; and I am inclined to think that on a level even more mundane than *The Memoirs of Saint-Simon* the collectors of significant royal gestures in the halls of Versailles must have been at it with the energy of cockchafers. The difference was perhaps that during the Second World War people such as I were attuned to such driblets or nuggets of significance on all kinds of levels: I could draw certain conclusions about the importance (and the possible consequences) of an event from the way it was announced on the radio, including the diction and the tone of the announcer.

Like every kind of appetite, this kind of mental interest is not aseptic or objective; yet this kind of interest, and its absorption by the mind, go counter to the "laws" of the physical world. Like true love: when we love someone we want to love her or him more and more; when we are interested in something we want to know more and more about it. When a material vessel, or a human stomach, is full, one cannot add any more to it; but the human mind will absorb additional knowledge quicker and more easily when it is filled than when it is empty—as long as the slightest bit of imagination remains. What I did not know then was that imagination has its own history, part and parcel of the evolving historicity of our consciousness, which is probably the only kind of evolution there is, and perhaps—*contra* Darwin—the only kind of evolution worth thinking and talking about.

One night in August 1944—I was a soldier then, the lowest rank assigned to an anti-aircraft battery—the sudden thought came to me that perhaps everywhere in our world logic exists on three levels. There was the inevitable logic of things: that two times two amounts to four, and that the spring bolt that I had to affix to the empty nut on the flank of the recoil box either fitted that nut exactly or it didn't (which happened to be the case), whereby the entire recoil mechanism could not function. This kind of reality corresponded to the other, well-nigh inevitable condition that Hitler and

his allies could not win the war against Russia, the United States
and Great Britain, with their hundreds of millions, producing and
possessing fifty guns for each German one. And this was the kind
of inevitable, dumb hardness of things, the natural order of the
physical universe that determined, or at least circumscribed, the
most complex and sentimental human relationships, too (I was
aching for my lover and worried about her: we had not seen each
other for a week or so and I tormented myself sometimes with
thoughts of jealousy); wasn't it true that without our ordinarily
functioning sexual organs all of this lovely affair would not have
amounted to anything? There was, however, a higher kind of non-
material and sentimental logic: the young lieutenant of the battery
liked me (partly because of our shared anti-Nazi sympathies and
Anglophile illusions), wherefore he, unlike another gunner sergeant or officer, would not curse and blame me for not having the
proper spring bolt at hand; and since he knew the ineffectiveness,
at best, of our small-caliber gun—and, even more, the stupidity of
Hungary's waging war against the Allies—he did not much care for
that spring bolt. It was, after all, human beings who had invented
mathematics, and science that led to the invention of spring bolts
and guns; and what mattered was what they would do with them.
And so Hitler was bound to be defeated not merely because of the
mechanical and numerical superiority of his opponents; he would
lose the war because he had turned so many people of the world
against him. So, too, after all of these tormenting thoughts, our
sexual organs were not the matter that had driven K. and me
together (no, monsieur Rémy de Gourmont, there is something else
than the contact of two epidermises); there were all kinds of matters,
on another level, to which the very functioning of our organs, and
perhaps even of our physical desires, were subordinate. And there
existed yet a higher level that was not given to human beings to
know, but about which they could glimpse something on occasion:
that this world was full of awful injustices and sins, but that somehow and somewhere it was given to us to comprehend (comprehend, rather than know) certain divine verities that would assert
themselves, though, alas, only in the long run. Millions were killed;

millions were yet to be killed; but Hitler would lose the war. We ourselves might die; one day we will die. Long before that our love affair would end, for all kinds of reasons, including our heavy but, still, so intoxicating load of sin. I write down these fairly juvenile cerebrations; yet I do not even now think that they were entirely meaningless.

During that month of August 1944 I was confronted with a startling example of the wishfulness of thinking: with an example not only of the inseparability of what happens from what people think happens, but also of the condition that what people think is so often inseparable from what they want to think. I was at home, on half-a-day's leave, when a Hungarian general staff officer, a friend of our family, was visiting us. He was pro-German. He said that he had just returned from western Hungary, where the Germans had demonstrated one of their new miracle weapons to a Hungarian staff. American bombers flew overhead; the Germans got busy with a box-like device; they aimed a complex assembly of mirrors skyward, pushed buttons, and the bombers burst into flames in an instant. It was a Death Ray. For a moment my mother and I, anti-Germans, were startled and frightened. Then we knew: this could not be true, as indeed it was not. What was extraordinary about this was that our friend was a decent man. I have been thinking about this episode ever since. He had invented it all. What is that astonishing alchemy of the human mind that produces inventions such as this? He did not only wish to deceive us; he obviously wished to deceive himself—a case in which, for once, the *why* may be more evident, and less complicated, than the *how*.

Toward the end of the war the unwillingness to think among my countrymen assumed newer forms. Half a million of them threw in their lot with the Germans by joining them in their retreat to Germany, in part because they were willing to believe the worst about the Russians, in part because they were still unwilling to admit that Germany could lose the war. Other millions, such as I, simply refused to think that the German propaganda about the Russians might actually be true: I, for one, preferred to think that the very fact of Stalin's alliance with Churchill and Roosevelt showed that Russia had become a responsible and circumspect power. In any event, education and communications contributed, rather than reduced, this massive unwillingness of minds. If, on the one hand, many people did not really believe what they read in the newspapers, millions of others—especially first generations of newspaper readers—did, taking sustenance and substance for their preferred beliefs from the papers that were often excruciatingly vile. In this Hitler and Goebbels were right, alas: the repetition of half-truths and phrases eventually affects the minds of millions, not only by contributing their ideas but by forming the very patterns of their thoughts, in part by way of a phraseology that, by incessant repetition, becomes an element in people's minds. If living under censorship and dictatorship sharpened the minds of people, the inflation of words and phrases surely contributed to the insubstantialization of things, including the gassiness of so many minds. There were journalists and publicists during the Second World War who produced the substance of the hatred that led to the gas chambers; or, rather, that made many ordinary people indifferent or hostile to the fate of certain victims; and these journalists were criminals perhaps worse than the bureaucratic chemists or technicians who manufactured and dispatched the canisters of gas. The generalization of lying, wrote Montaigne, is enough to dissolve society. Like Montaigne, I was not (and am not) a puritan; but it was then that I began to think that people ought to be brought to account for what they publicly say and write, and not only for what they do.

But when a nation (or a tribe, or a family, or a party) is so much riven by the different wishes and ideas of opposing camps, one may discover, here and there, the delights of incompleteness: of imprecisions, of imperfect categories of thoughts—matters that may correspond to the difference between what is important and what is significant. It was not only propitious, it was satisfying to know that the earlier described and self-convinced Germanophile officer friend of our family did not sympathize with, because he could not comprehend, the Nazis' hatred for certain people. It was pleasant to meet a German infantryman who said that his favorite German writer was Franz Werfel. And it was amusing, if sometimes exasperating, to argue with my love, who wanted Hitler to lose the war (well, at least she did not want him to win it), while she insisted that Germany had a right to a portion of Poland, or who said that she would die for her family, while a few moments later she said that a married woman could do anything she wanted. On one occasion she turned on me with unexpected anger when I—perhaps moved by sentimentalism, perhaps by compassion—said something good about her husband. I knew then that women were not illogical— rather, they had their own, instinctive, emotional logic that may be imprecise, but not because it is incomplete.

The delight of misunderstandings: it was then that I learned how communications between human beings are never perfect and complete (which is why the computerization of human communications is idiotic, in the proper and original Greek sense of the word *idiot*), because *A* never hears exactly what *B* is saying; but that incompleteness provides the very charm of their relationship (very much including that of lovers who find themselves in the delicious situation of being able to talk incessantly about themselves). A touch of a different accent, the tone of a different voice instantly involve a myriad of other associations. This is why *A* does not hear exactly what *B* is saying; why *A* may be attracted—or repelled—by *B*. Only later did I understand that here lies the charm of knowing a foreign language well enough, being able to recognize not only the particular prettiness of some of its words and sounds and expressions but also the condition that the very same word from the same root may mean something slightly different in one language from the other. (Example: *honor* in English, *honneur* in French.) That difference is both more and less than a dictionary difference; it suggests different tendencies, aspirations, nuances. My lover and I occasionally talked in French. We spoke that language somewhat imperfectly; consequently it was then that we perfectly understood each other.

Our love affair had many dramatic and laughable, lovely and sordid episodes, living on till the end of the war and then dying down in a smoldering and sodden unattractive heap of ashes. But there was this matter that I understand now and that I had not understood then: that everything human has a history, love as well as war. The Second World War was a kind of war that would not occur again; and this was the kind of love affair that would not occur again. And not only because I was growing up: this kind of passion belonged to the sensitivities of a certain time, somewhat in the way in which the flawed romantic aspirations of Emma Bovary belonged to a certain period, wherefore *Madame Bovary* is not only a better but a more *historical* novel than *War and Peace*. I am inclined to think that Flaubert did not know this (he did not have to), while I now do. Looking back at the history of Europe before 1945, reflected as it is in its letters as well as in the memories of people, I think that this was the last phase of what Mario Praz, with perhaps undue exaggeration, called The Romantic Agony: when the desire of a man for a communion with a certain woman, something for which the words *love affair* sound mundane and inadequate, was the most important aspiration in the minds of sensitive men, seeking therein a spiritual fulfillment and a mystery. I think that this kind of aspiration belonged within geographical and historical limits, within the spiritual geography and history of Europe. Men in the English-speaking world were largely devoid of it; when Scandinavians like Strindberg stumbled across it, they did so in anger and despair; it was limited to France in the west, Hungary and perhaps Poland in the east, by the North Sea and the Pyrenees and perhaps the Po valley; and its rough chronological limits were 1770 and 1945. Oddly, or perhaps not so oddly, this contemplation of women by men as if they belonged on a pedestal did not satisfy women at the time, although this romantic-sentimental treatment— perhaps the last curious flowering of chivalry—surely attracts them in retrospect.

And, if love has its history, so have imagination, and happiness, and memory. During that memorable August of 1944 I experienced, for example, a beautiful air raid. The first radio warning came in the twilight of the summer evening. I found myself in the center of Pest, knowing that I should not be able to reach my unit in time, even with the best of will; but I was heading in its direction, together with hundreds of people hurrying across the Danube bridges. The tramcars had stopped, and the last dimmed lights were going out. I mounted the hill on the other side of the Elizabeth Bridge and reported to another battery, to be sure; the officer in charge stamped my leave paper and waved me away. On the rocks and grassy slopes of the hill people were sitting or lying down: they either could not make it to their homes or found it safer to stay up on that hill, away from the sea of houses. Night had now fallen: scented, dark and starry. The great plain of Hungary stretched out beyond that sea of houses. Far to the east the first searchlights began to probe the sky, sweeping back and forth. The final warning of the sirens sounded, and from that hill it died out like a long melancholy wail. Then we heard the low droning of the Russian planes approaching from the east. In a few moments the sky was lit up with the most brilliant of man-made colors; more brilliant and fascinating, because less predictable, than any festive firework imaginable. It was not a large raid; we heard the explosions, mostly on the eastern edges of the great city, and saw the fires flaring up and dying down in fiery acid colors, yellow and red and electric blue. The anti-aircraft guns were popping and bursting without cease (and without much effect). Then we heard a great celestial swish of rushing sound, like that of an immense but shallow waterfall: the fragments of the expended anti-aircraft shells were coming down from the sky, with myriad metallic drops on the tile roofs of the houses of Budapest. I was surrounded by the presence of terrible beauty. How different it was from other air raids when I had to dig among the rubble for bodies that were still warm, with the stunning horror of the near-presence of death compounded by the sweetish odor of pulverized brick that smells like decaying flesh! How different these things are in my mind now, when I remember so much more about the beauties of that evening than about that afternoon among the dead bodies in the rubble.

During that deadly summer I learned not only that death and life are close, but that so are happiness and unhappiness: that one can find happiness amidst the most wretched circumstances, but one must look for it. It was many years later that I learned that unhappiness almost always involves an amount of self-indulgence (and despair a large sinful dose of it). To wallow in one's unhappiness—or, more exactly, in one's choice of the idea of one's happiness—is easy, while happiness requires a certain effort of organization and even of planning. Happiness, like love, is a self-imposed task. It requires forethought and cultivation, including the cultivation and the consciousness of one's imagination, which is why this task is not easy. Perhaps it is because of this that the converse is true: there are people who experience few moments of real happiness in their conscious lives, their misfortune being anchored in the muddy substance of their stupidity—but that stupidity is not intellectual; it exists not because of the inability but because of the unwillingness of their minds.

I also realized that joy was seldom separable from anticipation, which was not only one half of pleasure but the path to it. Yet by joy I do not merely mean pleasure but something akin to the acute sense of the willingness to live: the wish for more life. And when that wish dies out . . . That this realization first occurred to me amidst such extreme conditions was a blessing. Many years later I read the superb book by Viktor Frankl, whose entire therapeutic and philosophic approach to psychiatry rose out of his experiences in a death camp. Those who wanted to live tended to survive; those who gave up hope tended to die; and who were those who tended to live? they who had something to look forward to, someone to live for. Reading this in my cozy book room in Pennsylvania, twenty years after 1944, forced my memories to spring to life. I knew how right he was: because human causality is different from mechanical causality, because our lives are not only pushed by the past but pulled by the future, by our own view of the future, which is how anticipation is the spiritual stimulant of the willingness to live.

And memory—which is the other side of anticipation, of the same coin—has its history, too. I learned this from Dante or, rather, against him. We had read some Dante in school, and I recalled these lines: *"Nessun maggior dolore / Che ricordarsi al tempo felice / nella miseria"*—"There is no greater pain than to remember times of happiness when in misery." But that wasn't so. When I was a fugitive deserter, hiding in that cellar, frozen and hungry, I thought that the opposite was true. Or, rather, what Dante wrote was no longer true because the consciousness of our memory was not the same as that of a medieval Florentine seven hundred and fifty years before. What gave us pleasure in that cellar was not only thinking ahead—thinking about what we would do when the war was over and we'd be free again, well-fed and perhaps even happy. It was even more pleasant to think back, to reminisce about scenes and events of the past, associations, colors, tastes, the primary and secondary substances of which were vividly clear in our minds, having acquired especial charm in the conditions when our days had been turned into fearful nights. To think then of the past with my love filled my mind not only with longing but with an ineffable richness. To think ahead was something different; somehow I knew that after the war, when we should be able to meet freely again, things wouldn't be the same. And they weren't.

The end of this story came after the siege, well after that last telephone call across the front on Christmas morning. Gradually life began among the ruins: the ruins of a city, and of our previous lives. This love, and this war, were over. She took a new lover. There was no place for me now in her life—or, rather, not the kind of place that I would want. There was no place for me now in the "new" Hungary—or, rather, not the kind of place that I would want. I left for America. I still have her photograph in one of my drawers and the memories of love and war in my heart.

CHAPTER 3

East and West

$\mathcal{J}$N THAT CELLAR I was waiting for the Russians. I was a deserter, with false military identity papers; if I were to be found out by the National Socialists or by the field gendarmerie I could be shot or hanged on the spot. I left my unit in November. We were about to be shipped westward, eventually to Germany, together with the retreating Arrow Cross government and the army, or what was left of it. To the east of Budapest the Russians were less than forty miles away. We thought that they would march into the city in a few days. Together with my mother and a dozen relatives and friends, we moved into that cellar, a subterranean office and warehouse owned by my stepfather. But the Russians progressed very slowly. They did not besiege the city until they had surrounded it completely, after Christmas.

On the night before Christmas the first Russians moved into the western hills of the city, on the Buda side. All day we had heard the dull thudding of guns from that unaccustomed direction. The city was dark, the Danube carried the corpses of Jews who had been shot on the quays the night before; but people were still carrying small Christmas trees and packages home. After the siege my former Italian teacher told me how the turn of the tide had reached him. He lived in one of the Buda suburbs. When he got to the square where he had to change to another trolley the conductor told the passengers that he did not know how far his car would go. The trolley screeched along in the dark. One could hear the cracking of machine pistols somewhere. He got out before his stop. He decided to take a shortcut to the hilly street where he lived. Suddenly a Russian soldier moved out from the trees. He grabbed my Italian teacher's collar. The Russian put his finger to his lips. "Pssst!" he said to his captive, and let him go.

That day, December 24, 1944, my best friend and I, two fugitive deserters, issuing from that cellar, chose to lunch at the Ritz. One of the reasons for this choice was that we were hungry and there were few places open; the other was a kind of dare. The Ritz was full of all kinds of people, many of them refugees and fugitives, some of them with papers as false as ours. We had a dish of dried split-pea soup, served in the china plates of the Ritz (I can see their gold rims and blue crests now). Some of the big windows were broken. There was no heat and no electricity. It was a gray and cold high noon. There was the continuous muffled thudding of the guns—a mere accompaniment to the feverish subdued talk at the tables. The dining room still had the atmosphere and the noise of the dining room of a European grand hotel, aquarium-like; more surprisingly, it still had some of the lingering bouillon scent of a first-class restaurant on a Sunday noon. Some of the waiters still wore white cotton gloves. We got home—home, that is, to that cellar—having escaped a police razzia in the nick of time.

Snow fell on Christmas Day again. We now knew (and not merely heard) that the Russians had encircled Buda. We knew this not from Radio Budapest but from the BBC, to which we could still tune in on our small battery-powered radio for a day or so. What was happening three miles away we learned from a studio voice one thousand miles away, from London, via Moscow. That was the technology of the twentieth century at work; but so, too, was my fantastic experience that morning, the episode I recounted in the previous chapter, my talking on the telephone to my love across the front, across a world war. That remains one of my significant experiences of that time: the automatic insensitiveness of a few remnant wires transmitting human voices and thoughts, the continuity of life because of the dumb indifference of technology, cutting two ways.

* * *

Continuities notwithstanding, the great change was coming. The siege of Budapest had slowly but finally begun. The Russians were cautious. Each day they advanced, through fifty, perhaps a hundred blocks. Each day the Germans moved back their remaining tanks and trucks, trying to stable them in the narrow streets of the Inner City. They had no anti-aircraft artillery left. When daylight came, the Russian planes began circling over the broken rooftops of the city, dropping bundles of small bombs on anything that moved, and on every kind of vehicle, including burnt-out wrecks. Gradually the scenery of the Inner City became a Last Encampment of the Third Reich, an Augean stable of what was left of militant metal. In the cellar we huddled, hungry and cold. After a week or so we began to hear the Russian loudspeakers at night: songs, proclamations, inviting the Hungarian soldiery to surrender. I was more than game to surrender: I had wanted to be liberated from the Germans for a long time, preferably by the British or the Americans, or now by the Russians, it mattered not which. There came a dirty gray dawn when we knew that the Russians were only half a mile away. There came three big rambling thuds, with their long, ominous echoes reverberating from the hills. The Germans were blowing up the large bridges across the Danube. It must have been around eight when I climbed up to the street level, impetuous rather than brave, in my soiled half-uniform, wearing my sheepskin cadet's coat, with the fake orders in my pocket (". . . assigned to the remaining garrison of Budapest for as yet unspecified duties"), worth nothing. I glimpsed a patrol of the feared and hated field gendarmerie, moving self-consciously with cocked machine pistols amidst the rubble in a street fifty yards away. I slunk back to the cellar in an instant. The Russian planes vroomed overhead, but somehow their bombs sounded farther away. The cracking and rattling of small arms went on, but there rose the sense of a strange, sea-like quiet beneath them. Then we heard voices from the street. Hush! we told one another. They were louder and louder voices, in a foreign language. Was it

Russian? It sounded Russian. Now those sounds multiplied. Two of us went up to the ground floor of the house. That was risky, but we no longer cared. And as we stood in the doorway, peering out, Russian soldiers came by, one by one. It was nine-forty-five on the morning of January 18, 1945. Zero Minute, Zero Year.

They came in single file, close to the peeling, bulging, crumbling, shot-pitted walls of the dark apartment buildings. The first Russian was the first Russian I had ever met, and the nicest Russian I was to meet for a long time. He was some kind of officer, wearing a tightly padded uniform, a fur cap, with large binoculars hung around his neck. He had horn-rimmed glasses and a large mouth. He looked like a Weimar-Berlin film image of a Red Army officer, the kind of Russian who speaks German, likes chess and children and Beethoven. As matters turned out, a rare kind.

An hour or so after the first Russians had arrived we packed together bits of our belongings and bundled up for a trek across the city, to the house, about two miles away, where my mother's parents were, coincidentally very close to my father; from there it was only a short distance to our apartment house. As we came out into the narrow street we saw that the city was destroyed. The two-story building opposite that I had seen bomb-damaged only two or three days before was now an entire ruin. Smoke rose from the rubble into the morning air. There were fires burning here and there and much noise, shouting, in Russian. When, after five minutes of slow trekking, we turned into one of the big boulevards, I saw a scene that I shall not forget. There were a million Russians around. Of course there were not that many, but this is what it seemed. The boulevard was littered and empty. A few burnt-out automobiles lay crumpled along the curbs. The torn overhead wires drooped down in angry loops. Many houses were afire. But the dominant impression was that of an ocean of green-gray Russians, all coming in from the East, a few among them cantering around on horseback, some of them zigzagging fast in open Jeeps (the first American Jeeps I saw) with their caps pushed back from their low foreheads, in

Soviet fashion. The mass of the milling soldiery was on foot, many of them round Mongol faces, with narrow eyes, incurious and hostile.

The German occupiers had come from the West. These occupiers came from the East. The Germans were close, they had come from close by. But now something elemental had happened: a green-gray flood had reached us from the great Hungarian plains, coming from the East, a great oceanic tide that had risen somewhere near Asia.

By noon the news about their looting and raping reached us through the whispers of acquaintances whom we brushed against during our trek across the city, sometimes through whispers of other trekkers on the street. But this was not even necessary: one could see the Russians robbing and destroying and rounding up people; one could see a kind of naked emptiness in the faces of some of them, and a low kind of twisted ugliness in the faces of some others, besides the narrow-eyed Mongols.

We trudged past the house where my mother was born; it was burning. She cried. Twenty minutes later someone asked her: "What are we going to do tonight?" "We'll play bridge," she said.

It was obvious that people whose very lives were threatened until the Germans retreated in defeat—fugitive soldiers, Jews, people with Jewish relatives, anti-Germans, democrats, resisters, underground Socialists, Communists, etc.—looked forward to the Russians' arrival. What was less obvious, and more interesting, was that the Russians were only a little less eagerly awaited by the aristocracy, by the upper gentry, by high officials of a former semi-feudal state, by landowners, by bishops.* Many of the very people whose properties and possessions and ways of life were to be liquidated by

---

*Gossip overheard in a Budapest cellar by its intended subject, an independent and elegant woman with a certain presence. A chambermaid: "She says that the Russians will be here soon and it won't be bad at all. Is she a Jewess, perhaps?" Janitor's wife: "Oh, no. She is supposed to be the mistress of the Bishop of Veszprém." (She wasn't.) Maid: "Oh! She must know what she's talking about."

the Soviets hoped for the Germans' defeat. Many of the very people who would profit from the Communization of Hungary—streetcar conductors, janitors, steelworkers, hired hands—still hoped for a German victory. So much for the Marxist theory of class consciousness. It was class consciousness, all right, but in the reverse order. To favor the Germans, to believe in their propaganda of anti-Communism, was poor form; it showed a deficiency in taste, education, culture, in one's knowledge of the world. Chances were that a common parish priest was a nationalistic anti-Communist; his bishop would be more *nuancé*. A few second-rate actresses had thrown in their lot with the pro-German party; a truly first-rate actress would not do so. A low-level bureaucrat would conform to the directives of the pro-German regime and follow it to Germany. A high-level official, more often than not, would stay, frequently in hiding, and wait for the Russians to arrive. To some extent (but only to some extent) this was not unlike the American upper-class syndrome during the war and even for some years thereafter: anti-Communism was so vulgar and primitive, it was represented by such unspeakable people that to be wary of anti-Communism was a natural reaction.

Unlike in the United States, in Hungary there were elements of a Greek tragedy in this. The radical Germanophiles during the war bitterly attacked the upper classes for being disloyal to the German ally, for pursuing a mirage, since the defeat of Hitler's Third Reich would mean that the Soviets, and not the Anglo-Saxons, would reign over Hungary thereafter. These Germanophiles and Nazi sympathizers were, sadly enough, proved right, though for the wrong reasons, while many of the best Hungarians were opposed to the Third Reich for the right reasons, because of their traditional and old-fashioned and often reactionary convictions of decency.

As so often with my native people, the wish was the father of the thought. Yet this phrase does not go far enough: like the father who carries within him the seed of his children, the wish was the flesh and blood of the thought, the wish *was* the thought. The arrival of the Russians would mean the end of the war, in Budapest at least.

It would mean the end of the German era. For a considerable portion of the people, including most of the remnant aristocracy, almost all of the self-ascribed aristocracy and the great majority of snobs, this was decisive. They would welcome the Russians because the Russians were the allies of the English. To arrive in London via Moscow was what Hitler had wanted in 1941. This is what we wanted in 1944, though for different purposes. Few first-class snobs in Hungary were not pro-English. There was some opportunism in this, though not much. It was rather romantic. Men and women who should have known better expected that very soon after the Russians occupied Budapest, British and American missions would arrive, replete with smart officers from London and New York, whereafter the new era in our national history would properly begin. There were newspaper reports about the Russians raping and pillaging; we stopped for a moment, read them and said to ourselves, it isn't true. It was printed in the German, in the National Socialist press: atrocity propaganda. We, on the other hand, were listeners of the British Broadcasting Corporation. *We* knew.

This willingness of people to deceive themselves was not especially new in 1945; but it was then that I learned how the lives of people, including some of their most essential choices, are often determined by their thoughts and by their wishes, even in times when their very lives depend on enormous external events and circumstances that they cannot control.

From this feverish period I can recall certain reactions of people to the horrors they had been living through. For months after the siege was over people would trump each other with horror stories about the extraordinary perils they had experienced. Ten days without food beat five days without food *and* water, etc. What was curious about this was that often the same people who kept repeating and embellishing the recent awful tapestry of their own experiences (and personal horror stories become bores by their repetition, as does anything else) would also embellish and take pride in stories about how exceptionally and how well they managed to live under the worst of conditions. The same man who was compelled to describe the details of a sewer burst by a bomb that suddenly flooded a cellar, drowning people before his very eyes, would also narrate how he and his friends, in another cellar, had a champagne party on New Year's Eve. I understand this dual inclination: remember my vivid memories of that lunch at the Ritz. I have been thinking about this odd conjunction since, and I think I have an explanation for it. We are fascinated by violent changes as well as by astonishing continuities in this world: we take pride in telling—telling, and not merely remembering—what we had been living through, together with a different kind of pride in telling—again, with flourishes— how well *we* had made out, compared to others.

But the converse of this inclination existed, too: the suppressing of memories, for all kinds of reasons. For example, the aim of Jews throughout Europe was simple: to survive the war. This naturally intelligent and pessimistic people never doubted the disastrous possibilities of anti-Semitism, either before or after the war. At the same time they never doubted that Hitler would lose the war, sooner or later. Until that time they had to survive. I am inclined to think that Hitler knew this. The Jews knew that Hitler would lose the war; and Hitler knew that they knew. Perhaps this is why his fanatical hatred for them burned with such fierce force until his very end.

In 1945 some of the Hungarians who had helped Jews when that was not only impolitic and inopportune but also dangerous, were bitter because of what they thought was insufficient gratitude on the part of those they had helped to survive. This attitude was not commendable, but it was at least natural. What was ugly, and inexcusable, was the lack of remorse in the minds of those Hungarians (another minority) who had assisted, by deed or word, or who at least passively rejoiced in the delivery of perhaps as many as four hundred thousand Hungarian Jews to the German gas camps. There are Hungarians, as there are Germans and Austrians even now, who simply—or, rather, complicatedly—refuse to believe that so many Jews were actually murdered in 1944 and 1945. And there was another curious phenomenon of memory. Unlike other Hungarians, most Jews did not seem to want to talk about their recent sufferings. Were they ashamed of their humiliations? Or did they think that their shattering experiences were too profound, too serious, to talk about? I cannot tell. What I can tell is that in 1945 both the Jews in Hungary and the accomplices of their enemies had this in common: neither wanted to think much about what had just happened.

Three or four weeks after the fighting was over, a young boy, a relative of our janitor, helped me load some firewood on a paralytic wheelbarrow of sorts. There was a faint sound of guns in the distance. He said: "The Germans are coming back." His face shone with seriousness and anticipation. I don't remember whether I told him that he was wrong, that there was no chance of that. I knew that he only said what many of my countrymen hoped, especially after their experiences with the Russians: they hated them and they hated everything that was connected with them, including the prospect of Communism. The Russians and the Communists were cautious: they declared that they had no intention of imposing a dictatorship of the proletariat, that they were principal proponents of democracy, that they wanted to secure it in Hungary; and, indeed, in early 1945 it did not seem that Communism, certainly not the 1919 variety, would be imposed immediately on Hungary. What seemed inevitable was that Hungary, for the first time since 1919, would be ruled by the Left, by some kind of government of the Left.

The fighting was not yet over when the first cabaret opened in Pest, in typically Hungarian (or, rather, Pestish) fashion: the title of the show, printed on primitive posters, was "Leftward Ho!" In 1945 people in Budapest, as in New York, believed that this was now the main thrust of history, the wave of the present as well as of the future. I did not. I believed then, as I believe now, that this triumph of the Left was artificial and superficial. I knew that most people disliked the Left, what it stood for, or what it pretended to stand for. The Left did not appeal to them because of the particular circumstances of Hungary, including the people who were its particular, and vocal, representatives; but also because of something deeper, because of its thoroughly false conception of human nature. I cannot honestly say, since I cannot honestly remember, whether I saw this as clearly then as I came to know it soon thereafter. What I knew was that the Russians had come to stay; but also that, all appearances notwithstanding, the Left was not the wave of the future, certainly not in the long run. The press, and almost all politicians, spoke of "revolutionary" changes in 1945. The changes were indeed revolutionary in the literal sense of the word, the wheel of Hungarian fortune having been forced to undergo an entire revolution; but there was little that was revolutionary in the minds of the people. Indeed, the greatest revolution—and by "greatest" I mean that more people took part in it than in any other revolution in the history of Hungary, and proportionately perhaps more of them than in any revolution in the entire history of the world, a large order, that—exploded eleven years later, and it was an anti-Communist revolution.

A certain existentialist attitude was current across Europe in 1945. In France and in Belgium during the war and especially toward the end of it, the *débrouilleur* was a fashionable figure: the person who made out. Yet he was not the kind of "hard-faced man who did well out of the war." He was not the kind of person who trafficked with Germans as well as with partisans, he was not a black-market new rich like the dairyman immortalized by Jean Dutourd in *Au Bon Beurre.* The *débrouilleur* was rather dashing and knowledgeable and brave: in cutting corners he could also cut a fine figure of sorts. He had a contempt—a healthy contempt—for bureaucracy, all authorities, regulations: a contempt for every kind of man-made system. He skipped over, rather than snaked through, obstacles and labyrinths of regulations, knowing in his bones that they were senseless and stupid, that unlike all definitions, including philosophical ones about essence, existence is all that matters because it is real—indeed, that the preservation of it means the preservation of God's gift: in sum, the existentialist attitude.

Now the knowledge of what is opportune (materially, rather than intellectually) is essential for the talents of the *débrouilleur*. Yet opportunists and *débrouilleurs* are different. The opportunist is deadly serious in his calculations, secreting them within his inner self; the *débrouilleur* is a brilliant improviser, taking nothing very seriously and, at his best, laughing even at himself. It is like rendering Liszt versus playing Cole Porter: the first the suitable subject for a shameless rendition, the other for sprightly improvisation. Of course there are occasions when *débrouilleurs* degenerate into mere opportunists, and the reverse. From close up, such developments are not especially attractive to contemplate, but from a certain distance they may be amusing, and perhaps even instructive.

After the Russians arrived, there were all kinds of interesting affiliations. The oddest kinds of people joined the Communist Party. They included a rich stockbroker friend of ours, a tough-minded capitalist if ever there was one. He was one of those hard-headed (rather than hard-faced) men who made out well not only after the war but during it, including the siege. One could always be sure that F. had a car when no one else had a car any longer, that he had a black-market supply of gasoline, food, fuel, clothes, *napoléons d'or,* etc. In short, a merchant adventurer, a master opportunist, a great *débrouilleur.* I had a certain liking for him, for he was not ungenerous; he had an appreciation for good books, and a fine cynical sense of humor. I told him that he was wrong to join the Communist Party and I tried to explain why. That it was morally wrong, and bad form, I did not say, partly because he was an older man, and also because I knew that it would cut no ice with him. I explained my theory of the antiquated nature of Communism, and of its evident failure in the long run. He listened patiently, but I saw that he was a bit bored with it; it was too theoretical for him, too idealistic perhaps. Yet he was not as hardheaded as he thought he was. The few advantages of his Party membership were not worth the game. He thought that his quick and shameless adjustment to the powers at hand would provide for his independent comforts in years ahead; he convinced himself not only that Communism came to Hungary to stay but also that his kind could stay in Hungary under Communism. He was wrong. He mistook the wave of the present for the wave of the future—the occupational hazard of opportunists, including the most talented ones. He eventually retreated from Communism into *débrouilleurism:* in 1949—after two years of unnecessarily protracted expectations and anxieties—he bought himself a legal exit passport for a large sum (obtainable for much less money to non-Communists two years before) and emigrated to Australia, where he would die on a ski slope at the age of sixty.

In the dark December of 1944 I brushed against one of the self-conscious secret resistance conventicles that—alas, too late—were finally sprouting in Budapest and that, for once, were mostly composed of what could be called professional intellectuals: university people, journalists, officials of the former government, men and women on the fringes of cultural diplomacy. The leading figure of this group, J., was in his thirties, the son of respectable Calvinist gentry, dark, saturnine and handsome except for his buck teeth, a former *boursier* of the Horthy regime, with the then relatively rare accomplishment of speaking English, having visited the United States on a government study grant before Pearl Harbor. An older friend had brought me to his wife's apartment. J. announced that he was a Communist. This was before the Russians arrived. I was impressed. His announcement suddenly suggested a new kind of Hungary in which *this* kind of man might be an important personage as a Communist. I thought that J. was a very knowledgeable Machiavellian, a younger statesman of sorts, who would soon reach some kind of high position in a new Hungarian regime and employ his Anglo-Saxon contacts profitably, not only for himself but also for his country *because* of his Communist affiliation. I was impressed with the cleverness of this kind of calculation which, as I later found, was not unique. J.'s wife was a theatre critic, a high-strung intellectual, whose brother, a prominent National Socialist journalist, helped to hide a number of Jews during the last months of the National Socialist mob rule, whether out of truly changed humane convictions or out of a judicious and balanced concern for his own skin after the inevitable defeat, I cannot tell. Probably both.

After the Russians had arrived I met J. sporting a proletarian cloth cap, in Lenin's style, day in and day out, in the streets as well as inside their unheated apartment. Perhaps because he had studied the 1917 strategy of the great Lenin, J. struck out for a great career not so much within the Party itself (his membership in which he did not cease to flaunt) as within the organization of the Trade Unions; the Soviet track. He and some of his friends occupied a large grimy building, suitably situated in a grimy working-class district of Pest, where they established the Association of Trade Unions. The bureaucratic possibilities of such an organization seemed considerable. Hungarian trade unions, with their venerable Socialist past, were relatively few, even though they had been permitted to exist under the Horthy regime. The time was ripe, J. and his associates considered, to apply the union principle to all kinds of professions, especially to government and municipal offices—or, more accurately, the time was ripe to secure new and important positions for themselves through the impeccable instrument of Trade Unionism.

Besides providing leadership for my suddenly diminished family—my stepfather was hit by a shell on the street during the last days of the siege and died after three days of agony—I had not much to do. The university had not yet reopened; at any rate I had few courses to complete. Every day I trudged through the desolate city in ruins, to the headquarters of the Association of Trade Unions, where one of the attractions was the free bean soup distributed to the staff every noon. Very soon I suspected that not much would come out of this unionism. The older unions of printers and of metalworkers were already controlled by the Communists or by some of their grimmest fellow travelers, their organizations presided over by a former trolleyman by the name of Kossa whose very countenance—mean, suspicious and impassive—was sufficient to freeze the voluble J. into silence, which was no mean thing. Having glimpsed the two together, I sensed what was coming: Kossa had but slight regard for the Association of Trade Unions, very much including the latter-day Communist J. The order of the day was to let these people exist, as long as they had no real power, which, indeed, was the case, except that J. and his friends did not know it.

They were wholly preoccupied with their activities, having convinced themselves that playing at power was the same thing as the exercise of power—the occupational disease of bureaucrats and, even more, of intellectuals.

Very soon after arriving at the Association of Trade Unions I found that I had really nothing to do. Nor did the others. They, however, concealed this condition with a feverish activity of meetings, conferences, associations and "workshops" (I have yet to encounter a "workshop" that has anything to do with work), often behind closed doors. It was my first experience with the kind of intellectual bureaucracy that followed the phase of intellectual bohemianism as surely as other phenomena of the twentieth century followed those of the nineteenth. My colleagues were making paperwork for themselves; and they were taking their functions, paper functions, very seriously. After the siege there was in Budapest a shortage of everything, from flour to matches, even a shortage of water. Of paper, miraculously—or perhaps not so miraculously—there seemed to have been no shortage at all. Already on the second day of my appearance at the Association of Trade Unions I found that the most febrile kinds of intrigues were being constructed: confidential meetings behind closed doors from which certain people were excluded, others suddenly admitted; groupuscules with convincing nomenclatures were being formed and re-formed, all of them instruments thinly concealing the particular and hidden ambitions of the persons who called them into being. I soon found that the most secret ambitions and designs were also the most obvious. Yet the convention of the confidentiality was kept up not only by their perpetrators but also by the latter's bitterest and most suspicious rivals. It was an elaborate game of bureaucratic *Kriegs-spiel;* unlike the war games of military staffs, however, the sand tables were not reproductions of the actual terrain, they were criss-crossed by paths that may have come from somewhere but that surely led to nowhere. Indeed, within a year the Association of Trade Unions was gone; within five years J., the Early Communist, found himself in prison; another five years later he was acquitted, whereafter he was appointed to an important position within the government organization of export-import, having finally acquired the official limousine and the diplomatic passport—a Communist pilgrim's progress, a not untypical Hungarian career during the middle of the twentieth century.

Late in March the Americans arrived—an event that I must describe in some detail. According to the arrangements made at Yalta there was to be an Allied Control Commission in each of the former satellite countries, composed of Soviet, British and American representatives, a political and a military mission. The Russians, of course, ruled the roost in Budapest, and everywhere else in Eastern Europe (just as the Americans ruled similar commissions, say, in Rome). In retrospect, this American and British presence in Hungary was so ephemeral (the mission left in 1947 after the peace treaty was signed) that in the long and tragic history of my native country it is hardly worth mentioning at all. This remains a fact; and yet, oddly enough, it was not quite that way. Something of that air of American omnipotence in 1945, the impression that the United States, in an unprecedented way, was the greatest power in the world, transpired throughout the globe, lightening even the gloomy and depressing skies over Budapest. Americans had an influence in Hungary well beyond their numbers, and beyond their political limitations. There were perhaps not more than two hundred Americans, less than one hundred of them in uniform; yet somehow their presence in the capital seemed to be as evident, and sometimes almost as ubiquitous, as that of the Russians, especially in what had remained and what was beginning to revive of downtown, very much including places that both seemed and were expensive.

This condition, of course, was inseparable from the sudden and passionate Americanophilia of my countrymen, many of whom translated all of their expectations accordingly, by which I mean patriotic as well as personal expectations. I must say something about the latter. Months, perhaps years before the war ended, hundreds, maybe thousands of people who knew some English day-dreamed about getting a job with the British or the American missions. On the morning when the first Americans arrived, a nervous, teeming crowd of people besieged the entrances of the building they were to occupy; I heard that some people had arrived in the freezing dawn hours to get a first glimpse of the promised Americans in order to rush at them from favorable starting posts. As the day advanced the siege by supplicants turned into a bitter struggle, each man or woman on his or her own. Three or four days after the Americans came I entered the American Legation on a self-imposed mission (about which anon). A man was ensconced in a kind of niche behind the reception desk. I recognized him: he was one of my father's acquaintances, a bachelor of middle age, a former agent of the Hamburg-Amerika Line in the dim dear Twenties, a kind of floater during the war, regaling us with his reminiscences of Cuxhaven and Cherbourg, asserting that he was just the kind of person whom the Americans would need badly and employ profitably the moment they arrived—this despite the fact that, so far as I could ascertain, the little English he spoke was, if not altogether nasty and brutish, certainly poor and short. Now he hardly returned my greeting. His features had frozen into the kind of snarl with which a hungry dog is prone to protect his recently acquired bone; he was pale with the kind of suspicion with which men are prone to protect recent additions to their self-importance. I learned later that not only had he literally forced his way into the American building to be *en poste* an hour or so before the first American arrived, but that he, who had had no particular interest in Communism before, would eventually volunteer his services to the Communist political police in order to ensure that his clerical position at the American Legation remain fixed and secure at a later time when most Hungarian employees of the Western legations and missions would be forced to relinquish their jobs. To be associated with the Americans meant everything in the world to him; there was nothing he would not sacrifice for it, including old friendships, loyalties, self-esteem. He was not merely an ambitious man who had plenty of gall; he was the kind of man who had courage enough to be a coward. As I suggested before, he was but an extreme case of a syndrome that was widespread.

Presently just about every American, whether high officer or private, became the acquisition of a Hungarian wife or mistress. The head of the military mission was a major general, former governor of Oklahoma, who had his son posted to Budapest, where the latter was promptly annexed by a young bourgeoise, his father's ambitious secretary who had fought for her desk on the first day and won it by gleaming tooth and red-lacquered nail. They were subsequently married and left for the United States on a special military plane. What happened to her in Oklahoma I now wonder; at the time her story was a miracle tale, one of the *fabliaux* of 1945, Zero Year.

I would have liked very much to be annexed to the Americans or to the British, but I did not participate in the crush and rush of the first days, not so much because it would have been demeaning but because I had suffered from intellectual ochlophobia, the fear of crowds, since an early age. I thought I'd write my own ticket—a resolution that, again, involved me in an enterprise in which nobler and baser purposes were mixed. Having recognized the futility of my association with the Association of Trade Unions, I spent a night at home, literally burning the candle at both ends (candles were rare and electricity still nonexistent), composing a political memorandum in English that I intended to hand over to an American diplomat of the first rank. The memorandum consisted of information that I thought was not available elsewhere, items involving misdeeds by the Russians or the Communists. (I recall two principal items: one of them dealt with the murder of Bishop Apor of Győr, an aristocratic prelate who had distinguished himself in protesting against German and National Socialist brutalities as well as in protecting his flock; he was shot and killed by a Soviet soldier as he attempted to save a woman whom this Russian was about to rape in the cellar of his episcopal palace; the other dealt with the names of certain Communists who were camouflaged as members of other political parties.) My idea was very simple. I would inform the

Americans about such matters, not only for the benefit of my country but also of myself, since they would then learn that there were few, if any persons in Hungary, who understood political realities, expressed themselves in English and, generally speaking, were as knowledgeable as I—a recognition from which all kinds of advantages could ensue.

Somehow I had secured a list of the entire American personnel in Budapest, wherefrom I deduced that the person I ought to contact was the First Secretary of the Legation, a man by the name of Squires, since I was sufficiently aware of diplomatic practice to know that with such matters one should not confront the Minister or the Chief of Mission, at least not in the beginning. Accordingly I presented myself at the Legation about a week or so after it had established itself in Budapest. The line of supplicants and applicants had not much thinned, but the very fact that I asked for Mr. Squires by his name seemed to have made an impression on the Hungarian receptionist lady who, after a moment of hesitation, took the small envelope containing my visiting card on which I had written, in impeccable English, something like this: "The bearer of this card would like to have the honor and the pleasure to discuss certain matters of interest with Mr. Squires." I was admitted to Squires's office. He must have thought that I was about to offer him an array of interesting secondhand jewelry for a song. I did not know this then, but I understand it now. I vaguely remember him: he was a large, affable man, not quite as diffident as a British counterpart of his may have been, but reflecting, rather, the peculiarly American compound of being both perplexed and incurious at the same time. I babbled something in English about how important it was that the American mission be properly informed about certain important matters. I do not remember his saying anything. I put the memorandum upon the table. He said, "What can I do for you?" or words to that effect. On a coffee table I saw copies of *Time* and *Life* magazines. I hadn't seen their likes for many years. I said something to the effect that I would be only too glad to furnish him with the most confidential, and accurate, kind of political information about developments in Hungary if he would let me have a small supply of these superb American journals. He told me to help myself. I felt that I had just achieved a great, an unimaginable coup. I clutched several issues of *Life* and *Time* to my chest. I floated homeward in a cloud of triumph. In our unheated dwelling, grimy and redolent with the saddening odor of poverty, I faced the ruined beauty of my Anglomaniac mother. "Guess what I have!" I said. My mother turned radiant. She could not believe my luck.

Squires was one of those rich Americans, from a good family, who had entered the Foreign Service in the Thirties because it was a more interesting career than banking: a type that, I am sorry to say, has disappeared from the ranks of the American Foreign Service by now. This I recognized later, having also learned that his main interests included liquor and polo, a kind of period mix that makes me almost nostalgic. He seemed not very much interested in Hungarian politics, perhaps because he was smart enough to know that there was not much that the United States could or even should do. He was also enough of a man of the world to know how to disembarrass himself, in a smooth and professional way, of this young freak who, for all he knew, might be a Soviet or Communist agent. Eventually—and I cannot now remember exactly how—I found a less unwilling recipient of the kind of information that I had to offer. He was Rear Admiral William F. Dietrich, the third in command of the American Military Mission: an honest and erect navy officer of the old school, a practicing Catholic who abhorred Communism without at first openly saying so, who would not only welcome my confidences in a fatherly manner but who, a year later, would be a main instrument in getting me out of political trouble, arrange for the transportation of my only suitcase in his personal car across the border to Austria, whereto I escaped, and who would furnish me with the kind of character reference that ensured my receiving a priority visa to the United States once I presented myself to an American consulate in the West. In short, he may have saved my life.

By the time Admiral Dietrich and I had become friends, in the summer of 1945, I knew many of the Americans in Budapest, at least by sight. There was not, as far as I can remember or ascertain, a mean one among them. Every one of them was benevolent, including those who, according to later evidence, were more than considerably crooked. There was, as I can now see in retrospect, a paradox in this situation. To us the Americans seemed the brightest, the smartest and the best among all the human types who were to be found in Hungary in those crucial and tragic times; and, indeed, in many ways so they were. In any event, they were the living sources of untold and unaccountable bounty, material and spiritual: they had plenty of dollars, they were unrestricted, they were free. Eventually it dawned upon me that these Americans in Hungary were even more fortunate than were the Hungarian recipients of their available benefits. In 1945 an American in Hungary, whether in or out of uniform, found himself to be privileged beyond the dreams of avarice and of glory. American money, because of the poverty and the inflation raging in Hungary, gave him freedom to buy or do anything with ease. He was coveted by every woman because of the single virtue of his Americanship. I can recall only two types of Americans who left unpleasant memories. They were not members of the American missions. Sometime in the late summer of 1945 the news that a visit to ruined Budapest promised certain paradisiacal prospects for certain American visitors must have begun to circulate in certain circles in New York. Cognoscenti (*Am.:* wise guys) such as the publisher of *Esquire* magazine would arrive on a visit, hugely enjoying the pleasures of the flesh that were easily available to them in this downtrodden and beggar-poor country. There was something obscene in this, especially when they later described their visits in the style that was typical of *Esquire* at the time and that, alas, has become typical of most American magazines since then: the kind of prose whose principal purpose is to tell what kind of shoes, what kind of cheese, what kind of people and what kind of sexual compositions are "in"—a concept of connoisseurship that is public, not private: for what is the use of the discovery of a superb little wine from an unknown vineyard, or of a superb ruined city where formerly aristocratic privileges and pleasures can be secured for peanuts, unless the fact, even more than the subject, of one's discovery can be displayed in public?

The other kind of unpleasant visitor was the sort of emigré who, having left Hungary before the war, and being well on the way to a lucrative or spectacular career in the United States, usually in the capacity of either a Moviemaker or a Scientist, would arrive in Budapest from a paramount studio or from a rockefeller university, often in the resplendent uniform of the U.S. Army or, more than often, in that of the U.S. Army Air Forces, full of a compound of arrogance, unease and contempt for the miserable and despondent people of Hungary. I particularly remember one of these tatty birds of passage, already beyond the prime of his life, decked out in the regalia of an American colonel or brigadier, shuffling his flat feet across the lobby of the American mission building, outside of which he kept his waiting relatives, who were speechless—almost, but not quite—in their wondrous contemplation of this apparition from their own flesh. I read about him a few days later: he was professing the right kind of leftward opinions of the time. His sour countenance seemed to reflect his opinions: Hungary got what she had coming to her, that is, the Soviet occupation, the best thing for a people who had been stupid enough to be allied to the Germans. Years later in America he became a scientific adviser of the Eisenhower administration, one of the scientist-spokesmen for the production of bigger and better hydrogen bombs. In an interview he gave in the Fifties I read: "I know what Communism means: I know what the Soviets did to my unhappy country."

The British were a slightly different story. There were fewer of them, they were diffident and also more aloof. Because of geography and tradition, and because they were the early standard-bearers of the world war against the Third Reich from the outset, we thought, before Year Zero, that the British, rather than the Americans, would be the chief Western power in our part of Europe after the war—which, of course, did not turn out to be the case. They were much less impressed with the charms of Hungary and of Hungarians than were the Americans; they acted as if they knew that Hungary now belonged to the Soviet sphere of interest, and that there was not much left to do. It seemed to me, at the time, as if they were in command of some kind of superior reserve knowledge about the ultimate fate of Hungary: it rather seems to me now that they had few instructions that were relevant. My first meeting with them was sad. I was plodding home on a late March evening when the suddenly warm and liquid air and the brightness of the twilight promise the pleasantness of summer for people in more or less normal conditions, while for others this development of implacable warmth and of light serves only to illuminate one's wretchedness and misery—March, and not April, being the cruelest month, at least in my native city. I knew that the arrival of the British and American missions was imminent. Suddenly, rounding a bend on the empty boulevard, I came upon two British officers, with red tabs, one of them carrying his cane, taking a brisk after-dinner walk, no doubt. I stopped. "Are you British?" I asked. "Oh, it is so good to see you"—or words to that effect. We exchanged a few words, and they went on. I was only twenty-one years old, but even then I felt that this encounter had the sad tinge of a long unrequited love. So they had come, after all—even if it was too late, after so many years of disappointments, after so many years of waiting, of hope, of tragedy. I sensed a kind of embarrassment as they went on. We, who loved the British in 1940—memories that even now give me a *frisson*—imagined their future victory: the triumph of a British-led Europe where freedom, decency and a kind of easy elegance would exist anew. But it was not to be such a world.

At any rate (certainly at any rate of exchange) the British were poorer than the Americans. Their mission and their social life were less opulent. On the day of their arrival, like the Americans, they were besieged by job seekers, by all kinds of people who wanted to be associated with them. They hired few people; they preferred to hire certain recognizably frayed women of the former aristocracy and the gentry. Perhaps this had something to do with habitual British snobbery. They were poorer than they had ever been, but as snobbish as ever. I thought about this for a long time, coming to the tentative conclusion that, for the British, unlike for other peoples, snobbery is the outcome of diffidence as much as of arrogance, perhaps even more. They were unwilling to get involved with men and women whom they could not place and on whom, on occasion, they might have to depend. It was all restrained, modest and cold, with a slight touch of being almost shabby. It was all contrary to Hungarian expectations. Our best people still expected the British to be the Great Power in Europe, counterbalancing the Russians, to intervene eventually in Central Europe and in Hungary. In certain circles, including J.'s apartment, people passed around editorials from the London *Times,* taking deep draughts of encouragement from some of them, which in the late spring and early summer of 1945 contained, on occasion, carefully worded criticisms of certain Soviet actions. When on a Sunday afternoon in late July the news came that the English people had repudiated Churchill and elected a Socialist government some of my older friends reeled: it was one of the bitterest of blows.

Still Anglomania lived on. One of my pathetic memories of Year Zero includes a wedding reception in the fall. A Hungarian girl whose family I knew, the only daughter of an impoverished, gray-faced doctor, had fallen in love with a British sergeant—or, perhaps because he was British, she convinced herself that she had fallen in love with him. He was a decent sort, a North Englishman from Newcastle or Sunderland, with the long, knobby face of his class which, as I instantly recognized even before he spoke, was that of the lower-middle variety—but this his bride, and her family, did not (or perhaps did not want to) know. I can see him still in the living room of the doctor's apartment (the reception was held at home), furnished with the remnant scatteration—German china, Bohemian glass, faded runners, grayed lace, a worn rug—of a destroyed bourgeois past that once had belonged to a world that was civic, fussy, stuffy, but, after all was said, reasonably honorable. For a moment in its long and misery-ridden history, a corner of that room was lit by the bride's nervous smile. Some of her unsophisticated relatives, too, were smiling. The luck, the fortune, to be married to an English soldier at this time, to be carried off as a bride to England! I, and perhaps some others, knew that there was something very wrong with this: that her progress from this broken-down boulevard apartment with its low-bourgeois bibelots to a gas fire-grate somewhere in the Midlands was not necessarily up. After all, for someone born in Hungary even the ubiquitous cooking smell of paprika and onions frying in cheap lard—especially ubiquitous now when it could no longer be confined to kitchens—was preferable to the coal-smoke and sultana-cake and weak-cocoa odor of mid-England; even in a Sovietized Budapest the sun would shine in June with a laughing fury; and even the broken remnants of a past, that grand piano whose chords had long lost their twang and whose polish had long lost its shine, and the doctor-father's *Collected Works of Goethe* in the glass bookcase, were symbols of matters that would not exist where this girl was about to go. I confess that I felt, at the time, less compassion for her than for this decent and good Englishman, who stood there uneasily and self-consciously cracking jokes with two of his pals, blokes who had come to enliven the festivities, representing England. He was getting roped into something that was embarrassing and difficult. I doubted whether the marriage would last a year. Perhaps he did, too. The bride, well-tutored, articulate, Hungarian, did not know it. So much for the reputedly superb wiles and sophistication of my countrymen and my countrywomen. In a very Hungarian way, the wish *was* the thought, again and again.

There was also more to this. I have often thought that the personal relations of men and women who belong to different nationalities, rather than to different classes—especially when they try to comprehend each other in a language that for the one is his or her native one, while for the other it is not—is a subject not only for low comedy but a potentially profound subject for drama or even high tragedy which few, if any writers have yet attempted. It involves conflicts that issue not out of differences of class or out of differences of libido (perhaps the least important of all differences) but out of something much more important—it issues from differences of nationality, residing in deeply rooted matters such as habits of speech and, therefore, of thought. While it is true that the underlying subject matter of the modern novel, of the principal literary creation of the bourgeois age, may dissolve together with the dissolution of social classes, which is the main reason why contemporary versions of a Jane Austen or a Trollope or a Balzac are no longer possible, a fine and profound account of the tides of passion, of the incomplete understandings (and of the happily no less incomplete misunderstandings) between, say, a Frenchman and an English-woman or between an American man and a Hungarian woman, remains to be written, and not on the level of superficial comedy, either: in this respect the readable Pierre Daninos, the linguistic Fabergé art of Nabokov and even Nancy Mitford at her best will not do.

At their best, the English understand Europeans, but they do not really wish to know them. At their best, certain Europeans know the English, but they cannot really comprehend them. But enough of these paradoxes. A day or so after *ces noces tristes*—no, that would be too elegant, too romantic for what had really taken place, which was *noces ternes, en haillons, attristées*—something else happened that remains peculiarly lodged in my memory. The girl who worked with me as a part-time secretary and who was also a part-time secretary to an English officer, asked me what at the time was certainly an unusual question. Did I know of a Catholic priest who would be willing to baptize an Englishman? The English officer for whom she was working was an odd bird, she said; he was so quiet as to be a veritable recluse, he did not seem to like parties. Now he told her that he had taken instructions; he wanted to be baptized a Catholic as soon as possible, preferably tomorrow. She had no Catholic background or interest in religion, she did not understand this. I thought quickly of some of my priest acquaintances; for a moment my snob reflex rose to the surface of my mind; I thought of one or two of the Anglophile abbés, the habitués of the pseudo-aristocratic and anti-German salons before the collapse; it would take some time to find them, but I would find them all right. She sped off to the British mission, returning in an hour or so; the officer did not wish to wait, the event should take place tomorrow or at the latest the day after. I went to the Basilica, within walking distance, looking for the curate. He asked something about papers about which I knew nothing. Suspicious and not very cooperative at first, he agreed in the end. Tomorrow, before the second Mass in the early morning, he said. Late in the evening the girl sent a message to our apartment (we had no telephone) to the effect that she had to accompany the officer to the Basilica in the morning; that the officer wished to thank me and that he wished to know whether I would come to introduce him to the curate. I told her that this was quite unnecessary; the curate would be waiting for them; besides, I had no great desire to get up that early to go to Mass on a weekday morning (my Mass-going was, at best, very irregular in 1945); I was irritated with her; then I agreed.

I arrived at the depressing square in front of the Basilica a few minutes late, on a dark and dank and depressing morning. An English officer was coming down the steps. The girl, tagging behind, caught up with him and said something in his ear. (I had missed the Mass, which must have been speeded up for the curate's convenience.) The officer looked at me, briefly nodding his head. His face expressed something that I still remember: a kind of infinite seriousness. He went on, leaving the girl behind; he turned left into a desolate street; in a minute his figure disappeared in the morning fog. "A strange man," the girl said. *"Különös ember!"* I didn't think so. He had given me, us, the whole world, the impression that he wanted to be alone. He was alone. I suddenly felt a great surge of compassion, of sympathy for this lonely small thin figure. It was, to begin with, a novel experience. Perhaps for the first time in my life I felt sorry for an Englishman. I was sorry for this lonely officer, but I was not sorry out of condescension; it was the kind of sorrow that, strangely enough, is composed of human admiration together with human love, the kind of sorrow for a lonely follower of Christ. Many years later I came to feel, and I still feel, that English Catholics are a breed apart, perhaps the most serious, because in many ways they are the loneliest Catholic Christians in the world. Twenty years later I sensed this very strongly when I had taken it upon myself to fly to London at the time of Churchill's funeral, with my little son. The day after the funeral we went to Mass in a Roman Catholic church in Kensington. "It was not a very attractive church," I wrote in my diary, "set back between the brown brick houses. It was full of people, a few Poles, but the majority of the congregation was English, infinitely serious English men and women with their children. Living through the last phase of the Protestant episode, of the long, unhappy chapter of Roman Catholicism in England, with some of the old suspicions and mistrust melting away, these English Catholics, perhaps better than any other Catholics in the Western world, know what it means to be Christians in a post-Christian land. . . . In this people [the English] who ushered in the modern age there is still a near medieval strain, a strain that has been part and parcel of their Protestantism, of their puritanism, of the industrial evangelicalism, of their English socialism. It is there in this living strain of English Catholicism which, in the twentieth century—curious paradox in the spiritual history of England—has become one of the strongest subterranean streams of a particular Englishness. To be hounded by heaven is one way to put it—but it was not only the Francis Thompsons who sensed this. . . ." The English officer was going away, alone: a representative of one of the victorious Powers of this world, especially enviable in these small and sordid surroundings of defeated Hungary; he, for reasons known only to himself and to God, had chosen the religion of the defeated of the world, of sinners and sufferers; he had taken the Via Dolorosa on his own.

I have now filled page after page about the few hundred Americans and Englishmen who were temporary residents of my native city at the time. But how about the Russians, of whom there were hundreds of thousands around, who ruled my country and all of the surrounding countries then, and ever since that time? The Russians? Well, there is not much to say about the Russians. They were everywhere and they were nowhere. I have no inclination to describe them in detail. All kinds of funny, and some not so funny, books have been written about them, about their childishness, their primitiveness, their brutality—about the Russian soldiers who tried to shave out of flush toilets, mistaking them for washbasins; who gulped down entire bottles of eau de cologne, mistaking them for perfumed vodka; the most desirable object of whose robberies was a watch, but not just any kind of watch: they were entranced with the kind of toy watch that had something like Mickey Mouse on the dial face.

During the eighteen months that I spent under Russian occupation I did not meet a single Russian with whom I could talk more or less intelligently, and not one who spoke an intelligible French or English or even German. They all seemed to have been stamped out of a mold: their minds even more than their bodies. Under Soviet rule the eternally passive masses of the Russias had been activated—up to a certain level, in certain ways. They were taught to read and write; they were taught to think in public categories, for the first time in their history. They had acquired a new skill: they had learned words and phrases that were public answers to public questions. They were more than satisfied with this achievement: a verbal achievement that rendered them civic and "cultured." Yet this was exactly why intelligent conversation with them was impossible. It was exasperating, especially for someone who was impatient by nature. During and before the war I had occasionally talked with Germans who were Nazis. What made me despair then was their arrogance. They had an answer for every question, which went something like this: "Maybe so, but there are hard realities in this world which we have come to understand, whereas you are unwilling to admit them." (Examples of these "hard" realities: the inevitable "right" of a land-hungry people to conquer and colonize; the "inevitable fact" that the thinking of a Jewish scientist was necessarily inferior to that of an Aryan one, etc., etc.) When one talked to Russians one found that they had certain answers to certain questions, beyond which they were totally unwilling as well as wholly unable to go. The Germans had prided themselves on having found a satisfactory accord between the public ideology of their folk and their private thinking. The Russians seemed to be quite unaccustomed to private thinking. There was public thinking; and there was private behavior. That there were enormous discrepancies between the two did not bother them, since they did not recognize this at all. I think that the Soviet soldier who had just robbed a passerby of his watch or overcoat would, if asked, wholly agree with, or perhaps even be able to repeat, the slogan that he was a citizen-soldier of the most disciplined, most scientific and most progressive army of the world: the Red Army of the Soviet Union.

There is but one incident that I have been thinking about often since that time. The apartment house opposite ours had been sequestered by a group of Soviet sailors and their officers. They kept the lights blazing and played the gramophone at full volume day and night: their love for ear-shattering noises was to be matched only by American teenagers. Down the street a young Jewish man had returned from deportation. He was alone; his family, I understood, had been killed. He decorated the wall underneath his window with slogans in Cyrillic letters welcoming the Soviets and proclaiming their glory. One of the few possessions that had survived his family was his collection of ship models: he displayed these proudly in his small apartment, to which he invited the Soviet sailors, especially one of their warrant officers, a good-looking young Russian who would come to his apartment and play with the little ships for hours. This young man had some money and food, and entertained these Russians handsomely. One day we heard a lot of noise, shouting and slamming, at high noon. I looked out the window at an ugly scene. The young man was out in the street, shouting desperately, banging at the door that had been slammed shut by the Russians. They had gone into his apartment, taken his entire collection, thrown some of his stuff into the street, together with its owner. That was bad enough, but even worse than their brutality were the broad grins on their mugs. They thoroughly enjoyed the pitiful powerlessness of their former admirer and friend. They were splitting their sides at the sight of his lamentations: his repeated petitionings produced bursts of enormous laughter. They had nothing but contempt for him because he was helpless, because he was weak, because he was a fool, perhaps also because he was a Jew.

It was one of the ugliest scenes I witnessed during that ugly year; I have always found the humiliation of a human being to be the most shattering of scenes. This contempt for human weakness was something typically Russian; I had seen other expressions of it during

Year Zero. Years later I read in one of Dostoevsky's novels about a Russian who, having cheated a fool out of a thousand rubles at the horse fair, said upon his return: "How I despise that man!" Many years later some of Solzhenitsyn's accounts of social life in the *Gulag* rang a bell in my mind; his searingly angry description of how in the Soviet concentration camps the roost was often ruled by common criminals who were even worse than the policeman guards and who, because of their brutal contempt for any kind of human weakness, were respected and depended upon by the prison administrators themselves. Which was worse, I thought at the time: the Germans who had arranged for the murder of people such as this young man in obedience to what they thought was a principle; or the Russians who would rob and murder out of impulse, not only for no particular principle but for no purpose except that of enjoying their power over the temporarily powerless? I could not tell, just as I cannot tell which is worse in America: the robber who stabs the store owner after his robbery, or the gang member who stomps his victim for no purpose except that of enjoying his savage power over him.

Unlike the Germans, the Russians seemed to me to be a people utterly without pride. At their worst, the Germans were shameless; among the Russians one could occasionally sense the shamefulness of the brute. They were probably less inhuman than the Germans at their worst, but their humanity appeared only on a few unexpected occasions, somewhat like the sentimentality of a suspicious peasant. In 1945 I lost whatever respect I had for the self-professed Christianity of Tolstoy and Dostoevsky; among the Russians I found not only the Catholic convert Chaadayev but agnostics such as Turgenev or Chekhov infinitely more humane and Christian than these great bearded fake puritans belonging to the Russia that produced Rasputin. What impressed me even at that time was the Russians' deep-seated sense of inferiority. They, the conquerors, seemed thoroughly stiff and uneasy at the receptions of the American mission. In spite of their elephantine and hideous power they would react to the slightest kind of criticism; they insisted that respect be paid to them on any and every occasion; all in all, they were very unsure of themselves, perhaps especially in the presence of Americans for whom, I am sure, they had an emotional kind of admiration that they tried their best (and also their worst) to suppress. I was not at all surprised when, a few years later, Stalin began the ridiculous campaign proclaiming to the Soviet peoples and to the world that the inventors of the telephone, the airplane, etc., etc., had not been Americans or Europeans but Russians.

It was mainly, though not exclusively, because of the Russians that the distaste for Communism in Hungary was so extraordinarily widespread. I thought then, and also much later in the United States—arguing with Americans about this in vain, until I was blue in the face—that Communism was not much of a danger, that once the Russians removed themselves from a European country they occupied, Communism and Communists would vanish therefrom. The very fact that something was propagated by the Russians, the very fact that something looked or seemed Russian, made it repugnant. Other European peoples who had lived under Russian rule decades before, the Finns, Baltics, Poles, had had this experience. In this respect German rule, precisely because it was more civilized on the surface, probably would have harmed Hungary more in the long run, for then the culture of the nation would have become more than considerably Germanized. As matters turned out, after more than forty years of Russian occupation, the Russian influence on the culture and civilization of my native country has been zero.

This brings me to the deficient appeal of Communism and of Communists. During Year Zero I could see who were the kinds of people who joined their Party. The brightest among them were the opportunists such as the earlier-mentioned J., or the capitalist friend of my family who chose to join the winning side because it was the winning side, *pur et simple.* (Among opportunists no less than among revolutionaries there is such a type as *un pur:* the person who will allow no compromise to sully his dedication to the supreme cause of opportunism.) Oddly—or perhaps not so oddly—the Russians, forever eager to be appreciated, especially by people who were smart, had a respect for such opportunists, much more than they had for the motley variety of convinced Communists. What struck me at the time was how many of the latter were—how should I put it?—inferior types, poor specimens of humanity, men and women whose very faces and whose very bearing showed evident marks of humiliations in their lives, people with a deeply embedded sense of personal, rather than cultural inferiority. All of us suffer from the wounds of some kind of humiliation, all of us nurture at least one complex of relative inferiority in our hearts; but there are some people who allow these sentiments to grow to an extent that they became a dominant factor in their personalities and aspirations, and this seemed to be the case with most of the Communists I met in 1945. They were unsure, suspicious, narrow and bitter: in sum, preternaturally aged—as was indeed the philosophy of Marxism, that cast-iron piece left over from the junk heap of nineteenth-century ideas. (Compared to them, the Nazis I had known, including Nazi intellectuals, seemed young. A Nazi intellectual was the kind of person who would rather be vulgar than boring; with the Communists it was the reverse.)

This was true in a physical sense, too: most Communists were physically ugly, some to the point of being repellent. Sometime during the summer of Year Zero I met Georg Lukács,* one of the few famous Communist intellectuals, who had just arrived from Moscow. He, too, had the appearance of a tired survivor from another age: a leftover from the Weimar period. Everything about him was drooping and sliding down: his glasses, his eyelids behind his glasses, his ears, his nose, his large cynical mouth, his coat, his cravat, his tobacco-stained hands. His countenance, curiously like that of many other Weimar intellectuals whom I would later encounter in America, reminded me of a crumpled ashtray. He knew German better than he knew his native language, which he spoke with a weary coffeehouse accent. His conversation, or what I remember of it, consisted mostly of tired *Kaffeehaus* witticisms with

---

*I am no relative of this man, with whose name mine has been sometimes, and disagreeably, confused. His international fame was resurrected—or, rather, artificially inflated—by Anglo-American intellectuals circa 1960. Few people have bothered to read him in his native Hungary.

which he tried not only to lighten the customary Marxist platitudes but also to cover up the condition that he knew remarkably ("remarkably" being the *mot juste*) little of what Hungary had lived through and what Hungarians were thinking. His last contact with his native country had occurred more than a quarter of a century before, during Béla Kún's regime, which, for him, were halcyon days. In sum, an intellectual fossil.

Most of these still-believing Communist intellectuals moved by inclinations that were Trotskyist rather than Stalinist. Of course they would go to any lengths to deny this. This is, too, why I was not at all surprised when, on Stalin's orders, a few years later the police government of Hungary began to get rid of some of them in the most cruel and brutal manner imaginable: no matter how cowardly and conformist, they were after all, international Communists, not dumb Muscovite minions; they were not particularly good at being both brutal and vulgar, unlike their Russian masters. This was also why I was not surprised that most of these surviving Communist intellectuals were in the vanguard of the 1956 Rising, when they had—finally—realized that the rule imposed on them was so stupid and senseless as to be intolerable. They also realized that "intolerable" is what people no longer want to tolerate. In 1956 they took tremendous sustenance, intellectual and spiritual, from finding that, for once, what they said and thought was in harmony with what the vast majority of the downtrodden people of Hungary, whom they had for so long shamefully ignored, were thinking and saying. What they did not realize even then was that this salutary condition was not the result of their own spiritual courage. They could get away with it for a while when the Russian government, too, was beginning to bend, unaware of the condition that revolutions tend to break out not when the terror is harshest but when it has begun appreciably to lessen. But that is another story.

What made me pessimistic for the long run was that their masters were very different from them. The Russians who gave them orders gave a very different impression: they were young, not old. Years later I would run across Soviet men and women who seemed not to doubt the superiority of their system because they were not thinking about it. One day, many years after Zero, while waiting for interminable hours at Le Bourget airport, I watched a Russian airline pilot walk and talk: superficially handsome, with a large, naked face, a believing Russian and the prototype of the Soviet machine-man, half mechanic, half Cossack, like the writer Sholokhov. Unlike European Nazis, unlike European Communists, the bearing and the expressions of this man were both vulgar and boring, which did not bother him or the surrounding Aeroflot personnel in the least. His was not the last gospel; but he represented both the power and the glory of the immense Soviet Union, at least for the time being.

A conversation in 1945 with V.B., a young and not unintelligent baroness. "Well, we were at the top long enough. It is their turn now." She is wrong, for a number of reasons, the principal one being that *they* are not really the lower classes. *They* are merely another ruling group, essentially lower middle class in origin, one kind of bureaucracy replacing another. What she said is not ignoble, but it is a rationalization. It is a rationalization of one's misfortunes, not of one's misdeeds. It is a rationalization of resignation and not of envy. It is the opposite of sour grapes: sweet wine (i. e., *pourriture noble. Edelfäule*).

During the second half of 1945 my position as the secretary of the Hungarian-American Society kept me busy, together with my remaining university studies. We had an impressive membership, in quality as well as in quantity; the people who hoped for their salvation from the United States were numerous beyond reason, and so were some of their expectations. In October the cultural section of the American Legation planned a reception at which they would show some films; they asked me to help prepare a guest list, including some of the professors from the university. The professors, with notably inspiring exceptions, were not the bravest of men. I went to see some of them, including a professor of mine: an intelligent and saturnine man who had few illusions about the Americans or the British. "Why should I go there?" he said to me.

"What for?" I babbled something until suddenly the most obvious matter came to my mind: there would be plenty to eat, lots of hors d'oeuvres, at a time when most people in Budapest, very much including scholars on a fixed and almost worthless salary, went hungry day after day. I felt that I could not say this in so many words to this distinguished scholar. I said simply that there would be "a sumptuous reception." He indeed showed up, together with at least two dozen of his colleagues who previously, for reasons politic, professed to restrain their public admiration for things American, including the Hungarian-American Society. There *were* lots of tea sandwiches; they disappeared fast. I can still see the gray, gaunt scholars approaching the buffet table first carefully, slowly, and then nervously repeating this progress, faster and faster, until it ran like a film moving jerkily forward: it was comic and tragic at the same time.

More pathetic were the non-material expectations that people nurtured about the Americans. One of the top positions—executive vice-president or chairman of the board, I forget which—of the Hungarian-American Society was occupied by L., a professor of astronomy, whose main claim to this post had been his former Rockefeller or Carnegie Fellowship with which he had visited the Harvard Observatory and become friends with its director, Professor Harlow Shapley, about whom he would often talk with joyful expectations. One day I happened to run across the title of an article in *The Atlantic Monthly* written by, lo and behold! Harlow Shapley. I got it out of the American library, thinking how pleased L. would be. Next morning, as I read the article on a crowded trolley car, I was astonished to find that this eminent Harvard astronomer was a fervent admirer of the Soviets and a political imbecile. I said that much when I gave the article to L. I saw that he did not want to believe me; indeed, later in the day I saw that whatever liking he may have had for me (it was not much) had just about vanished. To this day I do not know whether he thought that I wanted to shame him, or whether he did not know enough English to comprehend the idiocies in Shapley's article. I hope the latter.

There was A., an old family friend, a run-down member of the former gentry and a romantic snob, who told me repeatedly that he would like to meet American diplomats, especially members of their staff of a certain eminence, as he put it. This happened in the spring of 1946. By that time there was enough food around to allow for a kind of tea party. I told my mother, who immediately rose to the occasion, as I knew she would. Neither Admiral Dietrich nor Colonel Townsend was free on the designated afternoon, but I succeeded in corralling T., the Cultural Attaché of the Legation, a pipe-smoking American liberal with a toothbrush mustache of the kind that I later saw repeated above the lips of Brooks Atkinson and Harrison Salisbury, a liberal mustache of a certain period; he was also the first man I ever saw wearing shirts with button-down collars, the practicality of which has escaped me then and ever since. The conversation around our tea table was a disaster. T. mentioned Count Michael Károlyi, the quondam president of the Hungarian Republic in 1918–19 who had been instrumental in bringing about the catastrophe that befell Hungary at the time. T. asked whether Károlyi was an intellectual, as he had read. I said, yes, of sorts. Well, T. said, then it was true: Károlyi must have been a spiritual aristocrat if there ever was one, probably the finest kind of man Hungary could produce, and did we agree? A.'s answer was to the point: Károlyi was a traitor to his class and to his country. He asked me to translate the exact words into English. "A weakling." "A scoundrel." After this the talk degenerated fast. A. produced certain rare and exquisite cases from the repertory of Russian atrocities, whereupon T. said that homesickness among the Russian soldiery ought not to be discounted. He quoted the latest issue of *Time* magazine, about American and Canadian soldiers having gone on riotous rampages in Le Havre or Cherbourg before their embarkation homeward. Later I told my mother that I thought A. had been a bit tactless, whereupon my mother remarked that she thought so, too, but then so was our American guest: "If this man had been posted to Dachau he would have probably told the inmates how Americans have been mistreating Indians."

In September Baron U., a great banker and capitalist, and a very genial man to boot, gave a party in his relatively untouched mansion in Benczur-utca, where he invited leading members of the government and of the political parties, including Rákosi, the potatoheaded unscrupulous boss of the Communist Party, back from Moscow. (I was not among the guests.) I asked F., U.'s relative—an older man, another former great industrialist and an officer of the Hungarian-British Society—why U. would do such a thing. "You are too young to understand, my boy," F. said. *"We* were brought up by the principle"—he said it in English—"right or wrong, my country." I was impressed by his response; I could not answer him and thought about it for a long time, feeling, however, that there was something wrong with this. Many years later I read Chesterton with delight: "My country right or wrong is like saying, 'My mother, drunk or sober.' " Still, Chesterton's aphorism related to an England, stiff and swollen with pride, in the aftermath of the mafficking and the jingoism of the Boer War. We, in Hungary, another generation later, were stiff and swollen not with pride and possessions but with hunger and hatred, including self-hatred. I was struggling against the Communist subjugation of my country, yet if someone had offered me American or Swiss or Portuguese citizenship I would have accepted it in an instant. "Right or wrong," I thought, *"my* country?" From this time on not much remains to be said: Year Zero was about to run out and I was about to run away from my country.

For a while it seemed that Hungary, even though remaining under the Soviet thumb, would not become entirely Communized or Sovietized. Most people thought that the Communists were not popular enough to rule by themselves; consequently, the country might continue to be governed by a coalition of the so-called democratic parties of which the Communists were members. I thought that, too; only I had come to the conclusion, early in Year Zero, that labels and names mattered little. What mattered was the possession of power, something that will always attract a sufficient number of people for its disposal. Within every one of the officially non-Communist parties and associations there were men and women who were willing to go along with the Russians and with the

Communists; they had some of the key positions; eventually they would be the local representatives of power, and this was what counted in the end. I also came to the conclusion, later in the year, that the British and the Americans would do little or nothing for Hungary; the Americans might do something, but at a time when it would be too late. I thought that not only the Communists but also the Russians were less sure of their power than it seemed. But I also knew that the Americans were not really aware of this—in a subdued way they may have respected the power of the Russians almost as much as the Russians respected, and feared, both American power and American prestige. In early October there occurred a significant event. In the city elections of Budapest the Communists lost. They had made the Socialists run on a joint ticket with them; even so, the majority of the people in this industrial city, including the majority of the working class, voted for the Small Holders' Party, originally a rural party and now relatively the most conservative one of the coalition. I was a member of this party, with its ungainly name, in the electoral success of which the majority of hopes now resided. One month after the Budapest election the national elections were to be held. The Russians now moved. Their commanding general called for a confidential meeting of the parties, including some of the leading Small Holders, telling them that there ought to be but one ticket in the election, that of a Democratic Front. The seats in the forthcoming parliament would then be distributed according to a prearranged schedule between the parties—the Small Holders were offered 47.5 percent of the seats. It was a sort of Russian ultimatum, to be decided immediately.

I was told about it by a family friend, Paul de Auer, a leading member of the Small Holders. A few of us had gathered in his apartment. We speculated that the Russians might be stalled at their game *if* the Americans were informed about this as promptly as possible, and if this clumsy Russian intervention were publicly revealed by the American press and radio. I volunteered to go straight to the Americans. My mission consisted of two parts: to tell the Americans what was up, and to try to ascertain whether they would protest accordingly and quickly against this Soviet interference in Hungarian politics. It was late afternoon; I bounded across the city in the rain; I found no one at the American Legation, but I caught Admiral Dietrich in the military mission building as he was about to leave. I was very excited; it took me some time to convince him that speed was of the utmost importance. I did not know whether I had succeeded in both of my tasks; I informed the Americans, but could not elicit any commitment from them. I now decided to lie. I rushed back to Uncle Paul's apartment. He had already gone to the headquarters of the party, where the matter was under discussion. I had great difficulty in pushing my way through the various anterooms of the old County Casino, which served as the headquarters of the Small Holders' Party. Finally Paul emerged, slightly irritated by my insistence. I breathlessly told him that I had talked to the top Americans, adding that I had reason to believe the Americans would intervene. I did this because I thought this piece of news might be decisive in tilting the decision in the party conclave in favor of the resisters and against the compromisers; I think that I did it, too, because it may have made me look more important and influential than I actually was.

It was a cold night; I lingered in the cavernous foyer of the building until, around eleven, the news came from upstairs: the leaders of the Small Holders' Party had chosen to decline the Russian suggestion; they refused to take part in the election on a joint ticket with the Democratic Popular Front, including the Communists. For months, indeed years afterward, I prided myself on my role that day, in having influenced, if only in the short run, the fate of Hungary, of Europe, perhaps of the world. Many years later I found out that the Americans had already learned about the Russian intervention independently of me; also that Paul had chosen not to announce my news at the party conclave, for a variety of reasons— *surtout pas trop de zèle.* The election took place on November 4. I voted, for the first time in my life and for the last time in Hungary. The Communists got 17 percent of the vote, the Small Holders nearly 60. I felt not much of a sense of triumph, rather the contrary: the composition of the new government reflected not so much the people's choice as the supreme reality, which was that Hungary belonged to the Russians. The key positions in the new government were allotted either to men whom the Russians wanted or to others whom the Russians would tolerate, at least for the time being, no matter to what party they might officially belong.

I convinced myself that the jig was up: or, rather, that it was not coming down, not at all. The year was drawing to its end; the atmosphere was chilly. I enveloped myself in a cocoon of self-indulgent gloom. My mother was not well. We had little money and little food. My personal life was unattractive, in more ways than one. On the day before Christmas I sat with my mother in darkness at noon, in our erstwhile dining room, with the electricity hardly flickering, with everything around us, including my mother's beauty, in ruins. The radio hissed and babbled while we were eating our soup. There was a program about what was going on citywide on this day. In a downtown square the staff of the American Military Mission had put up a Christmas tree. The voice that came on the radio was that of Margit Schlachta, the head of a Catholic religious order, a nun who was famous for her untiring, and sometimes heroic, efforts during previous years in protecting the victims of Nazis. She made a brief statement thanking the Americans for their gifts and then she suddenly said: "A little boy had come up to me just now. He asked me: 'Sister, what kind of soldiers are these?' My answer was: 'These are soldiers whom you don't have to fear.' " My mother burst into tears; so did I, I am ashamed to say.

I wasn't ashamed of it then. I was full of illusions about America, about the West. "The West": this term that the Germans, calculatedly and often shamelessly, employed in their propaganda toward the end of the war, began to have a real meaning for us only now, when we lay under the big hairy thumb of the Orient Bear. (No one in Hungary ever thought that we belonged to "Eastern Europe" before.) I knew how backward and unattractive the Communists and their Russian masters were, ridden with corruption and with their own sense of inferiority. I had not the slightest doubt that Americans were better, stronger, richer, more dynamic and infinitely more attractive. One day the Russians would retreat and the Americans would advance. But it would take a long time, perhaps decades. Soviet rule over Hungary was, for the time being, irreversible. I was right, for all that, but not entirely for the right reasons. My pessimism was, at least in part, a rationalization. I was convincing myself that things were turning not to the better but to the worse: that I had no future in this Hungary, that next year my university studies would be over, that because of my merits the Americans would give me a preferential visa, that sooner or later the Communist political police would reach out for me; in sum, that my situation in Hungary was becoming dangerous, that it was intolerable. In December 1945 some of this was still exaggerated. How much of my decision to skip was spurred by a sense of adventure, by a desire to escape these gloomy surroundings, perhaps even including the sad presence of my mother, I cannot tell. All immigrants lie, also to themselves. I was to be a political refugee *par excellence*; yet I know now, what I refused to know then, that in escaping to America my motives as well as my purposes were more mixed than I chose to think then, and for a long time thereafter. I was desperate and impetuous, pessimistic and impatient at the same time. "Intolerable" is simply what one doesn't want to tolerate.

Many years later, in the memoirs of a Hungarian political figure who, like many others, took the route of exile two or three years after me, I read a passage I have since thought about often. He related a conversation with a friend, a political colleague from the Small Holders' Party, with whom he had struggled against the Germans and their many followers but a few years before. Only now this man decided to go along with the Russians: he was prominent among the accommodationists, not the resisters. His friend reminded him that they had been sitting in the same restaurant only three or four years before, talking about the politicians who had thrown in their lot with the Germans, and who would be soon gone with the wind, destroyed or, at best, scattered in disgrace, which was indeed what happened. Wasn't he doing the same thing now: choosing the side of disgrace and of certain defeat? No, the other man said: the comparison was incomplete. Then the Germans were bound to be defeated, in a year or two at the most. Now the

Russians would stay for a long time. True, the Americans had begun to oppose them (this was in 1947), but the Americans had no staying power. Ten or twenty years would pass, and the Americans would give up this kind of struggle. They were an immature people; and they were going to have enough troubles of their own.

That, too, was a rationalization, I thought when I first read this, and I still think so: this man was trying to convince himself that, after all he had been living through, it was better for him to stay in Hungary and earn some kind of living under a Sovietish regime than to go abroad and be an exile in a foreign country. He, too, had just enough courage to be a coward. But of course he was not entirely wrong.

He was wrong in one sense, however, as indeed I was, coming from a different direction, and for different reasons. When I returned to Hungary on a visit in 1972, more than a quarter of a century after my escape, I found that the Americanization of my native country was nearly complete. The largest building along the once-destroyed Danube riverfront was an Intercontinental Hotel, a concrete pile looking like a large American airport building, furnished and inhabited by the clientele of the latter. A Hilton Hotel was being erected that would soon dominate the skyline of Buda. Hungary had become a democratized, industrialized and bureaucratized society, with hordes of young people wearing American blue jeans. The principal interest of the majority was cars. The only handwriting on a wall was not a political or even an obscene scrawl; it was the name of a famous American rock group. The red-white-and-blue pennant of Pepsi-Cola flew in many places, from sailboats on lakes to the doorways of restaurants. I saw large family parties ordering Pepsi after the main course in restaurants, with pride and panache, as if it were champagne. During twelve days in Hungary I saw less than a handful of Russians, while the city was full of Germans and Americans. In the better hotels and restaurants Russians were virtually nonexistent; if they ventured to trudge in, wearing dusty sandals and soiled open shirts, they were relegated to tables in the back, near the kitchen or the lavatory. More important was my realization that thirty years of Russian rule had left the culture and the civilization of my native country largely untouched. Russian fashions were nonexistent, Russian customs ignored, Russian art, Russian writing, both new and old, unpopular and left unread. After thirty years less than a handful of Russian words had been adopted or transformed into Magyar, while the everyday language teemed with new words that had come from the proletarian, the city argot, the Gypsy, the American or the computer-English languages. Of course this was but one side of the coin. The other side was the sovereign reality: the Russians were still the masters of the Hungarian state. Here, too, I thought, not much has really changed since Year Zero. The strange coexistence—or, rather, co-dominion—of America and Russia ruled the world, including Hungary. The levels of their influences may have changed, but the proportions remained largely the same. Had Hungary ended up on the western side of the iron curtain, she would have been spared much terror, brutality and suffering; yet, so far as her social transformation went, the end result may not have been terribly different. But that, too, is another story.

My story, that of Year Zero recalled, ends with a moral and with a failure. What I learned during that year was something I had found to be true well before 1945, under different circumstances, when the Germans had been dominant, and something that I was to find again and again, under even more different circumstances, in the United States. It was stated by Karl Stern in his spiritual autobiography, *The Pillar of Fire,* as he spoke about life under the Nazis in the Thirties; the same thing was true under the Soviets in the Forties. "In the 1930's," he wrote, "it first dawned on me that the great Dividing Line in Europe, in fact in the entire world, is not the line between Right and Left. All of us who grew up in the intellectual atmosphere of the Twenties were sincerely convinced that people who were politically to the Left of the middle acted under a moral incentive. Indeed, as I have said, in most radicals there had been during the early post-war period, underneath it all, a love of justice and a compassion for the multitude. Conversely, it was held that people were conservative out of material motives for conservation, no matter how much some of them were able to deceive themselves. In this respect the Nazi years taught us a lesson. It happened not infrequently that you met a friend whom you had known for years as a 'staunch liberal,' and he turned out to be eager for any compromise to save his skin. On the other hand, we saw people whom we had disclaimed as 'reactionaries' go to concentration camps and to the gallows. In the beginning it seemed confusing. But gradually the issue became clearer and it was obvious that the only thing that counts in this world is the strength of moral convictions."

How true this was, and how it corresponds with what I had seen! Only I wanted to have my cake and eat it, too. At the end of Year Zero my decision was made. I would get out, preferably to America. The next July I fled from Hungary. I was about to be smuggled across the Austrian frontier, with American help. At noon on the day I was to flee I went to say good-bye to my grandparents. "So you are going, after all?" my grandmother said. There was something infinitely sad about these words. *"Hát mégis elmész?"*

Once more, that afternoon, something gripped my heart. At Győr I left a bus and took a dirty, broken-down train for the frontier town where I was to meet the man who would take me across next morning. Passing through abandoned fields, torn-up sidings, ruined stations, that train wheezed forward during the hot, yellow dusk of a Hungarian evening in July. I saw a signalman in his pathetic, torn uniform of the Hungarian State Railways, with a thin and hungry face, stand in front of his signal house and give the customary salute with his signal flag to that rattling wreck of a train. At that moment I had an almost irresistible impulse to turn around, to cut my escape short. I knew it was my duty to return to my now almost manless family; the voice and picture of my grandmother swam before me in a small rising pool of tears. I felt not nostalgia and not homesickness but the deep impulse of a very human and solemn responsibility—surely to them, perhaps to my country, perhaps even to myself. As I just wrote, however, the compulsion was *almost* irresistible; and, no matter how true and deep their source, the small pool of my tears was shallow. Even now I sometimes think that to follow that impulse may have been the right thing to do. But I don't have enough of that stuff of self-sacrifice that I otherwise so much admire.

CHAPTER 4

New World, Old World

THREE MONTHS FROM THE day that I passed out of my native country, wending my way through a forest on the Austrian border, I came ashore in the United States at Portland, Maine. Owing to my recommendation letters from the American Minister and the American Military Mission in Hungary, the American Consulate in Paris gave me a visa immediately, but it took some time until I could get passage on a ship bound for the United States. A dockers' strike had restricted shipping in more East Coast ports, which was why the Liberty freighter on which I finally sailed from Bordeaux was directed to Portland. It was a warm October day. Remaining in my memory are the gray Maine rocks between which the ship was passing on its way to the port, the flatness of the horizon, the low skyline of the town and the thick woolen anklets of the young girls (bobby socks then) trooping through the streets. This may have been the first time I sensed that I was coming to live in a very old country inhabited by young people—the opposite of my mother continent, which is, by and large, geologically young but whose people are old.

Seven years later I was sworn in as an American citizen. When I walked into the Federal building at Ninth and Market streets in Philadelphia I found myself in a dark cavern of humid gloom. The corridors were formicant with municipal refuse. The court clerk had the expression of a malicious owl. A turtle-like judge pronounced a few dusty clichés. I was sworn in standing next to a

South African couple I had met in a Germantown bar some weeks before, when they had been unimpressively drunk. That ceremony was disconcerting. Yet it did not matter much, surely not at the time, the worst years of the Communist oppression in Hungary. I did not for a moment regret the loss (if that was what it was) of my erstwhile Hungarian citizenship. What mattered was the generosity of some of my American relatives and friends, who greeted my American citizenship cheerfully, welcoming me with small presents and an effusive spirit that was very American.

Thirty-six years after that event I still have ambiguous sentiments about being an American. When I talk about Americans or American things, whether here or abroad, I am self-conscious enough to find it difficult, or even impossible, to use the pronoun *we*. (Yet when some years ago a review in *The New Yorker* described me as "a noted American historian," this gave me a mix of amusement and pleasure.) I have often wished for the time before 1840, when one's American passport (then a beautiful quarto folded sheet of parchment paper) was issued by a state or city court and not by Washington, when one traveled and was identified as a Pennsylvanian as well as an American. But that is neither here nor there, being probably part and parcel of my liking for provincial affinities. What belongs here is that modicum of honesty which, I am sorry to say, I find missing in the recollections of many famous immigrants. "I am an American, born in Paris in 1929," I once read in an author's credit line, giving the impression that he was the smart offspring of cosmopolitan Americans of that time, whereas his parents' provenance was not American but Bessarabian, having come to Paris not from the eastern shores of the New World but from the eastern recesses of the Old. I also recall a successful immigrant savant of International Relations who worked his way up to become an American ambassador. He had been born in a provincial town of the Austro-Hungarian Empire, but he must have liked Vienna so much that it eventually became his birthplace. Some years ago Eugene Ormandy, the celebrated director of the Philadelphia Orchestra, received the Medal of Freedom from the President of the United States. To the reporters he said: "People always ask me where I was born. I was born at the age of twenty-one, when I arrived in the United States." Presumably facts such as that his name in Hungary was not Ormandy (being a near-aristocratic moniker), and that he had played a minor role during the sordid and short-lived Communist regime in Hungary in 1919 were now relegated to his pre-conscious memory.

The memory of immigrants is a complex story that still awaits its exposition by a knowledgeable and sensitive writer. It is complex because for so many immigrants, and even more for their descendants, the Atlantic was a vast psychic chasm, not a bridge between the Old World and the New. If they did not themselves invent the motives of their departure from their native countries, their descendants did it for them. Talking to my students and reading their family history papers year after year, I have been stunned by their sometimes willful ignorance of the provenance of their ancestors, even in instances when they possessed factual data about their grandparents' or great-grandparents' birthplaces in Italy or Ireland or Poland. A split-mindedness is at work there which I may illustrate by two examples. One of my students, Italian-American by name and looks, a third-generation American, wrote emphatically that she knew and wished to know nothing about her Italian ancestors. "We have always regarded ourselves as Americans, nothing more or less." A few sentences later she described one of her American aunts: "She is a full-blooded Italian." Another student, after having written in some detail about the dreadfully humiliating difficulties with which her grandfather, an Irish laborer, had to cope during his first ten years in the United States, went on to write a few lines later that her grandfather was blessed from the day he had set foot in America, where he was newly born.

I was *not* Newly Born. I was *not* An Immigrant. I was *not* one of Emma Lazarus's Huddled Masses. I was a special case: I came to the United States as the United States had allowed my homeland to become a part of the Russian sphere of Europe, having already then demonstrated my dedication to liberty and to the English-speaking nations. I kept telling this to Americans for years. They were not impressed. They listened to me sympathetically, but what

I said made no particular impression on them: an immigrant was an immigrant. They were right.

My naturalization (odd word, that) was expedited by the decision of the Immigration and Naturalization Service to classify me as a Displaced Person, a category that the American government established soon after the war, in order to cope with the millions of refugees, of the most various kind (Jews who had escaped Hitler's death camps were often put together with people who had helped the Germans in transporting them there), who were huddled in Western Germany, Austria and Italy after the war. I thought and felt and, on occasion, said that I had little in common with these untutored masses whom I, for one, had preceded by a few years. The very bureaucratic tone of the term Displaced Person grated on my ears. I was wrong. It took me years to realize that every displaced person, including myself, was a *bona et mala fide* immigrant; and that every American immigrant, beginning with 1607 and all that, was a displaced person.

Bona et mala fide: because the vast majority of immigrants had come with the idea of eventually returning to their native countries, an idea that later faded from their minds. This was true, too, of my generation of exiles, but for a different reason: we hoped that sooner or later the United States would force the Russians out of some of their Eastern European satrapies. I had doubts about that from the beginning; still, I thought that the word *exile* fitted me better than Displaced Person or Refugee or Immigrant. The psychology of exiles is interesting enough to fill an entire book. It involves not only aspirations and maladjustments but even dreams. Being an exile has its particular pains and pleasures. The first involve maladjustment in space as well as in time: the inability and, in some cases, the unwillingness to adjust one's mind to the conditions of the host country and to the national mind of its people. This is compounded by the inability to comprehend how one's native country has changed through the years, whereby even the most intelligent exiles can seldom free their minds from the categories and associations of the condition of their native country at the time of their departure.

There are, however, compensatory pleasures in the life of an exile. One of these involves the inflation of one's social status in the old country—a normal human weakness. A vignette of this may be found in the writing of the brilliant French reactionary Rivarol who, in the company of noblemen and noblewomen emigrés in a Hamburg boarding-house in 1793, listened to an aspiring newcomer referring to himself as *"nous aristocrates,"* whereupon Rivarol shot back: *"C'est un usage du pluriel que je trouve bien singulier"*—"This is a usage of the plural that I find very singular." In any event, an exile may find it possible to associate with such compatriots whose company in his native country he would have sought largely in vain. The pleasures of this kind of snobbery are easier to come by than in one's native country. Consequently, such social vanities may satisfy even such men and women who were not particularly addicted to social climbing in their earlier lives—as in the instance of a dear old friend of mine who declined my suggestion for a convivial evening in New York with the words, unexpected and strange from his lips: "You don't understand. I may be dining with the Prime Minister at the C.'s tonight." The Prime Minister, a thoroughly honorable man, had been the last constitutional prime minister of Hungary, but that was twenty years before; now he lived in reduced circumstances in New York, where my friend could meet him every day, had he wished to. On the other hand, the C. family *did* live on Park Avenue, a kind of salon of the *gratin* of Hungarian exiledom in New York. Another example of the magnetism of companionship was that of the man-about-town in Budapest now (temporarily) reduced to the status of a factory worker on Long Island, who would appear twice a week in the cocktail lounge of the Sherry-Netherland Hotel in New York, where a Hungarian pianist from Old Budapest was playing and where occasionally Hungarians would amble in. He spent a considerable portion of his paycheck on the glass of cognac and the cover charge; when I asked him why he did this, he said, "One can wave to people there."

Let me repeat: the psychology of exiles still awaits the genius of a master writer who will have to proceed from a position that is rare and difficult, since it must be equidistant from the small world of the exiles and from the larger world of Americans. He must be equidistant and at the same time thoroughly familiar with both, very much including their two languages with all of their nuances. In most cases, the mental life of an exile in the United States goes through three phases. During the first years he lives among other exiles. Then the slow period of his Americanization begins: gradually the number of his American friends and acquaintances and associations (including linguistic associations) increases, while those of his former compatriots decreases. Yet there comes a phase, many years later, when he rediscovers his native roots; among other things, he begins to reread the literature of his native country, and he is no longer unwilling to revisit his native country when that becomes possible. This evolution within the life of a single man is a condensed example of what often happens to immigrant families within three generations. The first generation is still steeped in old habits and ways of thinking. The second generation tears itself away, wishing to be as American as possible. It is the third generation that, fairly secure in its Americanism, sometimes develops a new (and, alas, often abstract or even false) interest in the country of its ancestors. This is different from the acculturation of an immigrant in, say, Britain or France, where he becomes more and more British or French as time goes on; but Americanization is both easier and more complicated than that. It is easier to become an American than to become American, and of course I mean something more than mere citizenship.

I know now that my claim of having been a special kind of immigrant was a distinction without a difference; but there was one difference between me and most of my fellow exiles. As I suggested before, I did not share their hopes for an eventual American liberation of Hungary, not because I was more of a political realist than they but because I knew Americans better than many of them did. Allied with my political pessimism was my conviction that Hungary was lost for a long time. This was one of the reasons I chose to make my academic career and writing into something more than becoming an interpreter of Central European history in English. It was one of the reasons, too, that soon after my arrival in the United States I chose to live among Americans. And this was the time, too, when my engagement to the English language matured into a pursuit of marriage—like all love affairs, full of satisfactions and frustrations, of surprising sudden understandings and depressing misunderstandings: a cohabitation and a concubinage that grew to an extent where I began thinking and counting and dreaming in English, though feeling in Magyar, nonetheless. As Horace said, *"patriae quis exsul se quoque fugit"*—"for a long time the exile flees not only his native country but himself."

Soon after my arrival in the United States I realized something that should have been dear to the heart of reactionaries: this country, in more than one way, was older than Europe; in other ways it was behind Europe. This was not the solitary recognition of a young man attracted to paradox. My generation of Displaced Persons, most of us anti-Communist exiles, took heart from the condition that around 1947 the American government and people at long last "awakened" to the danger of Communism, adopting—belatedly—ideas that to most of these exiles were familiar. In other words, the Americans were catching up with us. For me, some of the consequences of this catching up were welcome, while others were distressing, but that belongs to the next chapter. Together with my fellow exiles, I believed that the source of the belatedness of this American awakening was American simplicity and naïveté. Most of them—one example being Alexander Solzhenitsyn, whom I otherwise admire—believe this even now. I no longer do.

In any event, naïveté and innocence, hypocrisy and optimism: they seemed to abound and flourish in the American air: mental conditions of a New Old World, different and yet here and there reminiscent of beliefs that had burnt to ashes in Europe during the world wars and even before. That in 1945 and after, America was past its age of innocence, that American optimism, too, was more superficial than it seemed made, as yet, no difference: not to me, and not to Americans who would realize the insubstantial nature of their optimism later—alas, so often with deplorable results. What was wonderful was the existence of all kinds of freedoms that had vanished in Europe, surely in my native country: a divine freedom from regulations, governments, police, the freedom to move, to seek and find employment, to wander around, the astonishing prevalence of all kinds of goods, including books in libraries that you could take home to read, the absence of curiosity on the part of authorities and people in what you were doing. I soon found out that this absence of curiosity was not quite identical with trust, that it amounted at times to a lack of interest and at other times to suspicions (not only about what you might be doing but of what you may be thinking); yet, on balance, these things did not matter much against the often thoughtless generosity of America and Americans, against these widespread and prospering survivals of practices of the nineteenth century. I was now in a country where I had not the slightest fear of the police: except for their uniforms, which were assertively martial (especially those of state troopers), the police were what they had been in the century before—paid and dependable protectors of civic law and order. One day in 1948 I found a government envelope in my mail, out of which came a check: my tax refund. That in the United States it was not the state but I who reported my taxes due, that I had the opportunity to figure out that the taxes which had been withheld from my salary and which I had never seen may have amounted to a few dollars more than what I owed was curious enough; but that someone in the government actually paid this sum *back* to me, on my word alone, was something wondrous and unexpected, something that had to be seen to be believed. It was around that time that one of my older friends, a Philadelphia lawyer, said that while he was entitled to many professional deductions from his income tax, he took hardly any of these because he would not fiddle with what he owed his country. I believed what he said; I was properly impressed; but somehow I thought even then that this kind of ancient patriotic and patrician probity, admirable in principle, was increasingly rare. America would soon be catching up with Europe; such conduct would not, because it could not, last.

Very soon after my arrival in this country I realized that Americans were a conservative people. With all of their belief in Progress

and Science—beliefs that were typical of the nineteenth century—
they were loath to change their minds, while they were changing
and exchanging their material possessions incredibly fast: proof of
the opposite to the established notion that Americans are material-
ists. But this business—busy-ness—of American materialism was
complicated: since most Americans *thought* that they were material-
ists, consequently in some ways and on some levels of their thinking
they were. These levels did not, however, mean different levels of
consciousness. The American mind was split on the conscious level,
not between the conscious and the so-called subconscious. It was
split vertically, not horizontally. The same Americans who had
entertained an entirely materialist philosophy of the world, including themselves, were the same people who believed in American
idealism, thinking (and not only saying) that theirs was an idealist
nation, probably the only idealist nation in the world. This characteristic American split-mindedness was, in itself, a very old mental
inclination, harking back to the Middle Ages. I have written elsewhere about the medieval facet of the American mind: this, too,
does not belong here, except perhaps to say that people who have
illusions about the Middle Ages are conservatives, not reactionaries,
as indeed people in the Middle Ages were conservatives and not
reactionaries. The reactionaries were the men and women of the
Renaissance who, for the first time in many centuries, discovered
the virtues and the beauties of a Greece and Rome long past and
wanted to emulate them. When D. H. Lawrence wrote that the
Puritans had revolted against the freedoms of Renaissance Europe,
he was surely more right than wrong.

The churches were full in America in 1947. Whether the religious
beliefs of Americans were profound, whether their sermons were
up-to-date or Victorian or fundamentalist does not matter here:
what matters is that churchgoing was still an essential feature of
American Sundays, in the cities as well as in the small towns of the
country. And when I came to Philadelphia that year, to take up
residence and work in that city, I was surprised as well as charmed
to find a place where many of the appearances and the habits and
the minds of people were reminiscent of a near-Victorian England:

slow and solid, provincial and content, in red brick houses with small gardens in the back. The lives of people in the beautiful Philadelphia suburbs filled me with wonder, as did some of the provincial habits of many Philadelphians. Here I was in an American city where, unlike in England, some people kept on reading Trollope. (It was—and it probably still is—easier to find a second-hand Trollope in Philadelphia than almost anywhere else in the world.) In 1947 Philadelphia was still something of a Victorian city, with Victorian susceptibilities, and inhabited by plenty of people with pseudo-Victorian minds. I was (and am) not a Victorian addict; I find Victorian furniture, including the interior Victorian furniture of minds, fussy rather than attractive; but the philistine Victorianism of Philadelphia was so much preferable to the feverish and yet deadening superficiality of New York, where so much of the style and of the categories of intellectual life were, strangely, German rather than English, which is why refugees from Weimar Berlin had taken to it like ducks to water, since the New York of the Forties was, in odd ways, a fulfillment of their cosmopolitan expectations. But I was less than a refugee: I was a Displaced Person.

Displaced and lonely, I was looking forward to my first Christmas in Philadelphia. I had some business in New York, wherefrom I took the train back in the middle of the afternoon of the twenty-fourth of December. The train was half-empty. When I stepped down on the platform of Broad Street Station the dusk had already darkened into near-night. The sounds of the station echoed faintly under that large iron and glass roof. Old Broad Street was a real railway station, unlike Pennsylvania Station in New York, where you had to descend from something like Caracalla's Baths into the depths to reach your train, as if you were taking a subway. Old Broad Street Station was reminiscent of the grand Victorian terminals of London. Its high-ceilinged restaurant was empty, with a few stragglers and derelicts leaning over bowls of oyster stew, no doubt. As I crossed Market Street, oddly bereft of cars, unlike the hooting, shrieking New York streets on that afternoon, a few flecks of snow began to fall. I was going to a Philadelphia family for Christmas Eve dinner. Later that night the young woman of that family and I walked to midnight Mass. By that time the streets were dusted with snow. There was another Victorian touch in that scene, with the wintry streets and the cozy yellow lights in the brick houses. It was, of course, interrupted by sharp and acrid reminders of modern ugliness, to wit, the neon-lit White Tower stand on the corner of Market Street. As we approached the Cathedral on Logan Circle I saw that there was something wrong. The circle was empty; there were no cars in the approaching streets; the cathedral looked dark and forbidding. Indeed it was. The great bronze doors of the Cathedral of Saints Peter and Paul were locked tight as a drum. There was no midnight Mass at Christmas in Philadelphia. Cardinal Dougherty had forbidden it for many years, lest the people of Philadelphia be scandalized on Holy Night by the eventual sight of unseemly alcoholic merriment among his flock.

Many of the Blue Laws of Philadelphia still existed then. Consequently, date night in Philadelphia was Friday, not Saturday. On Saturday night bars closed at one a.m. For the next thirty-six hours no drink would be served in any public place in Philadelphia, which was a considerable strain on this displaced person, who lived in two rented rooms in Germantown, without kitchen facilities. For a non-Philadelphian a weekend in Philadelphia meant utter loneliness, Victorian loneliness, exactly in the way in which Taine had described London on a Sunday in the 1880s in his *Notes sur l'Angleterre:* large empty streets, funereal and forbidding. There were, of course, private islands of liquor and cheer in that gray sea: parties, parties. But I found myself beyond their coral fringe. There was the geographical problem: these islands of parties and clubs and cheer were all around in the suburbs, and my small boat had no motor; in plain English, I did not have a car. To go downtown wouldn't have made any sense: that downtown was empty, even for the sake of provender. Most restaurants were closed on Sunday. And how few restaurants there were in Philadelphia forty years ago! Most of them served tearoom food. There was perhaps only one restaurant with uniformly fine standards, that of the Barclay Hotel, with Caesar and Mario and Gustav, princes of maîtres. Public gourmets in

Philadelphia spoke with respect about one restaurant within sixty miles, Joe's in Reading, built on its Polish owners' dedication to mushrooms; but then there were few public gourmets in Philadelphia. Twenty years later the opposite came about: Philadelphia, like other cities of the Republic, was full of people who knew everything about restaurants, though not much about food.

But in the private houses and in the private clubs the opposite was true. Once in a while someone would invite me to a Philadelphia club, where the food was better than in the best London clubs (besides the splendid seafood from the Chesapeake there were old English elements: veal pies and trifles, for example); once in a while I would be invited to a Philadelphia dinner party, which for me was then (and which is still) the best place in the world to be on a Friday or Saturday night. There was something old-fashioned about that, too. In Europe, in England, the buffet, the *souper,* the cocktail party, had replaced dinner parties even before the last war, mostly because of the servant (or, rather, the non-servant) problem. In Philadelphia the chatelaine of the house, with a solitary helper, produced fine dinners and subdued conviviality for a small circle around the table. This was very different from the nervous haste and the straining at smartness at a New York dinner party. Foie gras and caviar there were none in Philadelphia, but drinks were aplenty, before, during and after dinner, which began late and leisurely, and went on enduring, like a Philadelphia reputation. It took me some time to recognize the Southern touch in Philadelphia, which in many ways—especially in its social life and drinking habits—has more in common not only with Baltimore but also with Charleston rather than with Boston, even though not many Philadelphians are conscious of this, having an occasional (and, to my mind, a greatly mistaken) sense of inferiority to the latter city. As Owen Wister once wrote: "Philadelphia happens to lie virtually on the border between two colonial parts of the country, distinct from each other; south of the Schuylkill the South may be fairly said to begin, and north of the Delaware the North."

For my first two years in Philadelphia I lived in Chestnut Hill and Germantown, in furnished rooms. How often I felt that I was in the midst of an atmosphere that had vanished in Europe long ago! The soft hypocrisies, the church-going, the unwillingness to recognize, let alone admit, anything unpleasant: they were like the taste of milk, the taste that I had abhorred in my childhood but that I began to like in Philadelphia. I remember that first taste, in October 1947. Up the hill the son of a friendly *grande dame* was chopping wood. I went out from my cramped little room to join him. It was one of those exhilarating sunny October afternoons that make the Pennsylvania autumn so beautiful, with a tinge of fresh woodsmoke in the air. We split wood for about an hour, after which we went into their large, empty, cool, white, china-cupboard kitchen and drank milk, after having spooned the cream from the bottle top. (Milk was still being delivered every morning from Montgomery County dairies in bottles.) "Guess what I did this afternoon?" I wrote that night to my beautiful, ill, trembling mother in Hungary. "I was cutting wood and drinking milk." I was back in a healthy, natural, outdoorsy past: back in time, and in America at that.*

A few weeks later I met someone who was to become a lifelong friend: a dear old Philadelphia lawyer, fairly obsessed with Natural Law, who devoted most of his time to an unfinished book concerned with the philosophical essence of Natural Law. He introduced me to a group called The Round Table, where once a

---

*I didn't remain a milk drinker for long. One evening a rich, handsome and Junoesque young Quakeress, a nubile graduate student at the University of Pennsylvania, invited me to her parents' house, grand in dimensions and furnished beyond the dreams of avarice. Among other things (this was before LP records, stereos and tapes) there was a music room, with a radio-phonograph occupying an entire long wall with thousands of records. For once, a Philadelphia house evoked memories of millionaires' quarters from Hollywood movies that I had seen. Listening to a record and to the crackling of oak logs in the fireplace I longed for a drink; but in that house they didn't serve any. ("Would you like some milk? Or apple juice?" she asked.) Then her younger sister came in, even more stunning and athletic. She was about to leave for Europe for the first time. This was 1948. I had visions of a rich and beautiful American girl making her way through Paris, Italy, the Riviera. I wanted to be helpful. And where was she going? I asked. "To Finland." "To Finland?" "We are going to build huts for Lapps," she said. I was, unlike Queen Victoria, amused rather than impressed.

month—after a dreadfully moderate dinner in a tearoom—Philadelphia lawyers, Episcopalians, and Catholics and Quakers gathered to read papers and discuss arcane theological questions that to them were related to the very immediacy of life.* On Sundays the Masses were thronged; people threw two money-filled envelopes or at least a dollar bill into the collection baskets. I had not seen anything like this in Europe, certainly not in Rome.

In 1948 I began to write my first book. Twice a week I went downtown to the library of the University of Pennsylvania. After wolfing down a quick and cheap and nourishing dinner in the then still antiseptic Horn & Hardart across from the campus, I entered the old Furness Library, a Victorian womb of knowledge if there ever was one. In the quiet gloom, under its fretwork and arches, I found book after book, periodical after periodical, that I wanted to read, and many others I had not known existed. The library was uncrowded. Occasionally I bumped into professors whom I knew and with whom I longed to talk about odd questions that had come to my mind; but usually they stepped away after a few moments, since most American professors were less interested in history than in historianship, then as well as now. This was no great loss. If I wanted some intellectual conversation I could get a good helping in the company of some of my lawyer friends, eventually in that of my father-in-law, who within the first hour of our acquaintance asked me about Napoleon's marshals. He knew the names of all of them by heart; but of course he was not a professor, and certainly not an intellectual. I loved him, and I loved his eldest daughter, whom I married in 1953. I was introduced to her in a house on Rittenhouse Square which no longer exists. The square was muffled in fog, and the few lights were brilliant in the night.†

*What impressed me even more was another kind of immediacy. One of our members once said that he remembered his grandmother's having told him that she had seen George Washington walking on Germantown Avenue.
†RIttenhouse and PEnnypacker (like RHinelander and MUrray Hill in New York) were still telephone-exchange names. And I was charmed, as I still am, by the shapes and sounds of old American place-names and family names: no, not by Indian or New England family names, not by Preserved Smith or

But my discovery of Chester County was even more poignant than my discovery of Philadelphia. One spring day a cursory acquaintance drove me out to a party at his brownstone farmhouse on a country road near Exton. The party included his former wife, a dark-haired young woman with a splendid posture and figure, and a racy American face in which I saw an Indian touch, all of her Welsh forebears notwithstanding. Alas, she was already engaged to her second husband-to-be, waiting until he could struggle himself free of his divorce proceedings. I found her extremely attractive, and we saw each other a few times that spring and early summer. She lived with her little daughters in a white Chester County farmhouse, at the end of a graveled lane off a highway, west of Exton. The porch of her house opened up on a large field, spinach-green in early May. It was there that I first smelled that inimitable scent of old Chester County houses: a potpourri of a faintly spiced mustiness wafting out from old walnut beams and herbaceous flowers somewhere in the kitchen. It was during our drives that I became enchanted with this deep green Pennsylvania countryside that I have loved, with an aching longing, ever since. Unlike other beautiful American scenes, this landscape was rich, humanly rooted, old, near-Arcadian. Oddly—and this in spite of the old and respectable tradition of Philadelphian and Pennsylvanian painting—no painter has done it justice, except perhaps for Daniel Garber and a few fine amateurs. (Andrew Wyeth, the celebrity now associated with southeastern Pennsylvania, is in essence a Maine painter: except for his stony textures, his landscapes and colors are essentially cold, early-spring, without reflecting the rich maturity of this land.) To describe this scenery further, its honest stone houses in the shade of enormous trees in a verdant and undulant and carefully cultivated land, to paint it with more words would make no sense here. I will say that it has something old-world about it. Unlike the

---

Leverett Saltonstall, but by Virginia, Maryland, Pennsylvania names, such as Barbour or Cadwalader or Truxton; not by place-names like Wounded Knee, but by Cinnaminson or Christiana or Sumneytown or Dauphin-Susquehanna, a station that flitted by one hot tropical night in the Philadelphia subway of the Broad Street Line.

Philadelphia suburbs that had, here and there, an English touch, in Chester County the land and the atmosphere it breathed (except during the unbearable, hazy, semi-tropical summer days of heat) were not unlike portions of Western Europe, resembling south-western German or Alsatian or Burgundian fields and hills; at any rate, solidly rooted and old. There have been other refugees in America who discovered elements reminiscent of their homelands in the eastern United States: Austrian refugees flocking to Vermont, for example. But this was different, not only because of the landscape but because of the human presence dotting it. There was no place and no reason here for chalets, and not even for a French- or English-type manor house. Chester County was old-American, a rich Arcadia still inhabited, here and there, by remnants of old gnarled people leading a faintly arcadian agricultural existence, unscarred by the physical and emotional ravages of two world wars, even though their lives had become motorized and gassy and on the cusp of television filling up the recesses of their minds. Eventually I came to live in Chester County with my first wife, struggling for years to convert the ruins of an old schoolhouse and to clear some of the wilderness—yes, wilderness, because of the subtropical burgeoning of a weedy, spiky, bushy, brush-infested vegetation—into the house and garden and field to which I added and added, living there for thirty years, where I fathered my two children, wrote twelve books, wherefrom I buried my first wife who died young, and where I married the second, who remains young enough to lift my spirits with her laughter every day.

So, from the ashes and cinders of the Second World War, it was good to find oneself in a place where so many of the decencies of an earlier age existed still. But there were disturbing elements in this American backwardness.

One of the disturbing elements was this: the new things of the New World had a way of getting old very fast. Some of this was not particularly American: a modern building or a plastic chair cannot age well; they are subject to instant decrepitude after their first encounter with grime or a visible scratch. But the cult of progress in America further contributes to this premature onrush of old age because of the American tendency to conform to whatever seems to be timely and prevalent in public, whereby so many American places and things and sometimes even people become, unwittingly, caricatures of themselves. When I arrived in the United States I had the advantage of knowing English fairly well and knowing something about America, so it was not an altogether unknown and unimagined land to me: in particular, I had seen so much of New York in American movies and picture magazines. Well, that was just it. Much of New York was exactly how I had imagined it: Rockefeller Center, Fifth Avenue, Wall Street, the Waldorf-Astoria, etc.—alas, there was no surprise left. They looked as they were supposed to look; they were straining to adhere to their image, indeed, to exaggerate it, which is the essence of caricature. On my first New Year's Eve in New York, where I lived for the first ten months of my American existence, I went to Times Square, which, too, I had seen in the movies and in the magazines and about which I had read in the newspapers. There expectability ran to excess, including the people who were whooping it up, grimly determined to be jolly, raucous and loud; for that was the way it was supposed to be, the way you were supposed to be on the Great White Night on the Great White Way. Later, too, I saw this tendency of places and people to become exaggerations of themselves not only on Times Square in New York but elsewhere, too, a resistless fate that can befall not only Las Vegas but Nantucket. I found it not only in the often celebrated speech patterns of New York cabdrivers but in the uncelebrated conclaves of businessmen or professors, when those small but essential differences between the expected and the unexpected, between the image and the reality, between the public and the private faces were missing. Philadelphia was different: the odd little streets, the quietness of the city in the evening, the utter unpretentiousness of it all. So were the people, because of their Philadelphian cultivation of an interior life, their privacy; for the sure way to avoid becoming a caricature of yourself is to avoid thinking too much about your appearance, about the image you wish to convey. At least one venerable Philadelphia institution has for its motto: *Esse quam videri*—to be more than to seem. (It does not always live up to it.)

But the difference that mattered was not really that between Old Philadelphia and Modern New York. What mattered was the difference in the process of aging, and the surprising and disconcerting impression that so many things in New York *looked* old. Much of New York was old; but it was not Old New York. The shattering iron clangor of the New York subway with its 1910 look and sounds, its catacombs suggesting Kafka, not Piranesi; the 1910 looks of so many of the office and industrial buildings, their steely rows of windows like the windrows of Theodore Roosevelt's teeth; the Wurlitzer sounds and atmosphere of the New York boulevards, as if this were not 1946 but 1910 or 1920, at the most . . . Odd things remain in my memory: a visit to an office building on Fifth Avenue, on the edge of the garment district, where a Jewish friend of mine worked. Opposite his office a door opened, in which someone was talking rapidly with a rabbinical figure in a long black coat, with a long black beard and earlocks. My friend said that these office neighbors were manufacturers of sleepwear and lingerie. When their door closed I saw the name of their company, in large gilded modern lettering: MOVIE STAR. These two words, I thought (or, rather, I now think I thought) connected this medieval rabbinical figure to modern America at large; they were the fixed bridge between the manufacturers of garments in New York and the manufacturers of dreams in Hollywood. They also annealed the Forties to the ideals of the Twenties; and, for being superficial, these connections were no less real.

Many Americans—and this was a surprise—looked older than I had imagined them. This was particularly so in the late 1940s, when American men still wore hats and undershirts even in the summer, when women wore longer skirts than in Europe, when American bathing suits were longer than European ones, when some older Americans still wore high-button shoes, and when certain American faces—druggists with their white dentures and steel-rimmed glasses, old waitresses with the faces of trolley cars, typewriter faces, smooth preachers' faces, sometimes even the smiles on young girls' faces—looked preternaturally old. There were entire classes of American women who inclined to age more rapidly than their European contemporaries. This had nothing to do with cosmetics or even with their physical circumstances; it had probably much to do with their interior lives. One of the few advancements in the twentieth century has been the prolongation of the sexual attractiveness in the lives of women, at least in the Western world, by perhaps as much as ten or even fifteen years. For the first time in history we live in a world where a woman in her fifties may still be sexually attractive (and not only to a sixty-five-year-old man writing these lines). Yet I saw so many pretty, fresh-skinned American girls suddenly change into middle-aged housewives before the age of thirty, probably less because of excessive physical wear and tear than because their youthful spirit of aspirations had given out. That the face is the mirror of the soul may be even truer in the twentieth century than before, something that has nothing to do with—indeed, in many instances it goes contrary to—face-lifting and cosmetics.

So I am back at the world of ideas, at the inevitable confusion of what happens with what people think happens—or, in a larger sense, at the inevitable intrusion of mind into matter. Some of the appearances of American things and people in the 1940s were old because their ideas were old; and when this aging was rapid and unseemly that happened because their ideas were not only old but corroded and decaying. This was true of the prose of the newspapers: of the prosaic moralism of their editorials as well as of the cheery vulgarities of their Broadway columnists with their ragtime revolver rhetoric, of which the fretful rhythm of the boulevards and the speech and thought patterns of certain people in New York were probably consequences as well as causes. Reading the *New York Post* on occasion I felt that I was in the presence of chemically cheapened and vulgarized substances of matter as well as mind. Its pages breathed an odor like the dreadful smell of hamburger grease floating out into the street from the steel counters of food shops. Besides hamburger grease the awful cloying smell of cheap candy in the subway arcades sticks in my nostrils and memory even now—associated, too, with the music of "Peg O'My Heart," one of the most popular tunes in 1947, a viscous mass of sound pulled by accordions toward a sentimental hell. Sentimentality, Wilde once wrote, is the Bank Holiday of cynicism. In the prose of Walter Winchell every phrase was such a holiday.

In 1946 the American upper class was still predominantly Anglo-Saxon or Anglo-Celtic. But New York was not in the least like London. Of its own Protestant patrician class little remained in evidence. The richest inhabitants of the Plaza were South Americans; the rich inhabitants of the Waldorf had round Herbert Hoover faces; the sage of the city was Bernard Baruch, the multimillionaire whose ideas had attained their shining successes in the high-button-shoe days of Woodrow Wilson, a large human survival of the Woolworth and Flatiron buildings whose features he indeed resembled. New York *was* a cosmopolitan city; there were, of course, opulent and elegant streets, townhouses and smart apartment buildings on Beekman Place, Sutton Place and Gramercy Park; but the arteries of old Protestant New York had become sclerotic, and by arteries I do not mean its streets but the movement of ideas in people's minds. There *was* cosmopolitan life in New York, but the *idea* of cosmopolitan New York had come from the movies. Midwesterners visited it as they would visit Hollywood. Their ideas of that sophisticated eastern metropolis coursed in their minds as they were jumping out of their large cars with their families, self-consciously loud and yet more than slightly anxious, immediately dependent on the all-knowing uniformed doormen of the Statler or the Taft, physically there and yet light-years away from the world of the New York aristocracy that had become Café Society and whose most successful catalysts were White Russians then.

But outside New York, too, across the vast United States, the presence of an outdated ideology prevailed. This was the unquestioned belief in Scientific (and therefore fatalistic) Progress, to which in 1945, and for some time thereafter, all Americans subscribed. American Christians and American atheists, Republicans and Democrats, political liberals and political conservatives believed in it, each in his own way. The trouble with this unquestioned and unquestioning belief was not its inherent optimism (after all, even gullibility ought to be preferable to distrust, and optimism to cynicism) but its outdated nature, left over from a previous century, consisting of endlessly reformulated applications of a mechanical utilitarianism, of the corroding cast-iron philosophies of Bentham or Spencer or Buckle or, indeed, Dickens's Gradgrind. Americans, including those who refused the Darwinian thesis about the creation of the world, were the quintessential Darwinists, not so much because they believed in the survival of the fittest but because fairly early in their history, well before Darwin, the sense of original sin had wholly evaporated even among the Puritans, replaced as this was by a faith in evolution, progress and science. The famous thesis of American historians, such as Professor Richard Hofstadter, to the effect that for about half a century Social Darwinism was the dominant and harmful American ideology was wrong. The most pervasive American creed was not The Survival of the Fittest (that was what Germans believed, not Americans) but of mechanical and inevitable Evolution, endless Progress. That belief had died out in Europe and even in England by the time of the First World War, not so much because of the first appearance of the first spate of post-scientific thinkers such as Dilthey, Bergson, Ortega (their great American confrère was William James), but because of the experiences of a generation. Having escaped those experiences, Americans were wonderfully fortunate; yet their fortunes kept them from the necessity of changing their minds about the relentless sunny march of Progress. Their belief in the acceleration of history actually slowed down the movements of their minds. Even Henry Adams, who claimed to represent some of the mind-set of the eighteenth century, concluded that history would now accelerate very fast, with the speed of a dynamic machine, toward catastrophe. He mistook the speed of communications for the movement of ideas: the first had become very fast, the second very slow. Apart from a few isolated, serious thinkers* the belief in an ever speedier,

---

*They were mostly to be found among intellectual Catholics who wrote for *Commonweal* at the time, or for seriously committed Catholics of *the Catholic Worker* movement. Thus the editorial in the August 3, 1945, *Commonweal*,

limitless and endless prospect of the world was as pervasive among
Americans in 1945 as it had been in 1915, including their grumbling
liberal intellectuals and moping academics. To question Science and
Progress was not only unthinkable; it was not to be thought about.
The unquestionable premise was not the Apostolic Creed; it was the
phrase *Science says* . . . When I said to my Catholic students that
whether the sun goes around the earth or the earth around the sun,
what difference does that make? they were nonplussed; and when
I went on to say that I do not believe everything Science says they
were shocked and uncomprehending. I had the strong feeling that
if I had said that I do not really believe in God they would have been
shocked, too, but far from uncomprehending: that was perhaps to
be expected from a European, even from a European Catholic. In
this there was no difference between New York and Philadelphia;
indeed, the trust in Science has lasted long in Philadelphia because
of the prevalence of nineteenth-century patterns of thinking in the
minds of Philadelphians.*

---

published but a few days before Hiroshima: "In trying to save the old nationalism by a new internationalism, we are on the threshold of a house not remarkably dissimilar from one the Europeans have seen destroyed over their heads.
We are about to go through what they have already gone through. Although
the materialism of our magnificent machine civilization is ultra-modern, everything non-material about us, our hopes and our ideals, our dreams and our
ambitions, our political thinking and feeling, is of the past. . . . Even from the
point of view of modern science, the American myth with its corollary of
infinite human perfectibility and limitless material progress is old-fashioned.
The philosophical journalists and religious writers of western Europe whose
political orientations would be considered reactionary by most American liberals and progressives are actually more advanced than the writers and journalists
of America. For they have noted that the probings of science downward into
the microscope and upward into the cosmological have reached a floor and a
ceiling: there are limits to man's freedom, imposed not by religion but by the
nature of man himself."
*From my diary, January 1983: "I lunch at the Philadelphia Club with D. and
his friend G., an old-fashioned Philadelphia gent. It is all very pleasant and
entirely aimless. At first I relish this contrast in tempo from New York where
I was yesterday; everything is slow and a little hesitant and utterly comfortable.
(Lunch not quite as good as it used to be there.) The conversation is civilized
and satisfactorily reactionary. But in the end the inevitable Philadelphian intel-

In 1945 the triumph of the United States and the Soviet Union revived the prestige of materialism. In their own ways both of these Great Powers represented philosophies of economic determinism. People all over the world adjusted their minds accordingly. Within the United States the progressive worldview dominated all political thinking, on the popular as well as on the academic level. Before and during the war Americans saw Hitler and the Third Reich—wrongly—as extreme representatives of backwardness and reaction. After 1945, as the cold war with Russia was crystallizing, they saw the developing world struggle not between two imperial states but between two economic ideologies, Communism and Capitalism, even though Stalin had nothing in common with Marx while he had much in common with Ivan the Terrible, and even though the United States was moving away from traditional capitalism fast. I had an early experience of that tendency in 1950, even before the age of the credit card. After my mother's death in Vienna I wanted to rescue the few remaining pieces of our old furniture that miraculously survived the war and the liquidation of our belongings. The shipping costs were large. At the very bank where I had a checking and a small savings account I applied for a loan. Having been brought up in a bourgeois world, impressed by the admonition that debt was a curse to be avoided, I answered the loan officer's questions: "Do you have any debts?" "Do you have charge accounts?" with a self-confident "No." "Well," he said, "we can't give you a loan then. You have no credit record." It was my first experience with the socialist and bureaucratic essence of what even now goes under the name of Capitalism in America, where a largely abstract capacity of creditability had come to count more than the actual

---

lectual inclination creeps in: G. talks *too long* about "digs," the discovery of new Assyrian clay tablets or, rather, their carbon-dating which, according to him, will revolutionize the dating of the Book of Daniel. This kind of reverence for the Facts Of Science, this carbon-dating of the Bible, this University of Pennsylvania Museum climate of the mind is part of the Franklinian Philadelphia spirit: these people cannot shake off their belief in Progress, at least not on one level of their minds, even while in their daily lives and human experiences they know better."

possession of assets or the record of personal thrift. (I must add that I got the loan in the end: one of my older friends, a Proper Philadelphian, spoke to his friend who was one of the bank directors. But this was Philadelphia, of course.)

My discovery of the discreet charms of an American bourgeoisie was a great compensation during my lonely years. *Bourgeoisie* is, of course, a European word that has been terribly misused, in the Old World as well as in the New. Most people cannot spell it without a mistake or two. Intellectuals have been consistently wrong about its very meaning. (Edmund Wilson wrote: "The writer who has made me feel most overwhelmingly that bourgeois society was ripe for burial was . . . Proust"—a revelation not only of Wilson's misconception of the term but of his own intellectual blinders.) At any rate, the bourgeoisie means something different from an aristocracy but also from the middle class. We in Europe knew something about the existence of an American class of millionaires, of a financial and social "aristocracy" in the United States; about the existence of an American working class whose standards of living were astonishingly high; and about the fact that between these two classes there was a powerful American middle class whose extent was amazingly large. But about the gradations, the various groups, the inclinations and the aspirations of this American middle class I knew almost nothing. Yet in Europe, too, I had begun to see that in a modern society the most significant differences were perhaps those between an upper and lower middle class, more significant than those separating the upper from the middle and the middle from the lower classes. These differences involved neither income nor profession, and perhaps not even recognitions of social status. They were differences of aspirations: they involved matters of culture, not money, and consequently, certain civilizational and political preferences (as I wrote before, during the last war the upper middle classes were generally Anglophile, while the lower middle classes were often Germanophile).

Those of the very rich in America whom I met during my first years in this country—they were not very many, but they were a representative sample—were not very different from the way I had imagined them. By and large, they accorded with the European image of the American millionaire. That there was an evident and visible difference between the new rich and the older moneyed families was obvious; that this difference favored the appearances and the habits of the older families was obvious, too, and nothing new. The troublesome thing about this American financial aristocracy was that their ways of life and their preferences were quite predictable. Unlike the remnant aristocracies in Europe, there were few eccentrics among them. The unorthodox and unusual and weird specimens among them tried to demonstrate their individuality; but among them, too, imagination was largely wanting. They simply (or, perhaps, complicatedly) took some secondhand pride in their acquisition and possession of opinions that were more liberal and more advanced than those of the common run of men, including their fellow rich. Since these ideas had been taken up from others, their bearers were seldom more than well-bred apostles of the *dernier cri*.

When it came to the American working class—a class that was more clearly distinct forty years ago than it is now—I again had some grounds for their understanding, since my teaching in a small Catholic college brought me into contact with them on occasion. I was happy to see their good-naturedness, their respect for learning, their strong sense of family and their religious habits, all quite different from most of their European counterparts. I was surprised to see the astonishingly limited scope of their aspirations, by which I do not merely mean cultural ones. They aspired to a respectability that almost never went beyond their own ethnic or social groups or even neighborhoods. That was evident, among other things, in the rituals of their celebrations, houses, vacations, recreations, manners. Again this was involved with that paucity of imagination which in the case of a workingman is certainly more excusable than in that of the leisured families of millionaires. More regrettable than that was their view of the realities of this world. This view, including its very language, depended on the repeated clichés of newspaper columnists, of movie people, of radio and later television personalities and comedians. The very history of the American working class amounts to the most blatant refutation of Marx. For many years they have been more conservative and less liberal than the American upper classes. They may have disliked the rich, but they felt no envy for them; social respectability among their fellow workers both circumscribed and constituted their ambitions. They believed, or at least they preferred to believe, that the United States was the greatest thing that ever happened in the history of mankind, that America was omnipotent and the only free country in the world, in the rest of which they were just about entirely uninterested (this lack of interest was evident, too, among second- and third-generation immigrants).

The intellectuals' attitudes toward the American working class were false and dishonest. I write "attitudes," not relations, because they had, save for a few rare instances, few relations with them. Those intellectuals (and they were numerous) who had sprung from the lower classes took good care that there should be no recoil. The intellectuals' ideas about the honest radicalism of the working-man during the Thirties—the "Waiting for Lefty" syndrome— were senseless rhetoric, hardly qualifying even for an illusion (an illusion does, after all, have an optical substance). One of the matters that disturbed me during the Fifties was the ignorance, fear and contempt that so many intellectuals revealed (though often unwittingly) when they thought or spoke about the American working classes.

In Philadelphia and in the Philadelphia country, then, I began to meet men and women among whom I felt instantly at home, though many of them did not instantly feel at home with me. These were members of what I call an American bourgeoisie. Most of them were Americans of English or Anglo-Celtic ancestry, Old Americans. I felt at home with them from the beginning, partly because of nostalgia: they reminded me of some things that had been destroyed in my homeland.

Their manners, their tastes and their behavior—in that order— were subdued and not assertive; their houses were more handsome and comfortable inside than outside; ostentation and pushiness were the prime social sins from which they instinctively recoiled; in spite of the dissolution of family ties and generational troubles that had already taken place, their sentiments and obligations to family and consanguinity remained, despite their difficulties, admirably strong. I found this cultivation of interiority and privacy refreshingly reminiscent of that bourgeois and patrician tradition in Europe that, after all has been said, had fathered the greatest civilization of the Modern Age during the five hundred years after the Middle Ages. Some of the standards of these men and women were English, as were their affinities, their literary inclinations, their instinctive liking for certain sports and for outdoor life, many of their social and drinking habits, the decoration of their houses and their gardens. Yet they differed from their English counterparts in two essential ways. The strivings and the snubbings of the English upper class, especially when within touching distance of the English aristocracy, were naturally absent among them, in part because of the absence or near-absence of such an aristocracy in America. More important, they were more generous and more courteous—and their American courtesy had an ineffable natural charm—than the English: that insensitivity and rudeness which is often but a defensive carapace of the shyness of the English was not very widespread among these Americans.

Who were (who are) these people? The sociologists' classifications of upper-middle, lower-middle, middle-upper, are distinctions without useable differences. The silly term *WASP,* made up in the 1960s, is also useless; so is the even sillier adjective *preppy,* current in the 1970s—even though, as in England, the schools these men (the men, rather than the women) had gone to did make a difference in their manners and in the circumference of their circles of friends. The penetrating eyes of novelists are often surer guides than the celebrations of sociologists and even of social historians. Yet the novelists, too, were preoccupied with surfaces, expressions and appearances, chronicling rather than comprehending the manners and habits and beliefs underlying them; pointing out the discrepancies between manners and morals but overlooking their essential connections. This was true of those novelists who set themselves up as the chroniclers of the manners of American upper-middle or lower-upper (call it what you will) society, writers such as John O'Hara or even John Updike or John Cheever, who saw these twentieth-century American bourgeois from the outside, a condition that in the case of a genius such as Balzac or Fontane made no difference; and when some of them were inside, they missed an essential point: the best of the American bourgeoisie were less curious and more indifferent to social status than were their chroniclers. A rare essence of maturity—that most difficult American achievement—was still a living presence in the lives and surroundings and manners of this otherwise open, sporty class of Americans, among whom I felt at home.

It took many of them a long time to appreciate—or even to understand—my appreciation of them. Many of them did not quite know why I enjoyed their company, especially since I was not a snob and my social aspirations were limited. They were not particularly intellectual and they knew this, sometimes uncomfortably so. (That uncomfortableness, too, was American rather than English.) I, on the other hand, found myself more at home with them than with many intellectuals. This requires explanation. Had I lived in prerevolutionary Russia or Poland this duality would not have existed: there the noun *intelligent* encompassed everybody with real or pretended intellectual interests, students and scholars as well as the more or less learned people among the middle class and the nobility: a small minority. In spite of their Latin roots, the nouns *intelligentsia* and *intellectual* were brought to England and America by immigrants from Russia: nouns that, perhaps for the first time in the history of the Western world, denoted less of a social class than a class of opinion. Having been brought up in Hungary I could not accept this. My parents, most of my relatives and my friends were intelligent people; many of them read many of the same books that scholars and professional intellectuals in Hungary had been reading; there was a measure of accord between their intellectual tastes and their brains. I did have acquaintances and friends who today would be called "intellectuals": fellow students with amateur literary or philosophical or artistic interests, critics, journalists, assistants at the university and occasionally professors. I enjoyed their company no more and no less—at times more, at times less—than that of some of my friends of the *jeunesse dorée*. Toward the end of the war my best friend was the son of a financial magnate who was studying agricultural science at the university: he was interested in all kinds of things, including clothes, horse racing, food, liquor and girls, while he was also one of the best-read people I knew. It was in the democracy of the United States where I found that intellectuals were a distinct and separate kind of people, self-isolated and suspicious of all other classes, including the American bourgeoisie, about which they understood even less than what the men and women of that class understood about them, which was not very much.

In my family in Hungary I had only one relative who could be classified as a professional intellectual: an uncle of my father, a noted professor of architecture, who died in the year I was born. My father, who was very talented, could have become a professor of medicine, but he, for odd reasons, was uninterested in such a career, even though he had published serious articles in medical journals on occasion. He also had a fine private library of several thousand books. Perhaps it was because of this background, too, that all my life I have resented being called An Intellectual. Perhaps archly, and perhaps especially in the United States I have preferred to say that I am a teacher and a writer. My acquaintance and eventual friendship with the men and the women of the American bourgeoisie were a great compensation for my frequent loneliness. These men and women—especially the men—were, as I wrote, not very intellectual. Yet their knowledge of people and of the world, assisted by some of their reading and by a modicum of their traveling, was sufficient to sustain their judgments and their tastes to an extent that my association and conversation with them were almost always pleasurable and interesting. Yes, I often longed for the company of people with whom I could talk about more detailed and sometimes more deep-going intellectual matters. I sometimes took pleasure—a false pleasure—in saying that in this country I had two sets of friends, taste-friends and brain-friends, the trouble being that my taste-friends had no brains, while my brain-friends had no taste. This was a conversational exaggeration, for two reasons. Many of my taste-friends had plenty of brains, and I found, too, brain-friends who had not only good taste but good and humane manners, manifest not only in the civilities of their minds but what Goethe had called the civilities of the heart. After all was said, it was those civilities of the heart that I cherished and still cherish the most, among the American bourgeoisie in the country around Philadelphia where I chose to live. For example—and it is one example that I shall not forget—their behavior during the dying days of my first wife reflected (by which word I mean that it shone with) a kindness out of goodness that went beyond the most exacting requirements of good manners. It showed a concern and a dedication that was equaled in its extent only by one or two of my close intellectual friends; and it was American, not English.

In sum, I found that with all that insufficiency of their intellectual interests, it was these people who were the best representatives of Western civilization in the United States. In many ways, and perhaps the most important ones, they, and not the intellectuals, were the carriers of culture, the *Kulturträger.* Finally (this, of course, took years to develop), I found that I could share with them some of those unspoken, or sometimes finely understated, reactions and judgments that form a substantial measure of the understanding among people with common preferences (preferences, rather than interests) and with a common background—in spite of the fact that my background, at least nationally (and therefore also rhetorically), was very different from theirs.

One thing that impressed me through the years was the quality of the American patriotism of these people. Their voluntary and at times self-abnegating willingness to serve their country in need was unlike anything I had seen in supernationalist Hungary. This appeared from their memories of themselves in the Second World War, and from other matters, too. They were probably the most patriotic class of people in the Republic (which had not been the case during the first ninety years of its existence). The same kind of patriotism turned many of them against the Vietnam War, in a different and deeper sense than were then the reactions of their children, since they were unencumbered by radical ideologies or by rationalizations of how to evade the draft. Duff Cooper once wrote that the jingo nationalist is always the first to denounce his fellow countrymen as traitors, the converse of this being that the true patriot is often the kind of person who is critical of, because he is deeply concerned with, the faults of his government or people.

They were not without their faults, the principal one of these being their intellectual disinterestedness, which was often married to their self-consciousness. Even their adherence to certain traditions was a matter more of custom than of cultivation; and while it is true that manners contain a strong measure of morals, at times—especially among the younger ones of that class—a touch of American-Indian wildness would break through the surface.* Their shortcoming was not only the underestimation of their own intellectual capacities but a consequent unwillingness to widen their circles of interests and friends, and—more important—the inability to free their minds, at least for some time, from some of their accepted categories of thinking. But how could I expect that these people, with all of their inherent virtues, would be *wholly* immune

---

*In 1949 I was invited (extra bachelors were needed) to a splendid coming-out party of a group of Southern debutantes on a country estate outside New Orleans. With a group of other young men I was flown there in a private airplane. I was exhilarated by the richness of that house and by the atmosphere. For me, a recent survivor of the Second World War, it was but a novel version of Waugh's description of a debutante party in the London season of 1923, in *Brideshead Revisited,* that I had only recently read then: ". . . substantial houses in the squares of Mayfair and Belgravia, alight and thronged . . . their music floating out among the plane-trees, couples outside sauntering on the quiet pavements or breathing the summer air from the balconies. Foreigners returning on post from their own wastelands wrote home that here they seemed to catch a glimpse of the world they had believed lost forever among the mud and wire . . . ." There was the dance music of the American high bourgeois period, those standard tunes such as "Mountain Greenery," "One More Time," "Dancing on the Ceiling." Later in the night, after much liquor had been consumed and the heavy clouds of boredom stood on the horizon, the band switched to Dixieland; and the pretty, demure Southern debutantes kicked off their shoes and began to dance and run about barefoot, more and more wildly, while the young men formed a circle and clapped them on.

to the decline of civilization? What Burckhardt wrote a century ago about the patricians of Basel (where he, more fortunate than I, found himself at home among his ancestral people, after having rejected a professorship in Germany among the other professors) applied to the American bourgeoisie: the danger was now that everything had become possible, "mainly because there are everywhere good, splendid, liberal people who do not quite know the boundaries of right and wrong and it is there that the duty of resistance and defense begins."

The year 1947 was a milestone in American history and in my own. I have sometimes thought of writing a book about it, without being able to find the perfect form, a new kind of historical writing that would meld two essential themes: the slow revolution in the American view of the world that became crystallized during that year, together with the appearance of a type of thinking that would be henceforth adopted by certain people—in accord with my anti-Dostoevskian and anti-Freudian and anti-ideological conviction that what ideas do to men is both less real and less interesting than what men do with ideas. But who would be the narrator? I could not think of one save in the form of a melancholy and pensive exile (not I: an imaginary older one), sufficiently knowledgeable to understand Americans from his own perspective, and yet disembodied and irritating because of his unavoidable omniscience. I am not a novelist; I cannot devise a plot, any plot; I am a historian because I find that what happened is not only more interesting than what could have happened: what might have happened is inherent in what did happen, the two are inextricably combined. I was thinking of describing Washington and New York in the hot spring and summer of that year, when American anti-Communism became institutionalized and when Washington turned, as it were, within a few months, into The Capital of the World.

Many historians, political scientists, journalists, memoirists have written books about 1947, more or less satisfactory ones, some of them tracing the origins of the Cold War from documents, establishing the political pedigree of the Truman Doctrine, the Marshall

Plan, the containment policy, NATO. (Dean Acheson, that para-
gon of American classy pomposity—and most American pomposity
is not classy but sanctimonious—entitled his memoirs *Present at the
Creation;* but he was present, I once wrote, not at the creation, but
at the packaging.) Yet in most of these books certain essentials are
missing. One of these is the curious psychic phenomenon, attributable again to the national habit of split-mindedness: the relief of the
government and of the foreign policy establishment, and perhaps
even of large masses of people, in having found a proper ideology,
without admitting that this meant the division of Europe with the
Russians. It was not only that within two years, from 1945 to 1947,
many Americans (very much including Acheson) turned from considering the Russians as the main ally to considering them as the
main enemy of the United States. It was less convenient to think
about the division of Europe than about the dangers of Communism. To think in terms of ideology rather than of geography
accorded with inclinations of the American mind. It was also politic
to declare (and Acheson in 1947 made certain extreme declarations
to wary Congressmen and Senators in that vein) that the Russian
imposition of Communistic governments in Europe meant that
Communism was advancing so fast that it had to be contained in
Europe and in other parts of the world, and that Communism was
the principal danger to the "Free World" (a new term then) and
to the United States. Yet Communism had come to Eastern Europe
principally, and in most countries exclusively, not through revolution or popular demand but through the presence of the Russian
army. That Stalin was not like Hitler, that Communism was different from Nazism, that the Soviet Union was different from the
Third Reich, that Russians were not like Germans was understood
by some people; but they, too, were hampered by the tendency of
many Americans to regard Communism as the monopoly of evil,
indeed, as the incarnation of everything opposite to what American
ideals stood for. Thus the policy of containment—contrary to the
very purposes of George Kennan, the author of the famous "containment" article—led to the unnatural division of Europe, to the
rigidification of the iron curtain and not to an eventual rectification

or gradual dissolution of it. Here was another element of relative relief, a not untypical result of the American political tradition of cumbrous compromises. The commitment to the defense of Western Europe meant that there would be no commitments regarding Eastern Europe, even though the latter condition was obscured by all kinds of rhetoric. Americans now believed that the Soviets, having installed Communism in Eastern Europe, were ready to debouch into Western Europe, which was not the case; Stalin believed that the Americans, having established themselves easily in Western and Southern Europe, were about to challenge his overlordship in Eastern Europe, which, alas, was also not the case. I write "alas" because, as an exile from Hungary, I wanted the Americans to do something about correcting the division of Europe: I knew that they would have been able to do so, and not only because of their then monopoly of the atom bomb, but because the Russians were afraid of American power and might; but I knew, too, that the Americans would not do so.

In this I was quite alone. The government was busy firming up the American presence on the western side of the iron curtain. The people were worried about the dangerous ideological infiltration of Communism within the United States, and not with the geographic presence of Russian armies in Central and Eastern Europe. The intellectuals could not care less about Eastern Europe, while they were bitter with the government (and the people) for having abandoned the ideals of Collective Security, International Collaboration, Progressive Democracy, World Government, The United Nations and Friendship with the Soviet Union—ideals of which so many intellectuals saw themselves as the high-minded guardians. The Eastern European exiles were taking hope from the fact that the American government had begun to help them (at least financially) and that it was finally taking an anti-Soviet position. During the next twenty years the government, the people, the exiles and the intellectuals gradually changed their views, the last the slowest. During the 1960s many of them discovered the "revisionist" thesis according to which twenty years before the United States had been as guilty for the origins of the cold war as was Stalin, since the

United States had been unnecessarily provocative to the Russians, challenging, among other things, their presence in Eastern Europe: a thesis that was not only incorrect but of which the very opposite had been true. That some kind of division of Europe could not be avoided, but that the geographic line of that division must be corrected was my view forty years ago as it is today. I never thought that the United States should risk an atomic war for the liberation of Hungary, or that the dissolution of the entire Russian empire ought to be the aim of American foreign policy. Russia was a great country, here to stay; she was made by Ivan and Peter, not by Marx and Lenin; the antecedents of Stalin and of his successors were the former not the latter; she was a powerful state, a historical and geographical reality, and not the incarnation or even the focus of International Revolution. For Americans, on the other hand, to establish themselves all over the world and to underwrite anybody and anything pretending to anti-Communism was as impractical as it was unrealistic; and, in a deeper sense, wrong. I suppose this is what one may call a historian's reactionary view.

On a superficial level American isolationism died away in 1947. The American internationalism that succeeded it was not such a radical or novel departure from it as it seemed at that time or even now. The latter was yet another version of that Wilsonian ideology that had, alas, established the intellectual framework of a grandiose and vague and abstract American internationalism thirty years earlier and that, despite its universalist pretensions, was not altogether different from American isolationism and American exceptionalism. (There are many things wrong with the internationalist idea to Make the World Safe for Democracy, one of them being that it is not that different from the nationalist idea that What Is Good for America Is Good for the World.) But developments in 1947 and after spawned a new type of mind and a new kind of occupation: that of the American internationalist bureaucrat. The time when American presidents found it necessary to select foreign-born intellectuals such as a Kissinger or a Brzezinski to explain the globe to them was still a quarter of a century away. In 1947 the reservoir of America's international representatives was still composed of educated native Americans of an older type who knew something of the world without having acquired an academic degree in International Relations. The willingness with which Americans took up their task of supporting Western Europe and also other impoverished or endangered countries, of being the prime representatives and leaders of Western civilization, did have something admirable about it: Americans addressed themselves to this with a dispatch and generosity that perhaps no other nation could have produced so swiftly, including the British. On the other hand, the Americanization of Europe did not really bring Europeans and Americans closer, except on widespread and superficial levels, while the consequent Europeanization of America, too, did not penetrate much beneath the level of the importation and the degustation of a variety of cheeses.

This novel American internationalism also produced certain disturbing elements in the imagination of Americans. There grew, for example, a national admiration for Secret Agents, and of all sorts of brummagem Hemingwayesque types, with their display of worldly-wise cynicism. The Hemingwayesque idea—or, rather, pretension—to the effect that some Americans know not only best how to shoot or fish or fly but also how to bed women and to outwit and beat their opponents throughout the world, became part of the American popular mythology, with the CIA man replacing the cowboy. An early example of this was the movie *Casablanca*, celebrating the supremacy of the American male because of his wonderfully American know-how. In this imbecile wartime picture Humphrey Bogart is the virile owner of the Bar Américain who knows everything about Frenchmen, Germans, Arabs, black markets, false papers, tricks with roulette wheels, vintages, champagnes and guns. He knows everything about human corruptibility as well as about how to deal with beautiful women. The great transformation from American Innocence to Worldly Expertise happened to Hemingway, too, who after fishing and hunting in Michigan, having discovered the varied pleasures of the Old World, began to take good care to impress Americans no longer with his innocence (something of the charm of which still remained in *A Farewell to*

Arms) but with his know-how: taking much pride in telling how to be at home at the Ritz, how to order the best wine, how to dine with the most celebrated toreros. Since 1947 I have seen—occasionally in Europe, but often enough in New York or in any fashionable American suburb—a new kind of American, one generation or two after Henry James: the Expert American, who wants to tell you which is the best hotel in Davos, what his Rolex cost in the Amsterdam duty-free, and how he is well known and can always get a good table at Taillevent. The few Americans I knew in Europe before the Second World War slid up and down on wooden skis and took pictures with Kodak box cameras. The Expert Americans carry their super-Nikons, and their ski gear is the most expensive in the world, made in America by Head, with the Head word displayed on the equipment in very big impressive letters. There is a direct line from Bogart (a Yale man) in *Casablanca* to the hero of Bill Buckley's successful spy novels, Blackford Oakes, another Yale man, an expert knower of vintages, old cognacs, young women (on one occasion he beds the young Queen of England), and of how to fight and defeat Communists. He is a CIA man. There was a time when "foreign agent," to Americans, meant something slightly sinister and alien. But after 1947 American foreign agents became glamorous figures on the screen and in print. I found it significant that Bill Buckley, who began his public career as a convinced isolationist and a suspicious opponent of the Blackford Oakes types at Yale (as his *God and Man at Yale* in 1949 suggests), became a convinced internationalist and CIA associate soon thereafter (and not only in his writing). In 1954 Graham Greene mistook the type of the American secret agent in *The Quiet American,* ascribing to him a kind of dreadful naïveté. Yet it was the amoral James Bond whom John Kennedy read with relish, and for whom in September 1983 Ronald Reagan pronounced his admiration at a press conference.

In 1948 or thereabout I read an excellent anthology of Americans writing about Europe, *Discovery of Europe,* collected and edited by Philip Rahv. But now I must write about the discovery of Europe by ex-Europeans such as myself. In this respect, too, my generation of exiles has been different from other immigrants, many of whom (this was especially true of Russian Jews and some of the Irish) had understandably little or no nostalgia for what they had left behind, who may have had their memories of their native villages or towns but who had little knowledge or interest in the Europe beyond that.

Soon after my arrival in the United States I had attacks of the European flu. This European flu was similar to that French flu which had afflicted certain people, including intellectuals, in England when they had been cut off from France during the Second World War. This flu consisted of a longing for France, for French scenes, tastes, odors, colors, landscapes, streets, houses and especially words. It was not only a nostalgia for French prose or for scintillating French conversation: the very names of the stations of the Paris Métro could be tremendously suggestive. I had similar symptoms of this kind of affliction in Hungary during the war and in the United States later, in my case involving an entire continent. Even now, when I can fly to Europe every year, if need be on a day's notice, a mere night flight away, the sounds and the shapes of place-names and railway stations in *Cook's Continental Timetable*, one of my most favorite books—Montélimar, Valence, St. Ramert, Vienne; Gloucester Eastgate, Bristol Temple Meads, Newton Abbot, Paington; Piacenza, Fidenza, Parma, Modena; Amstetten, Bischofshofen, St. Marien—fill my mind with a music that is so very evocative.

I must continue with a confession. It was not until I had lived for some time in America that I found myself to be a European. Sometime in 1950 I overheard my American hostess talking on the telephone: "We're having a European to dinner." I was startled. I had not thought of myself in that way. But gradually I found that I was very European indeed. I had not known that until I lived in the United States. This had nothing to do with nostalgia. It was, plainly, a matter of perspective, just as people will not regard themselves as Earthlings until they are exiled to the Moon or find themselves living among Martians. It is thus that in the New World—whether in the United States or Canada or Paraguay or

New Zealand—a Frenchman and a German, a Hungarian and a Rumanian instantly discover that they have many things, perhaps very important things, in their perception of the world, in common.

For my generation of exiles this Europeanness could be profitable. It was natural for our kind to go into the import business or international banking; such opportunities multiplied through the internationalization of American business and politics after 1947. In the intellectual professions, too, the natural thing for a refugee or an exile was to set himself down on the largely unworked academic turf defined by his provenance: to become the political or historical or economic expert of his particular homeland, interpreting it to American students, scholars, readers. This was particularly applicable to Eastern Europe, about which Americans knew relatively little and about which historical or political literature in English was not abundant. I, too, could have made an academic career for myself as an Eastern European expert. I chose not to do so, for several reasons, one of them being the undisciplined range of my mental interests, the other that besides my native language all the other languages I knew were Western European ones, and a mere Hungarian expert I did not wish to be. Yet another reason was the warning that a wise and respectable old professor gave me in Hungary before I left: he admonished me not to get involved with immigrant organizations and their politics.

It was in America that I learned more and more about Europe. In Hungary there had been no such thing as a course in European history at the Gymnasium or the university. Few books that I read in Hungary dealt with the history of the entire continent. It was in America, in those superb American libraries, that I devoured hundreds of books about the modern history of Europe, not only because some of them were necessary for the preparation of the courses I was giving in "Modern European History" but because for many years it was to Europe that my interests went back—or, rather, forward: for it was news from Europe (and not only from Hungary) for which I looked first every morning when I opened *The New York Times.* It was in the United States that I first read not only Jane Austen and F. Scott Fitzgerald but Chateaubriand and

Larbaud, not only Henry Adams but Tocqueville, not only Park-
man but Fustel de Coulanges. I read Belloc's *Path to Rome*, Stendhal's *Travels in the South of France*, Eileen Powers's *Medieval
People*, Goethe's *Farbenlehre*, Vico's *Scienza Nuova*, Vicens Vives's
History of Spain and the novels of Eça de Queiroz in Phoenixville,
not in Budapest. It was here that I soaked up much of my French,
all of the money spent by my parents on French tutors in Hungary
notwithstanding, or that I learned that there exist red Loire wines
and not only whites. It was in America, only in America, that entire
verities in the history of Europe opened before my eyes, that at a
clear morning hour I could tell my students things in that history,
correspondences and recognitions that crystallized in my mind then
and there. My parents were cosmopolitan people; I had traveled
with them in Austria, Switzerland, Germany, Italy, France and
England before the war. But it was from America that I first came
to Ireland, Portugal, Holland, Norway, Denmark, Poland and
Greece; it was coming from America that I found the Vivarais and
the Euganean Hills, the island of Sifnós and the Trollfjord in the
Lofoten. America made it possible for me.

Americans don't know this. They see us as natural sophisticates,
the sons and daughters of European civilization, supremely in the
know when it comes to calling porters or ordering wines, and of
course every European knows at least three languages as well as the
roseate windows in the cathedral of Auch, an eighteenth-century
cathedral, a rarity. But it is not quite like this. We are exiles, strewn
about America, displaced persons, refugees from the cruel Russian
flood after the last war. For many of us the discovery of Europe
began from American points of departure. It is in America that we
get the European flu, that nostalgia for places, compared to the
evocative power of whose names Proust's madeleine was but a bland
biscuit: Ste.-Wandrille, Vilshofen, Aosta, Pfäffikon, Les Andelys.
They evoke more than Paris or Vienna. In any event, they are
different from our birthplaces, Budapest or Prague or Szeged,
whereto we cannot return or, if we can, we go sadly, seriously,
without illusions.

So, for many years, I would say, and think, that I had become a

European through being an American: but this was not sufficiently true. Around the fiftieth year of my life I found the truer formula: Europe is my mother. America is my wife.

The dream of many exiles of my generation is home. Mother's home. Perhaps to live in Europe. Or to retire there, secure with the possession of an American passport and comfortable with American money. In my life there has been a delicious variant of a daydream: going to Europe with my American wife or with my American friends. To show Europe to them. When I returned to Europe for the first time in June 1954, with my American wife, my excitement and anticipation of that voyage (it was an ocean voyage then) were perhaps more acute than that of any other departure in my much traveled life, this revisiting and showing my wife the family mansion—even though one of its wings, the one where I was born and grew up, was walled in and closed off.

But there are disappointments to come. Europe is my mother, and I love her perhaps better than do the Europeans, those often ungrateful sons and daughters. Europe is the house of my mother, but my mother's house is not my home. I am an American, of European origin, which is not the best of all possible *combinazioni*. In 1964 I am a visiting professor in France. I give a lecture. I order a dinner. The French provincials are impressed—Some Americans have so much! They know so much!—until someone tells them that I am a Hungarian, living in America. Now they understand. This man is not a superior American, alas; he is an ordinary European, *bien sûr*. In Italy I attempt to talk Italian to cabdrivers, hotel porters, waiters. They are polite, suspicious, wary. Once in a while they drop their mask of courtesy and ask (when Italians ask you, they are really telling you something): "How come you speak Italian?" I explain: I learned it in Hungary, where I came from. They don't believe me. This man must have been here, in the war, in the German army? or in the American one? a suspicious person. But finally they identify my category, with the quickness characteristic of their minds: this man is an Italian-American who pretends not to speak Italian well, he pretends to speak with a foreign accent, the son of a bitch. In Greece I try out the few words remembered from classical-Greek classes; I put together words from posters, billboards, signs. At the end of our boat trip one of the sailors asks me where I learned that, how come I know the names of all the islands and the Greek alphabet? I tell him, but he does not believe me, and I overhear him later saying that this man's name really is Loukas, Ioannis Loukas, he is the son of some Greek-American, putting on the dog.

At other places, other times in Europe, men and women who know me have suggested, and sometimes said: "Of course you know this because you were born here. You're not like other Americans." They meant it as a compliment, as a kind of recognition; and I was irritated, I wanted to say to them that there are many Americans who know this or that better than they do, and sometimes I have said it. Is this better or worse than when I hear a Frenchman or a German spout that he likes America, and he soon shows that he likes all the wrong things about it? I don't know.

We travel in space and in time. If, instead of Portugal, we could visit the 1750s, the sensations of our recognitions would be the same. We would be fascinated and surprised by some things, repelled and disillusioned by others; we would encounter certain unexpected things that we would immediately recognize since we should have expected them; we would get used to other things and scenes gradually; in any event, the most interesting and vivifying experiences would involve crystallizations in our consciousness of things and ideas that, in some way or another, we have already known. In any event, 1989 in Phoenixville is not 1989 in Lisbon. When we visit Mother's place we fly back eastward and we go back in time, historical time, not clock time, and we will not elect to dine in a supermodern place and we avoid the Hilton like the dickens. We do not want to stay in a place where Mother's old furniture is gone, or where there is a photograph of her as a widow, with a callow young man, both in jeans.

I know that I am going back, and I know that I'm not going home. There comes a time during each visit to Europe, in Mother's place, on her continent, when I recognize that I no longer belong there, that my place in Pennsylvania is my home. This moment arrives resistless and unexpected; it is seldom the result of a sudden blue mood, of a *cafard* or of the *mistral,* or of a bad exchange with a vendor or of the Sunday-afternoon sadness of a seaside suburb. It comes from the recognition that it is better to be a European in America than to be an American in Europe, something that I also gleaned from the talk and from the faces of the flush American businessmen sailing back from Europe on the *Leonardo* twenty-five years ago, when the dollar and the America of Lyndon Johnson were still riding high, but then and there I knew that all of the talk of the domination of Europe by American business was mere blather.

Since then Americans have become poorer, and an entire range of manners that various Europeans affected before English-speaking tourists has grown threadbare, much of the servility and some of the respect are now gone, sometimes even the obligatory English announcements at airports and on airplanes are slurred through or even dropped altogether. But there are many traveling Americans who belong to the Old World now, when the once conviction of a chosen people, of an America devoid of sin, has weakened to unbelief; and Americans who know this are not less American for that. And when I sense the affection with which some of my American friends regard a European mannerism, a culinary custom, an odd way of expressing myself, a trace of *Gemütlichkeit* in our American home, I know that this is no longer due to some kind of exoticism in their eyes. Does one become American in order to be a European? Perhaps. Is it not through our wives that we become the sadder and wiser sons of our mothers?

Five or six years after I wrote this last paragraph I spent two months in my native city, reading and researching for a book. On a rainy March evening in 1987 I was at the residence of the American Ambassador in Budapest for a dinner, a dinner in my honor, to boot. In answering his charming toast I said something about having fled my native country with American help forty-one years before and that now I was being honored there by the American

Ambassador: that I was both moved and grateful for what America has allowed me to achieve, most of all the achievement of a home and a family in America which, at least in some ways, has been a reconstruction of some of the home that forty-one years before I had thought was lost forever. Yes, I said, "in F. Scott Fitzgerald's lovely phrase, America is the willingness of the heart." "Spoken like a patriot," the young Australian Ambassador said at the table. Of which country? I thought. A few weeks later, on another rainy evening in Budapest, I was waiting for a sprightly young American woman, the Consul of the United States in Budapest, for a drink. This was in the first-floor cocktail lounge of a new hotel, on the site where the old Ritz, destroyed in January 1945, used to be. This was 1987: a group of pockmarked Arabs, in dirty shirts, were chatting around one of the low tables. It did not matter. Through the large plate-glass wall glowed the lights of the Chain Bridge and the great historic shadows of Castle Hill rising over the Danube. I was in the presence of those rain-shrouded ochre shadows, of the historic, monumental Hungary, almost within touching distance; and how different was my situation from that of forty-one years ago! I was grateful for that, too. And then I suddenly realized why, besides my contemplation of that historic prospect, and of myself, the prospect of the hour to come exhilarated me. I had been spending several weeks in Budapest, reading and thinking and speaking Hungarian; and now I looked forward to the company of this pretty and intelligent girl because my mind was filled with an avid, a vivid desire to speak English.

How unpredictable is the history of nations! Perhaps even more unpredictable than the history of our lives. Forty-one years ago, and for many years afterward, I saw only two alternatives. Either Hungary would be liberated or—most probably—she would be lost behind the iron curtain, for a long time. Neither of these happened. It has become possible for hundreds of thousands of Hungarians to visit Hungary, going and coming, flying back and forth. I, too, have been back half a dozen times, for short visits. During one of those visits, in 1983, a melancholy recognition came to me. None of the people I saw belonged to my or to my parents' generation. I had virtually no relatives left in Hungary. All of my surviving friends and relatives live in the West.

I see them often when I come to Europe, in Milan or Zurich or Lugano or Munich or Brussels, it hardly matters where, because I include them in every one of my itineraries. I need them because I need to go back, to travel in time. When I meet them I experience a Hungarian immersion into a mental and spiritual pool of the past, my past. Most of these people are not of my generation but of my mother's, her erstwhile close friends. (She was a youthful woman and I was a precocious young man, drawn to older people.) These are the men and the women to whom I have come to feel closer even than to my few surviving relatives, for whose company I yearn with anticipation; meeting them congeals time into a high moment of happiness. This happens not only because we will talk about things and people in many ways that rest on a rich layer of sensitivities that are peculiarly ours. My being with them makes me deeply thankful to God for my existence now, in this world, for having allowed me this living and breathing connection with something more than abstract memories, with living men and women from a past that is long lost and gone but not irretrievable, no, not at all.

I began this section by saying that the dream of many exiles of my generation is home, and I must end it by saying something that few Americans know, which is that so many of us wish to be buried at home. Perhaps this is the first generation of immigrants among whom this desire exists. At times I hear about one or two friends and acquaintances—they include anti-Communist politicians and former aristocrats—whose ashes are brought back to Hungary. The Hungarian authorities allow this. Their burials are reported in the newspapers there. On the gravestone of one of them one succinct word is engraved: *Hazatért*—"Came Home."* I have no relatives left, only friends in Hungary now. I have two American children,

---

*This is touching but not very sad. The saddest report of this kind I read one day in the 1970s in *The New York Times.* A young American-born couple walked up to the middle of the George Washington Bridge one night, to empty the ashes of their European-born parents into the dark Hudson River, to carry their ashes back toward Europe.

one American grandchild and my second American wife. My Hungarian mother who died in Vienna in 1950, her unmarried older sister who died in Montreal in 1952, my first American wife who died here in 1970 are buried together in a grave of the parish churchyard of St. Mary's on the North Side of Phoenixville, around which stand small whitewashed working people's houses, on winter evenings resembling a northern Hungarian small town a little. I like to think that this tiny part of America, together with the house and the land where I have been living for more than thirty years, belongs to me and to my children and grandchildren. "Patriotism," Simone Weil wrote. "We must not have any love other than charity. A nation cannot be an object of charity. But a country can be such, as an environment bearing traditions which are eternal. Every country can be that."*

*_Gravity and Grace_ (1952), p. 222.

CHAPTER 5

Anti-Anti

I THINK IT WAS Kipling who said that to be born an Englishman means winning the first prize in God's lottery. I had won no such thing in any lottery, celestial or human; but I knew that I was blessed enough to have survived the war and to have played at least my Ace and Queen and Ten right, the Ace being my knowledge of English, the Queen my certifiable knowledge of portions of history and the Ten my uncertifiable understanding of some things in the world, with the result of finding myself in the United States and on the American side of the cold war. I remember myself on a cold morning in winter 1947, in the cold cavern below Thirtieth Street Station in Philadelphia. The New York train was waiting there, with its dark red Pennsylvania coaches. I gazed for a moment at that gold Twenties' lettering of PENNSYLVANIA. I thought how lucky I was being here, a world away from the Hungary that I had left behind. I was on the right side of the world. I was warm in my overcoat, wearing a smart hat, smoking an aromatic American cigarette, with *The New York Times* under my arm, ready to settle down on a comfortable seat, speeding off on an American express train to New York. This was different from the relief of a refugee's finding himself on the safe side. I was not only on the safe side; I was getting ensconced on the winning side, the rich side, the side of the present indicative, that is, of the near-future. A refugee, say, from Nazi Germany ten years earlier had fled from a frighteningly efficient country and people who at that time seemed to represent a wave of the future. I, a refugee from the Sovietized side of Europe, left behind an impoverished, dirty, run-down, semi-barbaric world. Nearly thirty years earlier Lincoln Steffens, returning from the Soviet Union, told the reporters in New York harbor that in Russia he had "been over into the future and it works." He did not see the future at all, which was right there before his long Puritan nose. In 1947 it was in front of my nose, too, which was at least one reason to congratulate myself.

But I was alone. Alone not only because I was bereft of my family in Hungary. Alone in America where, unlike most refugees, I had no relatives, friends, organizations to which I could turn. Americans were accustomed to a category of refugee who had fled to the United States during or before the war; but an anti-Communist refugee in 1946 and even 1947 was an odd apparition—he did not fit. During my first two or three years in America much of the intellectual climate of 1945 still lived on. Anti-Communism, to some people and to the large majority of intellectuals, was still disreputable, dangerous, perhaps even Fascist. The intellectuals' view of the world was still frozen in the categories of the American Twenties and Thirties. The best of them would say that, yes, they knew: Stalin was a dictator and all that; but, after all was said, Communism was still a progressive ideology; and its categorical alternative of anti-Communism, especially in America, was simply dreadful, represented by backward, unrefined, crude people: moneybags, rednecks, Catholics. When I tried to argue with the better kind of these anti-anti-Communists the best I could get was a faint, though inoperative, sense of goodwill as they heard me out: a little smile on their faces, showing that they sympathized with my misfortunes; but the meaning of these Hungarian misfortunes with Communism was untranslatable into American realities or even into American terms, just as an odd case of bad luck or of personal injustice, while regrettable, is surely insufficient cause to review an established rule of the law.

Still, there was at least sympathy on the part of these people; and the smile on their faces was, I think, genuine. It was cold comfort; but almost cozy when I compare it to the glacial climate with which

I was met by many liberal intellectuals at the time (or, indeed, for a long time thereafter). Their response to my arguments and, consequently, to me was dismissal at best and contempt at worst. Whether they were sure of themselves I do not know; I am inclined to doubt it. But they were certainly sure of the value of their ideas, like shrewd investors who pride themselves on the value of their investments—or, rather, on the knowledge that in virtue of these investments they have shown themselves to be smarter and better than others. They preferred to think that because of the superiority of their opinions they were people of superior taste and judgment. This was the essence of liberal snobbery, this determination to adhere to a class of opinions. If one's political and social opinions were not superior to those held by common people, then one was the kind of person whose tastes were bound to be common and vulgar, too: conversely, if one was a votary of Bertrand Russell or Pandit Nehru one would (or should) be an admirer of Sartre and Picasso. Soon after my arrival in the United States I was able to recognize these pervasive incarnations of liberal chic. I remember how a then celebrated city planner of Philadelphia told me that his favorite painter was Klee; he also defended Alger Hiss at the time. (Only a few months ago I read that he criticized—and rightly so—the erection of monstrous office buildings that would in 1988 tower above and obscure Philadelphia's famous French-Victorian City Hall; in 1932 he had proposed that City Hall be torn down and a modern parking garage be erected in its place.) I remember, too, how about 1948 at an upper-class liberal dinner party in Philadelphia I ventured to say that Roosevelt's view of Stalin had not been very realistic, and that I was harrumphed down by a high-powered social medico who, as I had gathered from his conversation, was a local snob of great assiduity and precision, qualities that I hope also marked his practice with his patients. Going home I was racking my brains as to what kind of man this American doctor reminded me of. Then it came to me: of the kind of self-satisfied bourgeois patron of the arts who in a fashionable seat at a fashionable concert or opera asserts himself amidst the applause by shouting a Bravo!

I have a sharp memory of another occasion. On a July evening in 1948 a friend drove me to an open-air restaurant in New Hope, Bucks County, at that time a favored summer habitat of writers and artists from New York. We were seated in a corner, next to a large table over which darted, leaped and singsang the loud and nervous small talk of a fashionable Broadway theatre producer and his retinue of friends: art dealers, actresses, critics, including a scatteration of rich men and women, supporters of the art world whom they had co-opted for social purposes—in sum, a representative sample of the Upper Bohemia of New York, a microcosm of liberal chic. It was a hot night: clouds of insects were buzzing around the lamps; fireflies gleamed over the dark river; some of these people were smartly got up, some of the women were pretty. It should have been a pleasant evening. It wasn't. I remember being filled with a bitter, instant fury. I could not help overhearing their conversation. Every bit of it was inane; much of it was vile. Their wisecracks were acrid, cynical and contemptuous of Harry Truman as well as of the morals and the brains of the "great unwashed"—that is, for the American people—and full of grim respect and nervous praise for anything that was revolutionary, godless and modern, including Communism. It was not only the stupidity of their opinions that made me seethe; it was the tone of their self-satisfaction. In spite of its rapid and agitated tone, their conversation was in reality monotonous, since it consisted of endless repetitions of the same themes. "The only ideas which interested them"—I cannot improve here on what Maurice Bowra once wrote about a dinner party among California bankers—"were those which they had in common and repeated like incantations to one another in the hope that this would make them feel good."

I must now recount, if only briefly, my encounters with the American professorate at the time. As I wrote, the better and more humane kind of liberal among them would occasionally hear me out with a little smile; but the faces of those professors to whom my opinions were alien were sheathed with a thin layer of gray ice. I was an anti-Communist, a Catholic and, philosophically at least, Rightist and not Leftist: such a reputation, in baseball terms, meant three strikes against me, to the effect that I was excluded from stepping up to the plate. In 1948, especially in the better universities, this professorate was predominantly Liberal and Leftist, many of them Henry Wallace voters, in their case less because of chic than because of their intellectual constructions about the nature of the world and of mankind, to which they had arrived from their admiration of the eighteenth century, having left the remnants of seventeenth-century popular credulity disdainfully behind.* Unlike the Upper Bohemians, they were not the avant-garde but the clerisy of the New World, Darwinist and Einsteinian to the last man and, if not votaries, at least profoundly respectful of the Webbs and/or Trotsky, Freud and/or Marx; anti-conservative, anti-Catholic and anti-anti-Communist.

In Philadelphia my few contacts with them included the functions of the World Affairs Council, a typical institution of American internationalism at that time. The purpose of that organization, instituted circa 1945 by the Council on Foreign Relations in the principal cities of the Republic, was to educate and assist Americans in "internationalism" (whatever that was, or is), with the help of imported talent or with local Experts and with the thrust of energy provided by socially ambitious people (the dreary term *upwardly mobile* was not yet current in the 1940s). The director of the Philadelphia chapter was a not unattractive divorcée around forty, with an unerring needle set in the direction of the magnetic pole of her social ambitions (from that directorship she went on to marry a local multimillionaire) and with a not less unerring caliper compassing the circumference of opinions acceptable under the auspices of the

---

*This is an important point. The American conflict between rational scientific intellectuality and emotional religiosity has been interpreted, to this day, as a conflict between the twentieth and the nineteenth centuries—as in the Scopes trial in 1925, with Clarence Darrow and William Jennings Bryan in the ring. The juxtaposition is false. What Bryan represented in Dayton, Tennessee, was not the nineteenth but the seventeenth century, gnarled puritan and biblical and populist survivals in the American mind; what Darrow represented was not the twentieth but the nineteenth century, the belief in the absolute, definite and exclusive truth of Science, a belief that was already outdated in 1925, even though few people knew it at the time.

World Affairs Council. With other professors I was invited to take part in panel discussions, open to the public, dealing with American-Soviet relations, the United Nations, World Government or whatnot. My opinions evoked the expectable uneasiness (or disdain) at many occasions; and my remarks were often deleted or at least partially censored in the bulletins of the World Affairs Council summing up this roundtable or that. This did not matter. My most vivid memory of my brief run with the World Affairs Council (after two or three years I no longer attended its meetings) concerns not my occasional verbal skirmishings but something that happened at the very end of a panel discussion. The session was over; the question-and-answer period was just about exhausted; we were ready to pack up our papers and leave; and there arose, in the back of the small audience, a genuine workingman on the floor, hesitant, shy and terribly earnest: the first (and only) workingman, member of the vast majority of the American people, whom I had ever seen at meetings of the World Affairs Council. Self-consciously and with some difficulty, he asked a question about the topic we had been discussing (what it was I cannot now recall). His hesitant question was not better but surely not worse than the usual spate of questions from the floor. He was earnest and almost pathetically infused with his respectful desire for more knowledge. He spoke slowly. Neither I nor my colleagues on the panel were, I think, impatient with him; but the director of the session, a youngish harebrained woman, was fiddling with her briefcase, looking nervously at the lamps still alight in the room. Only the brake of her manners kept her from looking at her watch until that brake gave out, too, and she looked at it demonstratively indeed. This man was obviously out of place, gumming up the works. For her the avowed end of this organization, to enlighten and educate the citizenry, included only such people who were already enlightened in promising ways, preferably along avenues of enlightenment on which traffic was moving smoothly, predictably and in one direction.

Having now described layers of liberals in descending order, I must descend further and say something about American Communists (whether Party members or active Communist sympathizers) of the period, even though I met few of them. Some of these few were not necessarily human specimens inferior to some of the liberal snobs I have just described; but I was struck by two conditions prevalent among Communists in America. One was that, with all of their different national and social backgrounds, their psychic makeup was remarkably similar to many of the Communists in Hungary. They were men and women whose bitter opposition to their national society was usually the result of some kind of deeply felt humiliation, an unnaturally self-nourished sense of inferiority. More important, and surely more contemptible, was the condition of their intellectual dishonesty. In the United States these Communists had every opportunity—indeed, after 1945 rapidly increasing opportunities—to read and to learn about the misdeeds of the Soviets, especially under Stalin's regime. Yet they refused not only to hear or read or see but to think about the brutal realities of Russia. Theirs was the crassest example of the condition that the unwillingness to think is a worse affliction than the inability to do so. My dislike of such people as the Rosenbergs or Lillian Hellman, persisting to this day, issues less from my distaste for their ideas than from my contempt for their management of those ideas, for their refusal to admit (to themselves as to others) that Stalin and his people were crude, brutal, dishonest (and anti-Semitic, too)—indeed, more so than those American anti-Communists whom these American Communists and their sympathizers feared and loathed with a fervor that deceived their own selves. They hated who and what they thought were the enemies of freedom so much more than they loved freedom—if indeed they had a love of freedom that went beyond their personal wishes. This was bad enough; but, in addition, their comprehension of who they thought were the enemies of freedom was often woefully wrong. Thus does the poison of fear and hatred infiltrate the minds of some people, bringing them together at the cost of their individuality. Allied with this kind of lamentable and harmful self-deception was their abstract view of the world. They admired, or at least professed to admire, the Soviet Union because that state was an ideological prototype: the first Communist classless society of the world. They were unable to see that a nation is a cultural, rather than an ideological prototype; that its character is the outcome of history and culture, rather than of ideology or of economic institutions; that the people of the Russias were not Marxists but Russians; that instead of having become the New Soviet Men and Women they remained, and were, very Russian indeed.

But then, and alas: the ideological way of contemplating the world prevailed among different Americans too, among people who were not at all Communist sympathizers or even doctrinaire liberals. Very soon after my arrival in New York I called on the impeccably dressed and mannered director of research of the august Council on Foreign Relations. I cannot now remember why and how this meeting occurred, except for its time—the winter of 1946–47—which is important, since by then the members of the American establishment, such as this well-mannered, well-meaning and intelligent man, had begun to change their ideas about Soviet Russia. They were the pilot fish, a few feet ahead of public opinion, aware that the course of the enormous American ship of state had begun to change. Yet there was not much of a meeting of minds between us. Knowing that I had spent three months in Western Europe en route to America, and perhaps also respectful of my credentials as a European historian, he kept asking me about the Communist danger in Western Europe. I was impatient with this, and blurted out something to the effect: "You don't understand. The idea of Communism is finished." I can still see the painful embarrassment on his face. What I meant was that the Fact and the Threat were the presence of Russian armed power in the middle of Europe, not the attractions of The Idea of Communism; that—unlike in the case of Nazism or Fascism—no Communist regime could or would come to power anywhere in Europe unless it was imposed by Russian armed force. Then I sensed that there was something wrong in the perceptions of even the best of Americans, not because they reacted to the Soviet incorporation of Eastern Europe only too late, not because their reaction would not go far enough, but because to think in terms of ideologies and economics ("Communism feeds on poverty" and all that nonsense), instead of in terms of

history and geography, was the dominant inclination of the supposedly pragmatic American mind.

I was a witness of the revolution of American public opinion
from Russophilia to anti-Communism that took place between 1945
and 1949; I arrived in the United States during the beginning of it;
I saw its development. Soon I found myself among odd allies. For
a while I took some consolation from thinking that the cheerful and
isolationist vulgarities of *The Saturday Evening Post* represented a
version of anti-Communism that did not really matter because of its
low intellectual level, while I took comfort from the earnestness
with which *The New York Times* in late 1946 and early 1947 began
to report and comment in detail about the brutal subjugation of
Eastern European countries by the Soviets, in the articles and col-
umns of Anne O'Hare McCormick, Hanson Baldwin, Cy Sulzberger, for example. Soon I realized that these intelligent and
worldly Americans, even though influential at the time, were a
small rivulet within the rapidly increasing and widening stream of
anti-Communist opinion and sentiment. A powerful undercurrent
within that big and muddy stream was the sometimes unspoken
resentment felt by considerable segments of the American population against the participation of the United States in the Second
World War. It is true that during that war the vast majority of
Americans had responded to their patriotic duties with admirable
discipline, and that there had been remarkably few examples of
treason or sabotage or "subversion" (whatever that word may
mean). But it is also true that the American alliance with Britain and
with Russia was not popular among many people, especially not
among German-, Italian-, Irish-, Slovak-, Croat-, Ukrainian-Ameri-
cans, together with isolationists of whatever ethnic origin. It is true
that, unlike after the First World War, after the Second World War
isolationism did not, because it could not, return. But the sentiments—sentiments, rather than opinions—that constituted the essential popular appeal of isolationism were still strong; and because
of the way in which Russia showed itself, the way in which the
world had turned out, these sentiments and opinions seemed jus-

tifiable to many people. "Haven't we always said that you cannot trust the Communists?" some of them said; and their opponents were uneasy when they saw that hard scowl on people's faces. Underneath this coursed the usually unspoken, but by no means absent sentiment: Germany had not been as bad as Russia. As Senator Taft said in 1941, the danger to America was not Hitlerism but Communism, "for Fascism appeals but to a few, and Communism to the many." He was entirely wrong; the opposite was more often true; but, no matter, this was what many Americans believed after the war and for many years to come, having convinced themselves that Communism was a much greater danger than "Fascism" (that inadequate term) had ever been.

Often I found myself in the company of such people in 1947 and for some years thereafter. Having heard or read somewhere that here was a recent arrival from Europe who was outspokenly anti-Russian and anti-Communist, certain people would find me, at times because they needed a speaker for this occasion or that. I responded to their invitations instantly, probably because of my loneliness. But very soon I found that I had as little in common with them as with their political opposites. We shared a few recognitions, but our differences were great. Most of these differences went back to the memories of the Second World War; some forward to the prospects of a third one. I did not think that it was wrong to fight and defeat Hitler; I did not think that a Europe wholly dominated by the Third Reich was preferable to a Europe whose eastern half was dominated by the Soviet Union; I did not think that Americans should support (or believe) everyone who claimed to be anti-Communist; I did not think that the United States should aim at the destruction of the entire Soviet Union. Having argued this with some of these people—and I was sometimes appalled how respectable their opinions sounded at the time, and how such opinions were, if not always asserted, at least suggested by respectable religious publications, especially German-American ones—I must say something for these people. They were usually less educated and intellectual than were American liberals, while their unwillingness to comprehend and to concede certain matters contrary to their preconceptions was as rigid as that of the liberals. On the other hand, if not very open-minded, they were more open-hearted than were most liberals. Personal relations counted more with them than the rightness or wrongness of opinions. The fact—or, rather, the reputation—that one was associated with a wrong kind of opinion meant instant hostility on the part of liberals; somewhat less so with my isolationist or populist or conservative acquaintances, even though in many instances I found that their views were utterly wrong, even dangerous, and said so. But this goes beyond politics and ideology; it is all mixed up with the diabolical alchemy of the human mind. I particularly remember a friend, a German-American professor, whose opinions and occasional writings against the adversaries of Germany, including Jews, were not only historically and factually wrong but often vile because they were suffused with the crudest of resentments and hatreds. Yet in some ways this man was a kind human being, and by this I do not mean only that, like Hitler or Himmler, he was kind to children and to animals. In his case, I think, the opposite of the Wildean aphorism was true: brutality being the Bank Holiday of his sentimentalism (which, when you think of it, is a German syndrome of sorts).

There was an important exception to my aggregate loneliness in those early American years. This consisted of my finding a home— at least, and surely, a kind of home—among certain Catholics. After I arrived in New York I had a small part-time and temporary teaching job at Columbia, where I met Professor Eugene Byrne, a historian of modern Europe, who taught at Barnard College. Having vetted me during a long evening in his house, where we talked not so much about history and academic business as about French literature and music (he was an old-fashioned historian), he introduced me to Ross J. S. Hoffman, of Fordham, who became my great friend for more than three decades, and a great contemporary in more than one way. His framed photograph hangs above my desk where I am writing this. In turn, Ross, who knew that I was in search of a permanent teaching job, brought me together with Erik von Kuehnelt-Lehddin, who was about to leave Chestnut Hill College and sought his replacement. Erik was one of the handful of anti-Nazi Europeans in America who moved in a direction opposite to most refugees: instead of staying in the United States he went back to Austria after the war (his wife's estate was in the Tyrol, in the western section of that then still divided country). His mind was unusually independent: he was an avowed conservative, a monarchist and an eloquent opponent of the ideology of modern democracy at a time when this was not only unpopular in the United States but virtually unheard-of. (He became more predictable later, when he became a columnist for *National Review*.) I admired the wide scope of his mind. On a frozen day in February 1947 I took the train to North Philadelphia, shivered on an empty platform waiting for the Chestnut Hill Local, at the end station of which I found a bus, crowded and cloudy with the wet woolen steam of the scarves, coats and socks of what I thought were pretty college girls. The bus took me to my interview at Chestnut Hill College, where I was thereafter given a contract to teach three classes in modern European history and one class in German literature for $2,800 per annum.

I moved to Philadelphia in September. As I wrote in the foregoing chapter, I liked Philadelphia immediately; I wasn't sure whether I liked Chestnut Hill College where, surely in the beginning, I was a callow young foreigner whom it was difficult to categorize, a round peg in a square hole. Some of my teacher colleagues were demonstratively aloof, sometimes revealing strains of a hostile suspicion. The nuns sailed along the corridors high-veiled, like black Spanish galleons. I was still an Anglophile; and the then still strong Anglophobia of the Irish startled me. But soon I was relieved to find that this was the place for me, for more than one reason. My liking for Philadelphia, the security of a permanent job, the possibility of being allowed to take on another part-time job in another local Catholic college (I needed the money because I had begun to support my ailing mother who, after great difficulties, made her way as far as Vienna) all played a part in my decision to stay. But the most important element was the kindness that was so easily and naturally extended to me by some of the older Sisters who governed the college. To an American Catholic religious a Catholic refugee from Communism in 1947 was a natural subject of compassion and charity. Yet their anti-Communism was neither bitter nor assertive. They had none of the inclinations to tell other Americans that "we told you so." I was a lonely refugee, not an ideological ally. What mattered to them was whether I was a responsible teacher and a Catholic, conditions that were spacious enough to fulfill with ease. They appreciated what I could give to the students, and they were willing to help me in more than one way. I sensed that Sister Maria Kostka, the president, Sister Clare Joseph, the rosy-cheeked registrar, an Irish nun of ineffable wisdom and goodness, Sister Loyola Maria, a *grande dame* of an academic dean, came to regard me as a stray young member of their family. So Chestnut Hill College became a sort of second home, rather than a professional niche or a step on the academic ladder, to me.

Very soon after my affiliation with Chestnut Hill College I kept hearing from academics that this kind of affiliation was a definite professional handicap, since Catholic colleges were, by their nature, inferior to other respectable American institutions of higher education. (As Peter Viereck wrote a few years later, anti-Catholicism was the anti-Semitism of intellectuals.) In some ways this was true: American Catholics at that time, including much of the American hierarchy, were not particularly intellectual; they were uninterested in and sometimes even suspicious of intellectuality. But this was not true of these Sisters who ran Chestnut Hill College at the time, whose respect for the humanities was well-grounded and, in many ways, solid because much of it was still old-fashioned, in many ways late-Victorian. Even in later years when the college, like everything else, had changed, I would sometimes (usually during wearisome faculty meetings, or between classes) gaze out the high windows on winter afternoons, and take a deep breath of comfort and sustenance from the sight of the solid, graystone buildings of the convent or St. Joseph's Hall, so reassuring because of their permanence, suggesting, at least to me, the surviving presence of an old, gloomy fortitude protective of an interior light and warmth. And there were intellectual Catholics to be found, among my colleagues as well as here and there, sometimes in the oddest corners and places, among the better students and professors and non-professionals. At the time these people were often called "Commonweal Catholics," because most of them read *Commonweal*, the Catholic intellectual journal founded twenty years earlier, with elevated literary standards and a political and social philosophy that was pristine and fairly unique in the United States, an American version of the Western European Christian Democracy. The important matter about *Commonweal* was not its liberalism, that it was more liberal than the ideology of most American Catholics; the important matter was its intellectual standards. Yet for most Americans these two matters were inseparable. For this was still a time in the history of the Republic when "intellectual" meant "liberal," that is, more broad-minded, more cosmopolitan, more thoughtful, more questioning and less complacent than the opinions assumed by the majority of Americans, surely by the majority of unquestioning Catholic Americans. *Commonweal* was a natural outlet for me; in 1951 I began writing for it and wrote many—perhaps too many—articles and reviews for it during the next four years. Then I ceased to write for it, even though we had no real quarrel or a sharp parting of the ways. I began to write *Historical Consciousness* and thought that I had little or no time for article-writing; but there was another reason, too. For *Commonweal*, too, I was a round peg in a square hole. I did not share its liberalism. This was less of an ideological difference than the difference of an entire, and I think important, historical perspective. The liberalism of the *Commonweal* editors was not an opportunistic one, even though sometimes they went to unconscionable extents to argue the compatibility of Catholicism with liberalism. The source of their liberalism was their progressive view of the world, springing from a respectful and intellectually avid appreciation of the Age of Reason, of the eighteenth-century Enlightenment, toward which they wished to guide other American Catholics whose categories and structures of belief were often automatic, unthinking, pre-modern and superstitious, representing a fideism before the Enlightenment—that is, of the seventeenth century and perhaps even earlier.* The *Commonweal* editors and writers did not see this in this way, but I did. They had been pre-liberals; I was a post-liberal. They were looking forward to the Enlightenment; I was looking back at it. And this is but another illustration of what I mean when I say that America was behind Europe as late as 1950—which is not a statement of intellectual smugness but the contrary, since I often wish that America *had* kept behind, instead of catching up with some of the worst habits of Europe during the last forty years.

But at least in one important matter *Commonweal* and I were and remained allies, sharing the same inclinations: in our dislike of the Second Red Scare that began to envelop the mental and political habits of Americans by 1950. Yes, I was contemptuous of Communism and Communists; and although I saw that the Communist threat existed only because of the Russian armed power behind it, I also knew that there *were* such things as Communist conspiracies in the United States (or, more precisely, conspiracies by Communists). "The penetration of the American governmental services by members or agents (conscious or otherwise) of the American Communist Party in the 1930s [indeed, until about 1947] was not a figment of the imagination," George Kennan wrote in his *Memoirs*. "It really existed; and it assumed proportions which, while never overwhelming, were also not trivial." Like Kennan in 1945, 1946 and 1947, I was vexed because so many Americans were not reacting, or reacted insufficiently, to the Soviet dangers. Three or four years later I found that I was disturbed because of their exaggerated and fervent and often thoughtless reactions. In sum, I had become an anti-anti-Communist. Did this mean that I had much in common with other anti-anti-Communists—with the frightened (and, alas, often cowardly) liberals of the time? At the risk of seeming arrogant, I must say no. Did it mean that I was a classic moderate, a

---

*Pascal: "If we submit everything to reason, our religion will have nothing in it mysterious or supernatural. If we violate the principles of reason, our religion will be absurd and ridiculous."

middle-of-the-roader, with my principled nose high up in the air, *always* opposed to *every* extreme stand or idea? Again, no; that kind of moderation does not suit my temperament: I like the English witticism, "moderation in everything, including moderation," the logic of its illogic. It took me some time to figure out (that ungainly phrase *figure out* is, for once, apposite) the essence of a consistency whereby I was compelled to prefer and to express seemingly—but only seemingly—antithetical opinions within a few years, something that I must explain a few pages later.

In the meantime—by this I mean most of the Fifties, a decade that so many writers and historians have recently come to regard as the zenith of what was good and prosperous in recent American history*—I suffered from the sight and the sense of what was going on in the minds of the people of my adopted country. The American anti-Communism of the Fifties was abstract, extreme, self-serving and false. It was abstract, because the attribution of every kind of evil and immorality to Communists was not only unhistorical but utterly unreal. (Many Americans saw Communists as late as 1955 in the shapes of Trotsky's Communists of a generation before: unkempt, bearded, diabolically clever anarchistic conspirators, addicted to the destruction of every kind of decency, poisoners of wells, corrupters of children, practitioners of every kind of sexual licentiousness—this at a time when the Soviet Union was ruled by a puritanical peasant [Khrushchev] and stiff slabs of military bureaucrats.) A clear example came to me one day in my classroom. This happened at the height of the McCarthy wave when, on occasion, I felt compelled, if not to interrupt, at least to illustrate my lectures on twentieth-century European history by telling my students how

---

*Here and there (as in the pages of my *Outgrowing Democracy: A History of the United States in the Twentieth Century,* written in 1980–83 and published in 1984) I tried to point out that, by a series of curious coincidences, the years 1955–57 may have been a most important turning point in the fortunes of this country during this century; but the meaning of this observation was missed by most reviewers and scholars. These coincidences ought, however, to be brought together, to bring attention to this historical hinge of fate, in a book with a title such as *The Turning Point*—another book that I will probably not write, though written it ought to be.

the dangers of Communism were, and indeed could be, exaggerated, for all kinds of pernicious political purposes. A girl in the class asked me whether it wasn't true that Communist agents were dangerous. I said yes. But weren't there many of them? she asked. I said, not in the United States, certainly not now. She insisted that there *were* many of them. (She did this fairly respectfully, not for the sake of arguing.) Then a thought came to me. I said: "There are thirty of you in this class. How many of you have ever met a Communist?" No one answered. "How many of you have ever heard a Communist?" Silence. "How many of you know *anyone* who knows a Communist?" Uneasy silence. (I took a gamble on that one, springing from my knowledge of the parochiality of the American Catholic middle classes: most of these students and their families knew few people who did not come from their own neighborhoods, geographical and social.) "Well," I said, "doesn't this show that there can't be that many of them around?" But the girl insisted. "Doctor," she said. "You yourself said that some of the most dangerous allies of the Russians have been people who aren't Party members, that they are hidden agents." At this moment *Deus illuminavit mentem meam*—the divine saving spark had come. "You mean," I said, "the example of a very clever and very dangerous Communist, who is told to mask himself and to deny that he belongs to the Party?" She nodded. "You mean that this man is so clever that he leads outwardly a normal and respectable life, and never says anything that is Communist?" More nodding. "You mean that this man *never says* anything that is Communist and *never does* anything that is Communist?" Emphatic nodding. "Then how come he is dangerous at all?" Uneasy laughter.

In addition to its abstract character, the anti-Communism of the Fifties was also extreme; and this extremism was not without its political dangers, dangers that resided—perhaps paradoxically—in the respectability of anti-Communism. As I wrote earlier, one of the cardinal stupidities in Marx's vision of the world was his inability to see how powerful and rampant is the desire for respectability in the human breast, and by no means only in the narrow little breasts of the bourgeois but also within the working classes, including the ample bosoms of their wives. Tocqueville noted this exactly one hundred years before the rise of Joe McCarthy. "The insane fear of socialism," he wrote in 1852 in a letter, "throws the middle classes headlong into the arms of despotism. . . . But now that the weakness of the Red party had been proved, people will regret the price at which their enemy has been put down." Mussolini and Hitler learned this early in their careers. Mussolini, who started out as a revolutionary, discovered that he was an Italian first and a socialist only second; thereafter he found that in order to come to power he had to make an appeal to that desire for respectability and to the conservatism that is deeply inherent in the minds of most people. The profession of Fascist opposition to socialism, Communism, anarchism and even to Italian republicanism made the king and the army accept him and people welcome him in 1922. When Hitler attempted a revolutionary *Putsch* in 1923, he failed. Less than ten years later he came to power because he convinced the ruling classes of Germany to be less worried about him than about Communism; and because of his appeal to the people of Germany who craved respectability and order.

Well, history does not repeat itself. The United States was not Germany; Eisenhower was not a Hindenburg; McCarthy was not a Hitler. Still, there were plenty of parallels—or, rather, of reminders. In Hungary, too, the hatred and fear of Communism had made many people go along with the Germans during the Third Reich years. These people were not necessarily those of the upper classes, who had reason to fear what Communism would do to them. Anti-Communism was a *given;* it was unquestioned, whereby all kinds of people, especially people who were not prone to question accepted and respected ideas, regarded anti-anti-Communism, in whatever form, as unpatriotic, disreputable, suspicious. Thus were old aristocrats accused of pro-Communist subversiveness because they seemed to be opposed to the Germans and to their nationalist allies. And there were plenty of politicians and intellectuals who knew how to swim with the tide. As in Hungary circa 1941, in the United States circa 1953 I could see the movements of opportunism and cowardly self-serving: intellectuals and politicians moving toward what to them seemed the winning side. This revolted me in America, for two reasons, one of them being that even during the worst years of the Second Red Scare there was no political terror in the United States. Unless they were or had been Communist Party members, few people were persecuted because of their political convictions; unlike in Hungary, the personal danger for sticking to your guns was minimal. The other source of my disillusionment was that these multiplying manifestations of prevarication and opportunism were precisely what I had *not* expected in an English-speaking and democratic country. (Because of different historical, cultural, national and linguistic traditions, the habitual ratio of fairness to unfairness, of honesty to dishonesty, of truthfulness to prevarication among, say, Englishmen and Rumanians or between Americans and Iranians is *not* the same. Nor is there much similarity between the kind of opportunism practiced by a Syrian and the kind practiced by a Scotsman. But among intellectuals of whatever nation, whether liberals or conservatives, Communists or anti-Communists, the ratio of opportunism to honesty seems everywhere about the same.)

In the winter of 1953 I wrote an article, "The Totalitarian Temptation," which was printed in *Commonweal* on January 22, 1954. There I wrote, among other things, that for an American Catholic to profess an opposition to Communism was no more and no less natural than for a Jew to profess his opposition to Nazism; but since American Catholics were far from being a persecuted minority, "for an American Catholic to bask in the respectable knowledge of anti-Communism in 1954 requires neither audacity nor determination, sacrifice, noble charity, inner fortitude, courage or wisdom. It connotes rather a temper of easy self-satisfaction." The argument of the article was that, not unlike in Germany in the 1930s and during the war, a split among American Catholics might occur. Because of their nationalism many of them might succumb to a totalitarian temptation, while some of them—again as in Germany and in other places—would be the principal martyrs and opponents of totalitarianism, including the most respectable and popular variants thereof. About this long-range argument I am as certain now as I was thirty-six years ago. What I am not certain about is whether I may have been unduly pessimistic at that time, because of the passing situation, by exaggerating the portents of McCarthyism: after all, McCarthy's fall from political grace began less than a year after my article was written.

Yet even now I am inclined to think that I was not altogether wrong. There were, at that time, phenomena that filled me with foreboding. One was the widespread misreading of Joe McCarthy, a misreading that has continued to this day. The standard view of McCarthy is still that he was an unscrupulous opportunist who hit on the issue of anti-Communism in 1950 because he was told by some of his friends that there was much political profit, "mileage," in it. Yet the key to McCarthy was not his decision, in early 1950, to begin his anti-Communist campaign. It was his decision, in 1948, to address himself to the issue of the so-called Malmédy trials.* That decision had an element of politic calculation in it: the victims of the Malmédy trials were Germans, and McCarthy's state of Wisconsin had a large German-American population. Yet there is every reason to believe that, as during his subsequent anti-Communist crusade, Joseph Raymond McCarthy (himself part-German) chose to speak and act not merely out of opportunism but out of conviction. To speak out in defense of former members of the SS and against their prosecutors was, after all, not the potentially most popular course even in 1948. At the same time it was not unpopular either—and McCarthy may have felt this in his bones—in certain places and among certain segments of the population who, as I wrote earlier, did not like the direction of American foreign policy during the Second World War. (The Republicans' winning slogan

---

*What happened was this. In 1944, during the Battle of the Bulge, a German SS unit infiltrated the American lines and at least in one instance killed American prisoners. After the war some members of this unit, including its commander, were rounded up and "tried" before an American military court, after having been mistreated and occasionally tortured by American counterintelligence personnel that included a number of former German refugee Jews in American uniforms. These flagitious illegalities then led to their vocal censure by an American judge, who consequently expressed his pro-German (and also anti-Semitic) opinions.

in the 1946 congressional elections suggested this: "Had Enough?")
This was the resentment against the coalition of internationalists,
liberals, Anglophiles, Jews, bankers and much of the Eastern
Anglo-Saxon elite who seemed to be in top positions during the
Roosevelt era and whose presence was still prevalent in Washington, a resentment that McCarthy wholly shared. He and his followers resented men such as Marshall or Acheson even more than they
hated Communists. McCarthy had the potential of a mass movement behind him. Fortunately his character was not strong enough
to sustain the burden of temporary setbacks. He was not German
enough to be humorless, categorical, disciplined and fanatic; and he
was Irish enough in his drinking, his black moods, his professions
of martyrdom, in his short-distance running and in his occasional
sense of humor. When his enemies finally got together to move
against him (not without hypocritical measures on their part), with
the result of passing a censure resolution in the Senate, arranged not
without difficulties (John F. Kennedy, a former secret contributor
to America First, chose not to vote against McCarthy), McCarthy's
spirit broke. A Hitler or a Mussolini would have taken sustenance
from such a censure; McCarthy was incapable of that. He sank into
self-pity and drank himself to death in less than three years. I will
admit that when my wife told me the news from our kitchen radio
I felt a twinge of sorrow for him: "God have mercy on his soul,"
I said.

Yet, I repeat: the elements of his strength and success were there.
To me, the danger was visible not so much from the evidence that
popular support of McCarthy was alarmingly widespread; the danger was, rather, inherent in the cowardice of his adversaries. By the
early Fifties the equation of patriotism with anti-Communism was
so overwhelming and unquestioned that few people in important
positions had the strength of mind and character to stand up against
it. To see the hapless Secretary of the Army quail and weasel before
McCarthy's crude (and often senseless) questions was, at least to me,
a reminder of how often demagogues and tyrants and totalitarians
have triumphed because of the weakness of their potential opponents. The phenomenon of opportunism was a result of that condi-

tion. Much of that opportunism consisted in the adjustment of minds to what seemed to be the prevailing climate of opinion. Through most of my life I have possessed—and been plagued with—an extreme, perhaps exaggerated sensitivity to such significant appearances of intellectual opportunism. Here are a few examples from the years 1953–55, before McCarthy's fall from grace —perhaps not the best ones but ones that remain even now in my memory. I found it at least faintly significant when reporters, tracking him down on one of his African safaris, could not coax Ernest Hemingway into making a clear statement against McCarthy. I found it sadly significant when William Remington, a former pro-Communist intellectual, was clubbed to death in his prison cell by criminals who claimed that he deserved what he got because he was a Communist. I found it revoltingly significant that an editorial in *Life* stated that McCarthyism was only a "venial sin," while Communism was a "cardinal sin." (Ten years before, that magazine had printed a full-page picture of Lenin with the caption: "This Was Perhaps the Greatest Man of the Twentieth Century.") I found it deplorably significant what a CIA agent said when he called on me during his rounds gathering information from Eastern Europeans. I told him that I had left Hungary seven years before and that I had little information beyond what he could find in the press, but that in the apartment house where I then lived there was a carpenter, a Jewish refugee, recently arrived from a remote and little-known part of the Soviet Union (Turkestan). He said that Jews were not considered "reliable."* I found it ludicrously significant when a

---

*I thought about this for some time, not only because of the stupid prejudice of that government agent but because of the very stupidity of his interviewing me. He had been directed to me by the administration of La Salle College, where he sought the names of potential interviewees from Eastern Europe. He ought to have known that I had come from Hungary seven years before and that I was not involved in emigré affairs; he also could have looked up some of my published writings, which he evidently had not done. In sum, there was little reason for this agent to interview me. Still, by doing so, he could fill out a report or a form and add to his quota of work. This was but another example of the procedures of "secret" agents all over the world. In order to ensure their positions they must fill their quotas, making work for themselves. It was this

student said that if a Communist were hit by a car outside the college it would not be right for a Catholic to call an ambulance (I must admit that I had coaxed her into that statement). And I found it, alas, expectable as well as significant that some liberal professors in 1954 began to profess views of Russia that, if not identical with those of McCarthy, were certainly getting closer and closer to those, say, of John Foster Dulles.

Varieties of opportunism, indeed . . . In April 1954 I was shocked to hear, with my own ears, George Sokolsky, a syndicated and well-known Jewish columnist and a Republican, tell the students in a lecture at La Salle College that "the worst mistake America ever made was to enter the Second World War. We goaded Britain into it, when we should have let Hitler unite Western Europe against Communism." Around that time I received a letter from a decent Catholic layman, an insurance agent in Southern California, who had read something that I had written. He was being publicly censured by members of his own chapter of the Knights of Columbus because he opposed their public support of one of their newer members, a man by the name of Artukovic, who had been the Interior Minister (that is, head of the police) of one of the most murderous and Nazified satellite governments during the Second World War, in Croatia. In 1955 an Archbishop Trifa, of the nationalist and autocephalous Rumanian Orthodox Church, an agitator and high council member of the Iron Guard in 1940–41 (when they hanged elderly Jews on butcher hooks in Bucharest), was invited to open the session of the Congress of the United States with his prayer. Twenty-five years later Artukovic and Trifa were about to be deported by the American government. Indeed, a bill was pending in the Senate to deport Trifa to Israel, where he would be tried for "war crimes." To me, this was as wrong as was his invitation to the prelacy of the Senate twenty-five years earlier. I mused about the changing conditions of whatever goes under the name of "pub-

---

kind of bureaucratic practice, even more than sadism and, of course, than ideological fervor, that explains much of the senseless and horrible collection of all kinds of victims during the Stalin "purges."

lic opinion" (which, in reality, is often merely simulated by the machinery of publicity). What changed during those twenty-five years was not so much popular opinion or popular sentiment but artificially engendered climates of publicity—that is, the propagation and the management of certain accepted ideas.

Sometime in the spring of 1954 my wife and I saw Joe McCarthy. The occasion was a "lecture" he gave at Rosemont College. We came early and sat in the first row, wherefrom I watched the Senator intently and, I believe, on one or two occasions I caught his eye. My wife and I might have been the only people in the audience who, rather demonstratively, refused to applaud him when his "presentation" was over. In the row behind us sat the owner of the *Philadelphia Inquirer* (later named Ambassador to the Court of St. James by Richard Nixon and bosom friend of Ronald Reagan), the President of the Pennsylvania Railroad and other Philadelphian notables. They smiled broadly at Joe McCarthy, laughed benevolently at his jokes and applauded him. Joe obviously enjoyed his reception, at times veering toward adulation, in spite—or perhaps because—of the circumstance that he did not quite fit into the scene. He was swarthy, sweaty, hairy, with feral gaps between his front teeth, in contrast not only to the well-dressed audience but also to the demure middle-class Catholic girls wearing white gloves, ushering the guests and then standing in the wings of the platform in virginal panoply. That the above-mentioned members of the Philadelphia financial (and, in some cases, social) aristocracy were not convinced McCarthyites I found possible even then; a year later I was sure that they wouldn't give him the time of the day. But their smiles and nods suggested more than good manners and courtesy; they were meant to demonstrate in public their agreement with his basic idea. Again, what interested me was not *what* these people thought but *how* they were employing their minds. In any case, my physical proximity to McCarthy only confirmed that this man was not, as some conservatives insisted, a conservative but a radical vulgarian.

By 1955 McCarthy's back was broken; and, as I wrote earlier, his failure to recover was his own doing—or, rather, non-doing. Yet the anti-Communist substitution for American patriotism went on for many years. In 1954 I was offered a visiting professorship at Columbia University for the coming academic year. I took the job eagerly: it amounted to extra money, to my first chance to teach a graduate class, it required only one weekly trip to New York, where I was given an office and a secretary in one of those 1910-type houses on Morningside Heights turned into offices from middle-class dwellings long ago. The office was dreary; the course was ill-advertised and wrongly announced in the catalogue. I started out with two students, both of poor quality; by the second semester I had none, but continued to be paid for doing nothing—a not infrequent situation in higher education. Perhaps I could have parlayed this appointment into a permanent professorship in Eastern European history, but I was indifferent to such an opportunity, for all kinds of reasons. I did not wish to concentrate on Eastern European history; I was distancing myself from centers of academic life; I had no desire to live or perhaps even work in New York. My wife and I had already chosen (we were married a year earlier) to move to Chester County, and to undertake the building of a house out of the ruins of an old one-room schoolhouse, a task that was as inspiring as it was burdensome, often to the extent of being painfully demanding. And when that house was ready for us to move into (barely ready, at that), on the edge of this green bower of what my sentimental eyes saw as an Arcadia in America, I learned that a few miles from us, on the top of the hill, Eisenhower's government had just then erected a Nike rocket station, one of a dozen in a wide circle around Philadelphia, in order to defend Philadelphia against Soviet air attacks. I was upset about this, not so much because it compromised my sentimental vision of having found a remote and peaceful cove in the American countryside *(beatus ille qui procul negotiis)* but because this was another evidence of the stupidity of a spendthrift government at a time when the chance of a Russian air attack on Philadelphia was not only remote, it was nonexistent. (The Nike stations were dismantled after a few years, ironically, at the very time when that other monumental stupidity, the so-called —and, as we now know, also nonexistent—"missile gap" had become another accepted idea, providing, among other things, the launching of the public career of Henry Kissinger.)

A year later (our house was still not finished, and the garden and fields were a weedy jungle) came the Hungarian Rising against the Soviets. There I sat in my house (or in my car) in feverish excitement, twirling the knobs on the radio, trying to get snatches of news every half hour, running out for the papers twice every day, hoping against hope that the revolution would succeed and that the Russians would retreat from Hungary; but unlike most of my fellow exiles, I also knew that the Eisenhower government would do nothing—by which I mean, nothing remotely reasonable—to ease such a Russian retreat. I was bitter not only because of the Russians' cruel suppression of the Rising of my native country but also because of the dishonesties of the government of my adopted one. When Eisenhower and Dulles said that the revolution was, for them, a complete surprise, they lied. It is true that they, and the CIA, had not instigated the Rising; but they had been very well informed of what was going on. Moreover, contrary to their pompous and self-righteous anti-Soviet declarations, they were relieved by the failure of the Rising because they did not have to revise their division of Europe with the Russians. (In turn, the Russians, and particularly Khrushchev, were relieved, too: for here was the definite proof that the Americans were not going to challenge the division of Europe.) Therefore 1956 was a turning point of the cold war, and of much else besides.

Unlike the government, the intellectuals were really surprised by the Hungarian Rising, one of their dogmas being that in a totalitarian state revolutions were impossible.* As usual, they were wrong.

---

*That dogma was expounded in *The Origins of Totalitarianism*, Hannah Arendt's celebrated book written in 1948–50 and published in 1951, to the reading of which many intellectuals, including most neo-conservatives, even now ascribe their conversion from Trotskyism to anti-Communism. In reality, that book was an ephemeral work of lucubration: ephemeral because of the intellectual opportunism of its author, who took what seemed to be happening in 1950 and projected this into a thesis, predicting the continuation of what seemed to be going on. In 1950 Stalin's regime had become evidently anti-Semitic; hence her thesis, according to which anti-Semitism was the inevitable ingredient of

What was more important, their belated conversion to anti-Communism was now in full swing. It was not only that former isolationists, "conservatives," American "right-wingers" had become dedicated internationalists, calling for American intervention everywhere in the world, some of them taken by the glamorous paraphernalia of global politics, including secret agentry. Many erstwhile liberals now found it politic and profitable to accept not only the doctrine that Soviet Communism was evil (which was, by and large, true) but that it was the greatest and increasing danger in the world (this after the evident demonstrations of the hatred for Communism by entire nations in Eastern Europe, and of the deflation of pro-Sovietism even among the Communist parties of Western Europe). By the end of the Fifties, many of the New York ex-Trotskyists had become neo-conservatives, even though they had not yet begun to apply that adjective to themselves.

It should now appear that I was much exercised by politics in the 1950s, but by the latest after 1956 my interest in politics decreased. I am not a political animal or a political scientist; my writing and teaching were primarily historical; and my interest in politics, too, was the result of my impatience with the inadequacy of the historical (and therefore, human) understanding demonstrated by politicians, bureaucrats and many intellectuals. This may have contributed to my beginning to write the first drafts of *Historical Consciousness* in 1955, but then I interrupted this long task in the winter of 1959–60 to write *A History of the Cold War*. That book was, more directly, the result of my concern with the inadequate historical understanding of the origins and the development of the

---

every totalitarian regime. But that was (and is) not necessarily true. More important was her second thesis, according to which it was in the nature of totalitarian rule to become ever more repressive and total, whence a revolution under totalitarian rule could not happen. A few years after the publication of her book came the thaw under Khrushchev and the Polish and Hungarian revolutions in 1956, developments and events that were living denials of Hannah Arendt's thesis—which, of course, did nothing to reduce her reputation among intellectuals, rather the contrary.

conflict between the United States and Soviet Russia. I chose to interrupt my work on *Historical Consciousness* and write this essay on the history of the cold war in order to attempt a practical illustration of some of my ideas (as proposed, in greater and deeper detail, in *Historical Consciousness*) about the hierarchy of historical forces, especially in the twentieth century. I knew that beneath the misinterpretations of present world political conditions lay inadequate and outdated perceptions of historical reality, of how and why things were happening, of how ideas moved, of how the very structure of events differed from the theories and structures and "laws" of biological evolution, indeed, from those of the so-called natural sciences.

By that time (the late Fifties) my recognitions had crystallized; I had become accustomed to think about thinking, including my own, and including (among many other things) that anti-anti-Communism of mine. I had become, as I wrote earlier, an anti-anti-Communist; yet (as I also wrote) I was not like many other anti-anti-Communists; I was neither a liberal nor a rigid middle-of-the-roader, an obsessive moderate. I was alone; but already years before I had gained sustenance from finding that my views of Russia and Communism were not unlike those of certain great men. Churchill, for example, in 1945 proposed a determined stand against certain Russian ambitions and against the permanent establishment of a Russian presence in the middle of Europe; but in 1953 he proposed that serious negotiations with Stalin's successors ought to be attempted in order to correct the unnatural division of Europe. In 1945 Churchill's proposals were rejected as being too dangerously anti-Soviet by the American establishment, including the then considerably pro-Soviet General Eisenhower; in 1953 he was rejected for being too pro-Soviet by some of the same people, including Eisenhower. George Kennan who, nearly alone among leading American diplomats, warned against the optimistic, sloppy and often intellectually flawed misreadings of Soviet purposes in 1944 and thereafter, by 1953 found himself compelled to attack the sordid practices and the ideology of the Second Red Scare, among other occasions, at Notre Dame University, in what should have been a memorable speech. I write "should have been" because he was ignored and misunderstood not only by Dulles's people but also by most intellectuals. Was it simply a sort of *Realpolitik* that explained this seemingly complete reversal of Churchill's or Kennan's propositions within a few years? No, there was more than that. Around 1952 I found a sentence in a letter by Metternich to the Spanish conservative philosopher Donoso Cortés. "An idea," Metternich wrote, "is like a fixed siege gun; it has the power to strike everything along a single straight line. But a principle is like a gun mounted on a revolving platform: it can turn and strike at error in every direction when it is anchored on a strong and permanent base." Well, men such as Churchill and Kennan were men of principles, not of ideas. Most men, like Eisenhower, were not; they would adopt ideas according to their circumstances.

This was one explanation—a valid one, I think—of what otherwise might seem puzzling, especially to people accustomed to thinking in terms of ideological categories. There was another, allied explanation: the difference of historical experience. Churchill and Kennan knew more about Russia and Russians than Eisenhower and Dulles; consequently, they understood some of the problems better. I, too, had my experiences with Russian power and with Communists; consequently, my thinking about the latter was less abstract than that of many Americans. In the mid-Forties I was more anti-Communist than they were; in the Fifties I was less anti-Communist than they were. Did this mean that I was more pro-Communist now? Not at all. *Pro-* and *anti-* (or *pro* and *con*) are categories taken from geometry and mathematics. *Pre-* and *post-*, before and after, are more telling: the results of historical experience. Yet not on all levels, and not always. An intelligent virgin may write a book about marriage that is more perceptive than a book written by a multiple divorcée. Conversely, I met many former Communists whose opinions and ideas were twisted out of reason because of their own experiences: with all of the zeal of a convert they were inclined to attribute every evil in the world to Communist conspiracies, about which they knew not only enough but too much; but, then, knowledge is a matter of quality, not of quantity.

And so, in the end, it is on this basis of non-quantifiable quality that I must explain "Anti-Anti." It involves the relationship of truths and half-truths. For a long time I thought that while Communism was a lie, certain kinds of anti-Communism, including Nazism,* were half-truths—whence their appeal to many people. But I also knew that a half-truth is more dangerous than a lie.† Eventually an explanation came to me, in accord not only with St. Thomas (half-truths are worse than lies because the sins of the spirit are worse than the sins of the flesh—and a lie is almost always, a product of weakness) but with Kierkegaard, who said that "numbers are the negation of truth." That I read many years later. Yet already during the Fifties I saw that a half-truth is *not* a 50 percent truth, but that it is a 100 percent truth and a 100 percent untruth compounded, mixed together. Mathematically speaking, of course, 100 + 100 makes 200—just as according to mathematical logic the negative of a negative is a positive (i.e., an anti-anti-Communist *must* be a pro-Communist of sorts). But life is not like that. There a hundred compounded with another hundred makes yet another kind of hundred. In the world of mathematics a 100 can be only one kind of 100—perfect, precise, absolute and unchanging. In real life there are all kinds of hundreds—warm, cold, hard, soft, blue, green ones. Moreover, they are never static but living, growing or shrinking, moving this way or another, toward something else. Much of this corresponded with those recognitions that led me to the writing of the more daring portions of *Historical Consciousness,* suggesting a

---

*I have written elsewhere that Hitler was an evil genius; that he had some good qualities, such as intelligence, insight, courage, etc.; but, as La Rochefoucauld wrote, there are evil people in this world who would do less harm if they hadn't some good in them. By this I do not mean that Hitler was "only" 80 or 50 percent evil. It was the misuse of those qualities with which God had endowed him that made him especially responsible historically, and reprehensible morally.

†And since a half-truth is worse than a lie (a lie is a product of weakness, and consequently is easier to identify than a half-truth) the kind of person who chooses to compromise his avoidance of the truth, who does not definitely deny some truth but invents a halfway solution, admitting *some* of it, shows a character that is weaker even than that of the unadulterated liar.

post-scientific view of history and the world, proposing history, rather than mathematics, as the principal form of thought for the understanding not only of ourselves but of the universe, inevitably dependent on the understanding of our human limitations of knowledge.

There are all kinds of reasons that $2 + 2 = 4$ is but one kind of truth, a man-made formulation. Mathematics is part of the history of man, a human creation, which, too, is why history is not part of mathematics. (There are certain physical subatomic situations where $2 + 2$ does not make 4, since these situations do not exist apart from our observations—that is, from our creations—of them.) And here, too, lies a difference between the Russian and the Western religious mind, the abyss between the following statements by Dostoevsky and by Kierkegaard. Dostoevsky said: "If anyone could prove to me that Christ is outside the truth, and if the truth really did exclude Christ, I should prefer to stay with Christ and not with the truth." To me, this is a horrible statement, an affirmation of faith wrought with despair, a denial of Christ's humaneness. Kierkegaard wrote: "If God held all truth concealed in his right hand, and in his left hand the persistent striving for truth, and while warning me against eternal error, should say: Choose! I should humbly bow before his left hand, and say: 'Father, forgive! The pure truth is for Thee alone!' " To us The Truth is not given to know, while we can glimpse all kinds of truths during our pilgrimage of life on this earth, in pursuit of it, consciously so. As the great German historian Johann Gustav Droysen wrote more than one hundred years ago; "History is Humanity's knowledge of itself, its certainty about itself. It is not 'the light and the truth,' but a search therefor, a sermon thereupon, a consecration thereto. It is like John the Baptist, 'not that Light but sent to bear witness of that Light.' " Isn't this especially timely during the second half of the twentieth century, at the time of the decay of entire civilizations, when our world is threatened not by the prevalence of injustice but by the monstrous propagations and by the so widespread prevalence of untruth?

* * *

Sometime during the Fifties the liberal intellectual consensus began to crumble, mostly because of the belated necessity of recognizing the ugly reality of the Soviet Union and Communism. But otherwise the rule and rote of the liberal and modernist inclinations in American intellectual life went on (consider only the so successful vogue of Abstract Expressionism among American painters then, or the dominant features of American corporate architecture, etc.). Seldom in American history was there such a distance between the ideas of intellectuals and those of the American masses. During the Fifties the slow, glacier-like movement of the masses away from the heritage and the memories of the Thirties began, a movement whose significance went beyond politics. The mid-1950s, as I wrote earlier, were a watershed in the history of the American people, in their inclinations, tastes, preferences and habits, on many levels. The emergence of the American conservative movement, beginning after 1953, was a consequence of that watershed. One of its early milestones was the wide attention paid to Russell Kirk's *The Conservative Mind* in 1954; the other the start of William Buckley's magazine, *National Review,* in 1955. This is not the place for a history or even for a historical sketch of the conservative movement in America. I will only insist that the history of politics is the history of words. As late as 1951 Senator Robert A. Taft, still the hero of Republicans and conservatives, a dry husk of a man whose presence was that of an apostle of accounting, refused to accept the adjective "conservative"; he was an old-fashioned liberal, he said. By 1960, the end of the decade, Eisenhower, the supreme opportunist president and general, said that he was a "conservative." That should sum up something: not the entire history of a decade but that of the beginning of the gradual landslide, culminating twenty years later in the national triumph of the "conservative" cause of a "conservative" president.

I kept apart from most of the conservatives in the Fifties. One reason for this was their narrow and ignorant ideological view of the world. Another reason was their more than occasional vulgarity.

With few exceptions, their intellectual level was abysmally low. Their humor was low-grade college humor, at best (the cartoons of *National Review,* for example, were just as ideological and crude as the Soviet cartoons of *Pravda* or *Krokodil*). Swift said that certain people "have just enough religion to hate but not enough to love." Many American conservatives, alas, gave ample evidence that they were just conservative enough to hate liberals but not enough to love liberty. None of them had the inclination to find (let alone voice) any disagreement with Joe McCarthy, whose crude populism and willful disregard for the American Constitution and its guarantees of civil freedoms were antithetical to anything that could be properly called conservative (just as Hitler has been the antithesis of anything reactionary). That the Liberal commentators of the period, such as Bernard De Voto and Edward R. Murrow, kept calling McCarthy a "reactionary," "to the Right of Louis the Fourteenth" does not cancel out the truth of this argument. Just as two wrongs do not make a right, the opposition of two stupidities does not mean that the truth is somewhere in the middle: what it means is that the atmosphere of discourse has been clouded and corrupted beyond reason.

This was the main reason that my interest in politics decreased after the Fifties. There was another, allied reason for this—again illustrative of the differences between mental and physical "laws." Some of the ephemeral ideas of the "Leftist," "radical," "revolutionary" Sixties were so absurd that I was inclined to ignore them instead of arguing with them: for while it is easier to wrestle down a weak body than a strong body it is more difficult to struggle with a weak mind than with a strong one. At least in one respect I was fortunate during the Sixties. Geographically, academically, intellectually, I lived so far removed from the fake radicalism and from the "revolutionary" play-acting of that period that my experience with its manifestations was remote, save for what I read in newspapers and magazines and what I occasionally saw in the appearance and behavior of grim young people in the streets. Yet I, too, opposed the Indochina War—together with many of the best and the worst of the American people at that time. Just about every one of my patriotic friends—including my first wife, whose sense of both the greatness and the tragedy of American history and American existence went very deep—opposed that war, for reasons that were more moral and deep than the motives of ideologues and the purposes of draft dodgers. They were appalled by the mounting evidence that America was doing something *wrong*. Not being a native American, and not being able (or willing) to avow that old American belief in American exceptionalism, my opposition to the Indochina War, while perhaps not altogether removed from moral considerations, was different. I did not believe that the United States should have been involved in it at all: it was the wrong war at the wrong time at the wrong place. Bismarck was once reputed to have said that the entire Balkans were not worth the bones of a Pomeranian grenadier; I thought that all of Indochina, South and North, Viet, Nam, Minh, Cong, were not worth the bones of a single United States Marine. I thought it unfortunate that few Americans were thinking in such terms. The fatal ideological bent was again dominant: so many of those who opposed American intervention based their opposition on the argument that the South Vietnamese government was corrupt, whereby it was but the easiest of steps for them to proceed to the assumption that the North Vietnamese were admirable people.

That was, of course, only one of the manifestations of the "radicalism" of the Sixties—in reality, the last verminous Leftist heave in American history. What I found execrable during the Sixties was not only the disastrous, destructive and customarily imbecile character of its temporarily fashionable ideas, but also the fraudulent assumption of their novelty. The Youth Revolution, the Pacifism, the Free Speech, the Direct Democracy, the Female Liberation, the Sexual Freedom, etc. "movements" of the Sixties were, like the miniskirt, stridently and artificially exaggerated and resuscitated versions of habits and ideas that had been current during the Twenties—of the Twenties that, in reality, were the last, and perhaps only, "modern" decade. Well before the Sixties I found that in the twentieth century—surely after 1945—we were living in a world of intellectual near-stagnation, that the movement of ideas had slowed down, something that Tocqueville observed and predicted in a chapter of *Democracy in America* with the title: "Why Great Revolutions Will become Rare."* What I saw in the Sixties was that the stagnation was now near-complete, with the pendulum of ideas moving back and forth without advancing at all—something that people obsessed with superficial appearances (and with words such as "progressive" or "revolutionary") mistake entirely, unable as they are to distinguish between motion and direction, or between position and tendency, their very seeing and listening having been impaired by public spectacle and public noise. "It is believed by some that modern society will always be changing," Tocqueville wrote in the late 1830s, in the second volume of his *Democracy*. "I fear that it will ultimately be too invariably fixed in the same institutions, the same prejudices . . . so that mankind will be stopped and circumscribed; that the mind will swing backwards and forwards forever without begetting fresh ideas; that man will waste his strength in senile and purposeless trifling; that, though in continual movement, humanity will no longer advance." During the Sixties many of the principal figures in the literary, intellectual, artistic, scientific and academic marketplace were not even silly ideologues but racketeers of publicity, not radical innovators but self-serving idea-jobbers—as, for example, those "revisionist" historians who, beginning about 1964, simply projected the acceptable dissatisfaction with the Vietnam War back into the origins of the cold war. Few people noticed the insufficiency of their thesis and the actual fraudulence of their "research." Much of the same was true of the academic—and immediately profitable—fads of "psychohistory" and "quantification." At times much of the American cultural and intellectual scene looked like a monstrous and absurd caricature of Weimar Berlin, though without the Nazis (or the Communists) in

---

*Example: the heroes of intellect and art, say, in 1924: Darwin, Marx, Freud, Einstein, Stravinsky, Picasso. Fifty years later this list was largely the same, with the puny variation of neo-Darwinians, neo-Marxists, neo-Freudians, etc. Now compare this to the climates of art and thought and of their most important and influential representatives in, say, 1824 and 1874—a very different world. Another, more evident example: "modern" buildings in 1924 and 1974. Etc., etc.

the wings, to be sure. In any event, it was artificial, without more than an ephemeral appeal to the masses of Americans, including their befuddled young.

But a great deal of harm was done, and not only of an ephemeral nature. This was why the conservatives and I drew closer together. I am not a publicist; few, if any, of my writings were directed to the contemporary scene; but around 1970 some of the articles in *National Review* or *The Alternative* or *Triumph* (Brent Bozell's traditionalist Catholic journal) were among the few breaths of fresh air and of common sense. Also, the composition of the conservative intellectual "movement" had changed. It was widening; the number of conservative journals and the intellectual quality of their contents grew; in some of the universities and colleges the presence of conservative professors (and of students) began to make itself felt. Last but not least, it was in these conservative journals that my occasional writings were welcomed and published. So, during the Seventies I wrote many articles and reviews for these magazines, whose editors and staffs, including Bill Buckley, treated my contributions with respect. I did not solicit their invitations and emoluments; in many instances I was satisfied to be published at all; in others I was grateful for their friendship and generosity.

But after the election of 1980 came the deplorable change. I had voted for Ronald Reagan because of my exasperation with the pusillanimities of Jimmy Carter. With his customary generosity, Bill Buckley invited my wife and me to the gala dinner in the Plaza Hotel in December 1980, celebrating *National Review*'s twenty-fifth anniversary. That Plaza affair was, in itself, a mark of the landslide of fashionable American opinion. The very names of those present showed that in the realms of intellectual, artistic, political celebrity the monopoly of the once liberal establishment was gone. The arrangements were in good taste, as were the speeches, because they were brief.* During the introduction of the celebrities a shower of

---

*The exception was the speech by Clare Boothe Luce, which was not only self-congratulatory but arrogant. She said that the twenty-five-year history of *National Review* and the presidential victory of Ronald Reagan were not a mere coincidence (true); that here was an example of the ultimate influence of a

applause greeted Henry Kissinger. I was sufficiently irritated to ejaculate a fairly loud Boo! heard only by my friends around our table.

A day or so before that evening Dorothy Day had died. She was the founder and saintly heroine of the Catholic Worker movement. During that glamorous evening I thought: who was a truer conservative, Dorothy Day or Henry Kissinger? Surely it was Dorothy Day, whose respect for what was old and valid, whose dedication to the plain decencies and duties of human life rested on the traditions of two millennia of Christianity, and who was a radical only in the truthful sense of attempting to get to the roots of the human predicament. Despite its pro-Catholic tendency, and despite its commendable custom of commemorating the passing of worthy people even when some of these did not belong to the conservatives, *National Review* paid neither respect nor attention to the passing of Dorothy Day, while around the same time it published a respectful R.I.P. column in honor of Oswald Mosley, the onetime leader of the British Fascist Party. (In 1987 it published a eulogy at the death of the unsavory gangster Roy Cohn.) Immediately after Ronald Reagan's election the probity, taste, judgment and standards of the American conservative publications began to melt away in the hot summer of their success—proof of the maxim that it takes greater character to carry off good fortune than bad. A repetitive and strident tone of self-congratulation, an inability to listen to, let alone consider, any kind of criticism—especially of Ronald Reagan and his friends—and a sharp, even crude tone of meanness now began to characterize the principal conservative journals of opinion such as *National Review* and *The American Spectator*. In spite (or perhaps because) of the increasing number of writers (and subscribers) willing to be associated with them, the very style of these journals worsened. They became repetitious, predictable and poorly edited. In 1983 I devoted a subchapter in my American

---

dedicated minority (partly true); that this dedicated minority consisted of the elite of America, leading the untutored masses toward the kingdom of light (untrue).

history, *Outgrowing Democracy,* to the history of the American conservative movement, including this sentence: "Here was a peculiarly American paradox: *the liberals had become senile, while the conservatives were immature.* Their intellectual—and moral—substance was not sufficient to fill the post-liberal vacuum." But my brief run (if that was what it was) with the conservatives was well over before that. I will, however, say that I do not regret our association. I may have burnt my bridges; but the fire was not an all-consuming one, and planks of that bridge still remain. I still have friends on the "conservative" side who, on occasion, will wave a friendly hello. So will I.

I am writing this in 1988, at a time when I, an early anti-Communist, have more sympathy, respect and goodwill for Mikhail Gorbachev than for Ronald Reagan. What a difference from forty years ago, when I was fretful and impatient with an America that was not anti-Russian and anti-Communist enough! I owe a last accounting of this to my readers—and to myself.

This change—if change it is—developed on three levels. I shall attempt to describe them in a sequence, proceeding from what is most obvious (but also least important) to what may be least obvious (but most important).

Forty years ago, as a Hungarian, I thought that my native country could escape its subjugation only through increasing American pressure against Russia in the affairs of Eastern Europe. I still believe that this was true at the time. But already in the year 1948 I knew this would not happen. Soon afterward I realized, too, that the only hope of correcting the fatal division of Europe lay in a Russian-American renegotiation of it. Consequently I came to believe that the best hope for my native country resided no longer in the prospect of increasing American hostility to Russia—that is, in a worsening of American-Russian relations—but, to the contrary, in an improvement of American-Russian relations, through a then consequent Russian recognition that their vital interests were not being threatened by the United States. This is as true now as it was thirty-five years ago. (It is not, however, a permanent "truth," since such "laws" in the histories of nations and in their relations do not exist.)

Is, then, the explanation of my change from anti-Communist to anti-anti-Communist the result of my Americanization? Have I become so much of an American that I have grown indifferent to the fate of my native country? No: this explanation contains no more than a half-truth. Yes: it is mainly my concern with my adopted country that reacts against the vulgarity and the shallowness of someone like Reagan and to some of the perils latent therein; but it is, too, my concern with my native country (and with my native continent) that makes me say to Hungarians and Europeans that Americans such as Ronald Reagan are not the Western world's knights in shining armor in virtue of their vocal condemnations of Communism and of their addiction to the unceasing increase of American armaments.

There is, however, something more important. It arises out of my vision of the history of the modern world. The principal power among men is still nationalism. It rests on the consciousness of one's nationality. As early as the late Middle Ages this began to replace religion as the strongest bond of community among large numbers of people. Later it was the framework of states that filled up with the content of the national masses. Marx largely ignored this phenomenon; Hitler, among others, did not. He was an extreme nationalist whose nationalism was wholly different from the older, moral character of patriotism that was rooted in a particular place and not in the racial or other tribal bonds of a people. And nationalism survived Hitler, in every part of the world, from Israel to Ulster. It has protean manifestations: nationalism varies from country to country more than socialism does. In America, too, nationalism remains the principal cohesive force—whence the dangers represented by its ideological perpetrators. These dangers exist because the appeal to nationalism is a normal and respectable sentiment—whereby not many people become aware when its propagation becomes unreasonable, extreme and immoral.

I wrote before that a lie is never as dangerous as a half-truth; and even a cursory reading of St. John of the Apocalypse will tell us that the Anti-Christ will rise far in this world precisely because he will speak half-truths and incarnate them. I am not saying that any American politician resembles either Hitler or the Anti-Christ, even though a reading of the Apocalypse tells us how the Anti-Christ will be well-combed and smiling and popular, not someone with disrespectable ideas, crazy hair and a spiky Luciferian goatee. What I am saying is that the American "conservative" movement possesses its own particularly dangerous and immoral inclinations, whereby its very employment of the proper adjective of *conservative* has been twisted out of reason. In an article in 1983 Jeffrey Hart, the managing editor of Buckley's *National Review,* advocated a public listing of those Russian cities that American nuclear rockets would pulverize in an atomic war. Then he went on to say that this novel kind of diplomacy (he called it "a new conceptualization of atomic strategy") "has numerous connections elsewhere. In one area after another, we appear to be entering an epoch in which reality will be defined increasingly in terms of abstract analysis . . . abstract analysis becomes the only knowable reality . . . we now appear to be entering a distinctively new phase, in which abstract thought will again become [as in the Middle Ages] a decisive part of our sense of the real." For at least two hundred years, beginning with Edmund Burke and Dr. Johnson, the commonsense conservative argument against abstract reasoning has been the best and the strongest weapon of conservative thinkers against the propagation and celebration of modernism. Yet the admiration of the mechanical and the abstract, of an inhuman technology and nuclear "power," has had a strange and particular appeal to many American conservatives.

In 1946 Georges Bernanos, the most profound and greatest Catholic thinker and writer of this century, wrote that the atom bomb was the triumph of technique over reason. About ten years ago the Italian poet Eugenio Montale wrote that "the substitution of the word, by something other than the word, by different means of expression, proves that man is tired of being man. . . . " I would say that man despairs of being man, and woman despairs of being woman, which is, alas, a deep predicament of our times. It is therefore that the intellectual task that I set for myself, mostly in my teaching but also in some of my writing, has been to insist that we must rethink the meaning of progress; that progress is not synonymous with change; that human destiny and therefore history consist of continuity and change; that the hope of the future must be with those who can detect those truer elements in human progress that are more and more evidently latent in our conscious recognition of our human continuity, of our connectedness with the men and women and children who were living on this earth before us, whose bones and dust and thoughts and spirit still live, enriching this earth and our hearts and our minds—in sum, with the evolution of our consciousness, which must be historical and, therefore, real.

CHAPTER 6

Teaching

HAD SOMEONE TOLD me before the age of twenty-one that I would become a teacher I would have laughed. In the Gymnasium and even at the university our professors were our enemies. This had much to do with the strict and stiff Germanic and bureaucratic organization and requirements of Hungarian schools and universities that, otherwise, were on a very high academic level: the standards of the Gymnasium graduation examination, at seventeen, were well beyond what is required of a graduate of a top American college or university now. It took me a long time to recognize that I had profited from this kind of schooling, after all: from six years of compulsory Latin, for example. However, our requirements were rigid and terrifying, not only because of their demands but also because of their arbitrariness. An unlucky theme, or the whim of a teacher, could decide one's grade. In order to get by, most of us tried to cheat as much as was possible, resorting often to the most inventive stratagems. As in Germany, this kind of education may have done much for one's brain but not much for one's character. The results are obvious in retrospect. When I look back at my Gymnasium and university classmates, I find no relationship between their achievements in school and their achievements in life: as many of the top students turned out to be bad eggs as did mediocre ones. (I was not a top student.) At the same time most of the poorest students did come from poor families, living in bookless homes, sometimes in rough conditions. So even then I knew what I know now: what mattered in Hungary, as in the United States, was not what one acquired in school but what one received, often indirectly, from one's family, at home. And it was therefore, too, that the few teachers and professors we respected were men of probity: gentlemen in the broad sense of that word, old-fashioned in their manners, steeped in their learning rather than in their occupational situation, serious but fair with their students. Most were older men. There was something timelessly clean in their very appearance: they did not exhale that airless smell out of the cramped circumstances in which many of the Gymnasium professors lived. At the risk of being pompous, let me say that even then we sensed—without really knowing it—the essential, the unavoidable connection (or, rather, interdependence) of integrity and knowledge.

Then, in 1945, there came a change—a small transitory episode in my life then, but something whose significance rises before me in retrospect. I was still a university student, but I had all kinds of secondary occupations during that awful year at the end of the war and the Russian conquest. I had a connection with the Hungarian Institute for Foreign Affairs, whose temporary office was in one of the relatively undamaged but unheated rooms of the Parliament Building. There someone suggested that I give a course in the English language, for a minimal tuition, for whoever wished to come. There came a gray, desolate, hopeless rainy day in late September. The room was crowded to the walls with people whose faces were full of hope. They were, for the most part, people of the defeated Hungarian Gentile middle classes, who at that time put all their hopes—and I mean *all* their hopes—in the English-speaking Powers that might as yet liberate Hungary from the Russians. The course ran for three or four months—I cannot now remember how and when my teaching there came to an end. What I remember is the unexpected satisfaction that my teaching there gave me. The sources of this satisfaction existed on different levels. There was the pleasure of purpose, at that confused, sad, downcast phase of my young life; I was, at least for a few hours each week, doing something useful. There was an element of intellectual pleasure: the sudden realization that by explaining things, my own knowledge was becoming clarified and reasonable—and not, as in a conversation, with the purpose of drawing attention to my person. (It was years later that, in reading St. Augustine, I found what this meant: that by giving out something we are not impoverished by it. Rather, the contrary; that the "laws" of the natural world do not apply to those of the human spirit and mind; that expressing something may lighten one's mind and even enrich it.) Finally there was the element of vanity. I was still a student, yet now it was I who stood in front of a table, writing on a board, my words sometimes avidly followed by this crowd of impoverished and hopeful men and women, sitting bundled up in their shabby overcoats, whose very presence in that once richly decorated but now suddenly antediluvian room invested me with a kind of authority that I never had before—in sum, the pleasures of vanity. I have now sorted out these unexpected satisfactions in descending order; but I do not for a moment doubt that the last and the lowest one of these, that of vanity, was the most important one, surely at that time.

I have written about my flight from Hungary to America earlier. In late 1946 I arrived in New York with few connections but with a few letters addressed to university people.* Almost immediately I had a part-time job at Columbia because of the large wave of students flooding American universities and colleges in 1947, veterans turning the GI Bill of Rights to good account (and I mean to good account: they were, by and large, admirably serious students, as all teachers of that period will remember). I taught a course in

---

*One of these was directed to a Master of one of the colleges at Yale, where I had an embarrassing experience. This kind, genial and cultured man had expected to receive a European scholar of respectable age and stature, putting him up in a suite where, the night before, a trustee of the university, a famous United States Senator, had stayed. Instead, he found himself face-to-face with a callow and nervous and unnecessarily voluble young man of twenty-three. He had also arranged a dinner with the principal fellows and professors, during which I babbled unnecessarily and made an ill-prepared little speech. I spent my last dollars on a bouquet of flowers that I sent to Professor and Mrs. French, and slunk down in the seat of the train to New York with the seasick knowledge of having given the unavoidable impression of an importunate fraud.

nineteenth-century European history twice a week. My reaction and experiences in those superheated classrooms in New York accorded exactly with those in that unheated antediluvian room in Budapest, one calendar year and one light-year away. I was sure now: I wanted an American college appointment; I could teach and have time to write. (What it was that I wanted to write I did not yet know.) I had all kinds of part-time jobs in New York to sustain me*; my part-time salary from Columbia paid me, of course, very little, but it contributed to my opportunity to secure a full-time appointment at Chestnut Hill College.

I am—sometimes—a bit of a gambler, wherefore I was not disheartened by the task of teaching, in English, including one or two courses about the contents of which I was not very sure. Lecturing, after all, has had for me much in common with another habit of mine, that gambling spirit of impertinence—impertinence, rather than daring—when it comes to speaking in a foreign language of whose grammar I might be uncertain and of whose vocabulary my knowledge is incomplete. There is a spirit of enjoyment when after a long time I attempt to speak Italian or Spanish; it is like walking a high-spirited dog on a thin leash. Like every beginning teacher, I began by preparing copious notes. Alarmingly soon I came to

---

*The first one was that of a translator (French-English) in a firm that was engaged in the rebuilding and selling of ships. Years later I learned that the owners and the chief naval architect of this firm had been engaged in an enormous fraud: they had been buying Liberty ships built during the war and which the U.S. government sold cheap with the provision that they were not to be resold to foreigners; what this firm did was to redesign and rebuild portions of these ships so that they could be sold under false names. My second job did not last long: the employer, an importer of Oriental rugs, wanted me to accompany him on his public speaking engagements, since he belonged to an organization devoted to the perfection of public speaking, no matter on what topic. He also wanted me to consider marrying his daughter, a moon-faced and sloe-eyed, sad and kind Levantine girl. My third job, like the first, was due to my knowledge of languages. The owners of this firm were horrified on learning that I was interested in teaching and writing. They had begun to train me in the intricacies of importing and exporting international wax. Consequently and disingenuously, I kept silent about the fact that, come September, I was off to Philadelphia in the morning.

think that I did not much need these and threw them away. I was a voluble young man, to be sure.

One thing still worried me in the beginning. Chestnut Hill is a girls' college. There I stood, day after day, in front of an audience of young rosy girls, some of them not more than two years younger than I. I write rosy because I found these American girls, en masse, very pretty. I thought that sooner or later there would be trouble: I would get interested in one of them and this, in a strict Catholic institution! I thought that I mustn't. Then I found that this kind of self-discipline was even easier done than said, since I evinced no temptations, not even on those rare—and they were very rare— occasions when a girl sitting in front of me showed a remarkable extent of leg and thigh. This was not a matter of the weakness of flesh but of spirit, because our chronological and biological proximity of age meant nothing: these girl-students were so much younger than I. With all their American goodwill and eagerness we had very little in common. All my life I had little interest in females with whom I could not much talk; until about the age of twenty-six I never had a love affair with a girl who was younger than I. In forty-one years of teaching I can remember only one girl in the classroom who appealed to me as a woman. I made a point of talking to her after class. She was a very intelligent girl: I suggested that she go on to graduate school. I am sure that my purposes were mixed: I wanted to keep in contact with her, and on one occasion I inveigled her to attend a history lecture or forum at a nearby university. This was shortly before her graduation; and a day or so later I found an odd, sad letter from her on my desk. No, she would not go on with her history studies, she wrote. This was a different country; what I was trying to do was a fine thing, but not really applicable to her world and at this time. It was too idealistic, too impractical.

By this time—it was around 1949—I began to realize something that kept bothering me for a long time: the oh, so limited aspirations of many Americans, and the extraordinary docility of the young ones among them. Their lightheartedness, their optimism, their explosions of energy: yes, I knew all of that American dynamism,

I saw its expressions every day. Yet so few of them aimed at anything beyond the brief radius of their immediate circle. It was not
only that they knew so little of life outside that circle. They were
not interested in looking, let alone going, beyond it; and those
among them who really wanted to rise in the world wanted to rise
only within the group of their friends and acquaintances. They
were afraid to think beyond their class—so much more afraid than
many young people in the restricted society of half-feudal Hungary
had been. Of course there were shortcomings in their intellectual
education that made them so incurious. But there was more to that.
I thought then, and I think even now, when social conformism
among young Americans is perhaps (but only perhaps) less than it
was thirty or forty years ago. They were not self-confident enough
to aspire to anything that, to them, was unusual. To these young,
often undisciplined and, on occasion, wild and strident girls, success
in life meant safety and respectability, with the emphasis on the
latter: respectability among people they knew and were to know.
And as the range of their imaginations and their ambitions was
limited, so was its time span. They all wanted to get married, the
sooner the better; and beyond the wondrous prospect of becoming
engaged and the dazzling white-and-gold glory of the wedding day
their contemplation of their future was so very vague.

Teaching was not always pleasurable; but teaching was easy. My
fear (the fear, I believe, of every beginning teacher) that I might not
have enough "material" to fill this or that fifty minutes evaporated
very soon. The problem turned out to be the opposite: I had (or I
thought I had) too much to say, wherefore I kept running out of
time. I needed money, and I taught a lot—on Saturday mornings,
in the summer, part-time at another college, a schedule that I kept
up for about fifteen years. Professors in higher institutions of learning were appalled when they heard that I was teaching that much,
sometimes eighteen hours a week. It contributed to their suspicion
that this kind of person cannot be taken seriously, he could not be
a good teacher. I think that they were wrong. They were right,
however, in their suspicions in one important sense: I cared little
about an academic career. I wanted to be a writer. I wanted to make

my money and my reputation as a historian whose works are read by more than an academic readership, at the same time maintaining—and possibly even elevating—the standards of professional historianship. It took me more than thirty years to realize that this was not going to work; but the story of that belongs to the next chapter, about my writing. What belongs here is my confession of my hopes that accompanied me for at least fifteen years of my teaching career. I hoped that, by the age of fifty at the latest, my main income would come from my writing, subsequent to which I might reduce some of my teaching. This did not happen. But something else was happening, something that developed slowly, something that was positive not negative, something different from a compromise, from an accommodation of one's life and career to the necessity of one's circumstances. I began to realize—gradually and slowly—that I *am* a teacher as much as a writer. In the beginning the principal purpose of my job as a teacher was that it enabled me to write. Thirty years later this relationship of means to ends was no longer so simple. I found that teaching was not only relatively easy but, on occasion, inspired by occasional impulses of intellectual pleasure. At the end of this chapter I shall say more about how my teaching helped my writing. Here I will only state the recurrent—and, fortunately still sometimes alive—pleasure of fresh mornings, driving alone on country roads, smoking my matutinal cigar, mentally planning the contents of my coming lecture whose sequence and organization are falling wonderfully into place, crystallizing in sparks of sunlight. I think that every writer worth his salt will know that this kind of pleasure does not exist when one is in front of one's typewriter. One may be driven to write; but the pleasures of writing (whatever those are) are something quite different, if indeed they exist at all; they consist in having written something, not in writing it.

One of the pleasures of teaching—it is, I hasten to say, a pleasure on a fairly low level—is that of having a captive audience. Vanity and irresponsibility are inherent in that pleasure. Vanity: because of the often serious, and sometimes even shining, faces of one's students; because of the sense of one's intellectual, institutional and almost tangible authority; because here are people who are actually listening to you, something that has become a rarity at this time of the twentieth century. During the twentieth century the capacity and the practice of listening have deteriorated. In all walks of life, in all kinds of circumstances, the capacity of attention has become disrupted and curtailed because of the incredible—literally incredible—amount of noise and sounds and music and words and slogans whirling around people's heads and ears. This condition is, in itself, a matter worthy of the attention of a historian. It is the condition that the very consciousness of people changes through the ages: not only their ideas or the subjects of their thoughts but the functioning of their senses and their minds as well. We have reason to believe, and evidence to prove it, that six hundred years ago, before the Renaissance rediscovery of perspective, people's eyes moved differently from the way they move now. We also know that, say, three hundred years ago not only did people hear different sounds but they used their ears and, therefore, their minds differently. Consider only the duration of sermons in the seventeenth century when otherwise there was so much for the simple people to do, at a time when their lives were indeed poor, nasty, brutish and *short:* we know, for example, that during the English Civil War the fact that the Puritan preachers' sermons were longer and better than those of the Anglicans mightily contributed to the popularity of the Cromwellian army. The converse of that mental habit, the inability to concentrate, has, of course, woefully affected our people, and perhaps especially the young, in the second half of the twentieth century. Millions have lost the ability to concentrate on anything, and especially to listen—the automatic responses of a secretary being but one last step ahead of the ultimate insult, the answering machine, that diabolical instrument which responds but does not listen to you. By insulting a person, you do, at least, pay attention to his existence; but by refusing to listen to him, you have refused to acknowledge his existence at all. Plainly, it is easier to talk than to listen—not to speak of what Goethe said: "To communicate our thoughts to others is nature; to assimilate what is communicated to us, with understanding, is culture." "In the intellectual order," Simone Weil once wrote, "the virtue of humility is nothing more or less than the power of attention"—to which allow me to add that attention has nothing to do with the subconscious: *nothing*.

Having a captive audience was a luxury. Here, for fifty minutes at a time, I could tell students about interesting things and they were actually listening to me. After nearly forty years of experience as a writer, having written thirteen books, I do not think that I have ever seen a person who was actually engaged in reading one of them. Do people really listen to a famous man who is on the radio or television? Yes and no. But in those classrooms, because of my authority as a teacher, they had to listen—and I could tell them, at my own choice and pleasure, many things.

I must say something here about the authority of an American college teacher. It is, plainly, enormous—in most cases unwarrantedly so. It is abused by many professors who otherwise cultivate a phony camaraderie with their students, a camaraderie that may include an entire range of execrable practices, from calling each other by their first names to a professor fornicating with a selected student. At first sight nothing could be so dissimilar as the authority of a German university professor and an American college one. Since teaching is a two-way relationship, that comparison is deceiving. What American students may lack in discipline they make up in docility. An old-fashioned German professor is often so remote from his students that he is a semi-divinity, an archbishop of learning, sexless. A modern American professor is a father figure, a male figure, and not sexless at all.* (Nor is an American priest, but that is another story.) I am not a Germanic type, but that American camaraderie, so often artificial, so often phonily democratic, had no attraction for me, not even at the beginning of my teaching career. I have never called my students by their first names.† I would have

---

*Example: the extreme—and I mean extreme—attention that American students pay to their teachers' clothing.

†Consider this *excursus* beyond teaching. Consider that by calling a newly met person by his first name you have actually reduced his individuality. He is now only one of a million Joes or one of ten thousand Josephines. His connection

liked, I would still like, my American students to ask me more questions, but this has not happened because of their docility and shyness. This was a loss but not a great one, since that celebrated American desideratum of a dialogue between students and teachers is often false. The lack of curiosity among students is, of course, to be regretted. Yet their unwillingness to say something or to ask questions is not always attributable to a dull shyness; they know that their knowledge is less than yours, and that's it. American students, indeed, American youth, admire and, yes, even love authority, perhaps even more than their German counterparts, though in different ways. During forty-one years as a teacher my students occasionally saw me, or heard about me, driving a truck,* going to the races, dancing at a ball, playing squash or jazz piano. They seemed to be fascinated with such tidbits of individual life: probably less out of curiosity than out of a want of imagination.

Want of imagination, indeed! A few years after I began teaching I grew conscious of something that I did not know before, that my teaching American students at this time of our decaying civilization has a dual purpose—a recognition that took some time to coagulate in my mind. The dual endeavor was this: I was teaching them history, but I also wanted—more: I felt compelled—to teach them a historical, that is, a human way of thinking: about the past, about human nature, about themselves. It took some time before the summation—that history is a form of thought—crystallized in my own mind. Before that I had recognized the obvious: that teaching involved unteaching. Yes, I was aware—and often appalled—by their dreadful ignorance of history. But I also began to understand that this involved something else than a mere lack of knowledge, that it

---

with his family name, with his ancestors and with his provenance has been severed. Alas, this is but one illustration of how the exaggeration of democracy inevitably leads to the degradation of human dignity.

*Cars! Cars! One day a student accompanied me to the parking lot. He said, "We are all wondering what kind of car you drive." ??? "We thought it must be a Mercedes or a Bug." I was driving a Pontiac convertible then. Whether he was disappointed or not I did not know.

involved a mode of thinking—not merely the subjects of their minds but the very functioning of those minds. I learned that teaching was more than the dissemination of information* because we must remind people as much, if not more, than to instruct them. What I have tried to remind them of was a commonsense historical way of thinking, a form of thinking that has not always existed, and the emergence of which may have been even more important (though seldom so recognized) than the emergence of the scientific method three or four hundred years ago—that historical thinking was, plainly, past-thinking, including the conscious knowledge of their own past; that they knew more about that past than they thought they knew; and that they knew more about history than science, which was natural, since it is science that is part of history and not the other way around. In sum, I have been teaching my students history *and* a historical philosophy—something that is the very reverse of a "philosophy of history," the latter often little more than a compound of gassy theories systematized by speculative historians.

I liked my classrooms. I taught in the same one for thirty years. It was in that classroom that important news came to me: the telephone message that my wife was in labor with our first child, the same kind of message with my second child, the news that John Kennedy had been shot, and, during one examination as I read my mail, the news in a sad letter from my aunt that my mother would

---

*Occasionally, I would berate them with a somewhat vulgar simile. "With you," I would say, "it is not only a matter of in one ear and out another. That wouldn't be so bad because anything going in one ear and out another means that it is passing through your brain, so that some of it will stick. That is the mystery of learning, you know. Think of the very best book you have ever read. How much can you remember of it? Perhaps one percent. But this doesn't mean that the other ninety-nine percent is lost. Yet with you it is not even in one ear because those ears and heads of yours are stuffed with all kinds of things: moldy phrases, bits of cheap information, old Kleenexes. Instead of drilling a hole in thick heads and pouring in new stuff through a funnel, what a teacher must now do first is to use something like a vacuum cleaner. I must unteach you while I teach you." At least I said *while*, not *before*, aware that unteaching and teaching are simultaneous.

soon die—moments not easily forgotten. I am now teaching in a less attractive and comfortable classroom, but that doesn't matter. What matters is that it was in these classrooms that I realized the melancholy truth, stated by George Orwell, to the effect that in the twentieth century we have sunk so deep that it is our duty to restate the obvious; and another, perhaps more exhilarating truth, stated by Jean Dutourd, to the effect that in this dreary century a little bit of common sense is enough to give the impression that one is a first-rate philosopher. At any rate, when I hear from a student or a former student that he or she remembers my teaching because of my "philosophy" (the inverted commas may be proper) I think that I prefer this to their telling me that they were particularly taken by my knowledgeable lectures in nineteenth-century German intellectual or twentieth-century American diplomatic history. This does not mean that I am more of a philosopher than a historian. The reverse is true, especially now when all that remains meaningful in philosophy is, by necessity, epistemology, and, moreover, an epistemology that is inevitably historical; for it is philosophy that is part of the history of mankind and not the other way around. First was nature, then came man, and then the science of nature (a moment's contemplation of which sequence should be enough to refute all the pretensions of the Darwinists); I am, therefore I think, therefore I am: a supersession, more than a mere reversal, of Descartes.

In any event, a student's grateful memory is pleasing to one's vanity, though perhaps not on the lowest levels of that fundamental human weakness. And there is another weakness attendant on having a captive audience: the temptation to irresponsibility in the classroom, which I often failed to avoid. I must confess that I often enjoyed it. Irresponsibility: because a professor, perhaps especially in America, can, and indeed will, say some things in the classroom that he might not say elsewhere—a scathing remark about a contemporary politician, for example. This temptation, in my case, was stimulated by my classes at La Salle College, where I was teaching boys, not girls: young men, not young women. My mother, extricated from Hungary, arrived in Vienna in 1949, cared for by her unmarried older sister; she was very ill. I had to support her out of my meager salary, I looked for an additional part-time teaching job, and the President of Chestnut Hill allowed me to do so. There began an altogether pleasant association with La Salle for thirty-four years, until the history department (some of them former students of mine) preferred to end it. I enjoyed the often solicitous friendship of the Christian Brothers who ran the school, their increasingly useful library with its excellent librarian, those early-summer faculty picnics rich with food and drink, so much more generous and easygoing than the stiff affairs of faculty clubs at prestigious schools; and I particularly enjoyed the students, sometimes rough-mannered and poorly prepared young men, the best of whom, however, were better than my best students at Chestnut Hill because, unlike the girls, they were avid for more learning. They were instantly, if perhaps unfortunately, receptive to the occasional crudities and vulgarities with which I felt free to pepper my language on sudden impulse, perhaps not for effect but for the sake of striking a direct point in a kind of rhetorical shorthand—a kind of language that I would employ before an audience of young men but not in a class of young girls. This was perhaps a minor weakness and not more than an occasional one. As time went on, I abandoned this practice, while I did not altogether abandon my occasional habit of exaggeration (a habit in my conversation, and not only in my lectures), again for the purpose of shocking my students into the instant awareness of something that otherwise would take too long to explain.

There is still another weakness of my teaching that I must confess. I am a lazy teacher—perhaps no more but no less than most college teachers, who are a lazy crowd indeed. I have always put most, if not all, of my energies into my lectures. I am punctual and precise about the requirements of my classes, their examinations, my reading lists and their administrative details; but there is an array of instruments at the disposal of a teacher that I have willfully neglected through the years. For one thing, in spite of my knowledge of their awfully poor writing habits, I require few term papers from my students because a conscientious reading of such papers would take an unconscionably long time. I know that, to do any good, I would have to correct every sentence and perhaps every third or fourth word, and I have not enough time for that. As it is, I, who am so convinced that history is a seamless web, who stress in my lectures the evident connectedness of art and customs and fashions and politics in history—that, for example, in the seventeenth century the French obsession with the mathematical nature of things was there not only in Descartes but also in the organization of their government and in their military engineering and in the topiary shapes of their gardens; or that there was such a thing as a First Empire style of painting and even of a Third Reich style of architecture—well, I do nothing beyond telling them that, without showing them pictures or films or whatnot. I know that "total history" is impossible, and that M. Fernand Braudel is a *faux bonhomme,* but I also know its webbed nature. Last but not least, I know how the lamentably weakened imagination of this generation is pictorial rather than verbal. Yet I do not find time to illustrate my lectures with pictures, filmstrips, movies, music—a kind of laziness, I think. But perhaps I really do not have time: I have too much to tell to that captive audience; and on the handful of occasions when I chose to darken the classroom and show a film I found myself sitting suddenly mute in the dark, in the position of a numb, and surely dumb, fool; a supernumerary, a superfluous teacher and man.

My admittedly reactionary view of history and of human nature includes the belief that continuity is as important as change. I find this to be true as I contemplate the ever-succeeding student generations during more than forty years of teaching. Yes, I know: there have been changes, and even important ones, among them. The students' clothing is different, something that is perhaps especially apparent in a Catholic girls' college. Yet their behavior in the classroom has hardly changed at all: their, at best, attentive and, at worst, rigid faces; their sometimes respectful, sometimes unthinking acceptance of authority. Some of their ideas may have changed, but the workings of their minds have not. Yes, they are ignorant about the world at large and about the history of their entire culture, meaning the provenance of just about everything to which they are physically and mentally accustomed: but they are not stupid. They are probably more ignorant and less stupid than were students thirty or forty years ago because they are aware, sometimes woefully, of their own ignorance, unlike thirty or more years ago when so many young Americans took an odd kind of social pride in the fact that they were not "brains."* Television and the dreadful decline of high school requirements have affected them profoundly. The world of books is unknown to many of them, whereby I reached the conclusion many years ago that what the American college must do is really something very simple (the goal is simple while its accomplishment is not): we must teach these young people how to read and write. Their very imaginations have become pictorial, not verbal—a subterranean slide away from the traditions of the last five hundred years that were irretrievably connected with books. Yet their respect for books may have increased, not decreased: I remember how, around 1950, people looked oddly at a young woman who in a Philadelphia trolley car was actually reading a book. This would not happen today, while at the same time my students' ability to read and their capacity to absorb what they are reading have decreased, together with their very appetite for reading. Yes, therefore I had to make adjustments in my teaching. I have had to take less and less for granted—alas, in a Catholic college, the very knowledge of the essentials of their religion, including the Gospels and the very episodes in the life of Christ, is often sadly wanting—and I have had to reduce my requirements. (Soon after the start of my teaching career in America I found that one of my tasks was to introduce these students to good books. I put a strong emphasis on my required reading lists, but while thirty years ago I could require my undergraduates to read seven or eight books per semester, I have reduced this to five or six.) Yet I do not

---

*When my first wife graduated from Springside School in 1944, one of the three top Philadelphia private girls' schools at the time, she was one of three of a class of about thirty who chose to go on to college: "brains"; the rest were "coming out," debutantes. I doubt whether there was a single Springside graduate twenty years later who wasn't trying to get into college—any college.

believe that my students are worse—by which I mean, worse human beings—than those whom I taught thirty or more years ago. I am inclined to believe the opposite; and not because I have become more resigned, or even more mellow, with age. Even now, twenty years after their "sexual" and "social" liberation, American college students are less cynical and less worldly than their European counterparts.

These are generalizations. Generalizations, like brooms, ought not to stand in a corner closet forever; they ought to sweep as a matter of course. There may be a particular reason they are excusable here. This is the uniformity of student vintages across the vast United States. Ask any sensible professor, from any kind of institution: which were the good years? 1946–52, 1958–65, etc., etc. This in a nation and in a society where the characters, the backgrounds, the provenance, the social training, the fashions, etc., of young contemporaries could not be more different: where a girl, say, from Bryn Mawr College would prefer the company of a male student from Zambia than that of her coeval from, say, Villanova University, less than two miles away—whom she would not meet and would not want to meet. During more than forty years in the teaching profession I have been amazed, again and again, by how my estimation of my students at Chestnut Hill, in this small, isolated, Catholic (and for a long time predominantly Irish-Catholic) middle-class college corresponded exactly, uncannily, with what other professors at very different institutions found among their students at the same time.

I have served as visiting professor at a number of universities during my teaching career. Some of these stints were agreeable, and not only because of the added income: I could go into some detail in subjects that interested me, since these visiting professorships involved graduate classes. Yet I found less of a difference between my graduate students and the undergraduates at Chestnut Hill than I had expected originally.* One of my visiting professorships was

*One exception was my professorship at the University of Toulouse, in France, where my students were singularly uncharitable of my halting—no, of my inadequate—knowledge of the French subjunctive, while they were appreciative, en masse, of my hazardous, and possibly even impertinent, attempts at wit.

at the Fletcher School of Law and Diplomacy in Medford, Massa-chusetts, in 1971 and 1972. The acting head of that institution was attracted by one of my books and was about to offer me a chair, with the consent of his professors of course. This chair would have meant twice the income for half the teaching I was doing at Chestnut Hill, but I was not tempted by it. I offered a compromise: I would fly up to Boston once a week and teach for two days, without having to diminish my teaching in Philadelphia significantly, and see what happened after a year. Whatever temptation I may have had evapo-rated during the first day. The professors whom I met at the recep-tion tendered me were a sour bunch. Medford, Massachusetts, was plainly awful—plain *and* awful. I began to dread these weekly expeditions—and I do not necessarily mean the necessity of having to rise before six, not even the heartrendingly ugly drive to the Philadelphia airport, perhaps not even the dirty yellow ice coating the Medford streets. I hated the poisonous warm fug and clattering din of the Tufts cafeteria, where I had to take my breakfast, a period place and scene of masses of unkempt, unwashed and sleepy-eyed students shuffling along in their Russian-style padded jackets in clouds of malodorous steam; the padlocks and chains on doors, entrances, gates everywhere, evidences of a universal distrust of humanity; the atmosphere of Cambridge, where I would go in the evenings in search of a place to dine; the darkness of Harvard Square, interrupted only by cold vapor lights; a kind of Nordic tropics, or Soviet America, or an American version of what was worst in the surrealist atmosphere of Weimar Berlin, much of it fake to the core, like the Baltic-Latvian compound name of Häagen-Dazs, the rich ice cream that my eyes met first up there in Boston. One night I dined at the Harvard Faculty Club—the only faculty club in America whose atmosphere produced a bit of wistful long-ing, as I imagined bins of claret kept there by a few old and well-heeled professors. But this impression, too, evaporated soon. My hosts excused themselves for the relative limitations of the menu, since it was the day of the week of the ethnic smorgasbord: Scandi-navian that week, Italian next week and Soul Food the previous week, they said. My plate was more than adequately filled by the stumpy New England ladies standing like sturdy little trees in white uniforms, with their marcelled gray hair, behind the steam tables, relentlessly smiling. I could imagine them with that smile during Soul Food day the week before, with perhaps an extra smile for the black professor of sociology, in his serious three-piece suit, who may or may not have preferred roast beef, but who must have thought that Soul Food was one of those things from which he had sprung with a determination of no return.

I came to the United States at a time when almost all American intellectuals and most American professors were liberals, to the "left" of American politics, supposedly full of a naïve and humane idealism. Their pride in belonging to a class of opinion was there; but it was a fairly low kind of pride. As Dr. Johnson's Imlac said in *Rasselas,* pride "is seldom delicate, it will please itself with very mean advantages; and envy feels not its own happiness, but when it may be compared with the misery of others." Yet what Johnson's Rasselas saw among intellectuals did not apply. Rasselas "went often to an assembly of learned men, who met at stated times to unbend their minds, and compare their opinions. Their manners were somewhat coarse, but their conversation was instructive, and their disputations acute, though sometimes too violent, and often continued till neither controvertist remembered upon what question they began. Some faults were almost general among them: every one was desirous to dictate to the rest, and every one was pleased to hear the genius or knowledge of another depreciated." This was truer of Hungarian and European intellectuals than of American ones, who did not really meet to unbend their minds or to compare their opinions; whose conversation was seldom instructive and almost never violent; who seldom, if ever, were desirous of dictating to the rest; and those who were pleased to hear the knowledge of another deprecated took ample care to camouflage their pleasure with rhetorical practices suitable to the subtleties of a Chinese court, even though their manners were not good enough to keep their jealousy in abeyance.

For a long time I thought that most American academics were hampered by their naïveté. They were more isolated from the world, they knew less of the world than their colleagues in other countries—a curious condition in a democratic country such as the United States, but so it was. It was not only that intellectuals were writing for other intellectuals, with sometimes deplorable consequences for their rhetoric, language and style. Their social life was restricted to the narrow circle of other intellectuals with consequences that were deplorable, too. It took me some time to recognize that this naïveté, with its attendant abstract optimism of the world—say, their early belief in the United Nations or in World Government or in the Progressive Left—was complicated rather than simpleminded. Mixed within it was a dose of corroding pessimism, the kind of despair that, at best, is a pathfinder out of a cemetery of dead untruths and, at worst, a pathfinder of cynicism*—something not entirely different from what Joseph Conrad wrote about Russians in *Under Western Eyes:* "a terrible corroding simplicity in which mystic phrases clothe a naïve and hopeless cynicism." The intellectuals' fear and loathing of non-liberal—or, indeed, any academically unacceptable—opinion was the intolerance of the tolerationists. This kind of airless isolation was already there a century ago in the progress—or, rather, devolution—of Emerson, who in 1837 had issued his famous proclamation of democratic learning in "The American Scholar," while thirty years later in his Phi Beta Kappa address at Harvard, "The Progress of Culture," he said that that progress depended on small "minorities," on the "few superior and attractive men," forming "a knighthood" of learning and virtue. (That this "progress" from the Open Workshop to the Ivory Tower was not much of a progress toward refinement should be obvious to those of us who recognize that life in an ivory tower may

---

*Example: Numerous American intellectuals and academics kept telling me, early in my American years, that to understand America I ought to read the short story by Shirley Jackson, "The Lottery," written in 1948. In this dreadful tale the villagers take great pleasure in having a yearly fête, during which they select one of their own and stone him to death—the villagers being ordinary Americans, presumably New Englanders, people of this most advanced democracy enlightening the world. What struck me was how this story, incarnating a hatred and fear of The People, has been devoured and admired by the people who were votaries of Progressivism, The Left, Liberalism, Adlai Stevenson, etc.

be as unsanitary as it is stifling.) For a long time this uneasy compound of optimism and pessimism, of naïveté and despair, did little harm to America, precisely because what was taught in the colleges did not matter much: what mattered was the college "experience." But by the 1960s the dependence of institutions and even of the government on intellectuals—consider only those presidents who had to have foreign-born academics from the very dubious "discipline" of International Relations, such as Professors Kissinger or Brzezinski, to twirl the globe and explain the world to them— became a fact. And it was then that the lack of responsibility among the professorate, amounting to a shameful abdication in the 1960s, became disastrous. It was they—more than the students, and even more than the bureaucratic administrators of their colleges and universities—who allowed, in most cases thoughtlessly, the elimination of history, literature, the classics, etc., from the requirements of colleges and high schools, about the latter of which they were ignorant as well as indifferent. Their ambitions, aspirations, intellectual energies were concentrated on their own bureaucratic situations and advancement, in committees, conferences, foundation grants, publicity within the academy. The habit of flitting from conference to conference hardly widened their knowledge; while it may have sharpened their ambitions, it narrowed their discourse. One of my most disillusioning experiences was a week-long conference in 1966, arranged by the followers of Michael Polanyi, an "anti-reductionist," funded by the Ford Foundation (about which Dwight Macdonald once wrote that it "is a large body of money completely surrounded by people who want some"). Soon after my arrival in the United States I decided to avoid conferences, finding them uninstructive and, more often than not, depressing. But here, I thought, was something worth going to. I would meet a group of people, from different disciplines, who were engaged in the same task as I (I had just finished ten years of work on my *Historical Consciousness*): in breaking through to a new recognition of our situation in the universe, in a rethinking of the conditions of thinking itself. I was sadly disappointed. Instead of a happy band of a moral minority, instead of a group of men and women who were interested in the same thing, I found that most* of these people were uninterested in anything beyond gathering additional security for their self-esteem. This kind of self-esteem was a puny one, wholly restricted within the radius of academic respectability; and that academic respectability was further constrained by ambitions that were less intellectual than they were bureaucratic. Most professional intellectuals are now hardly interested in anything beyond their "fields"; but even within their "fields" they profess to ignore what is truly exceptional and unpredictable. There is a sentence in one of Evelyn Waugh's last books that applies to intellectuals as much as it applies to politicians. "In a democracy," he wrote, "men do not seek authority so that they may impose a policy. They seek a policy so that they may achieve authority." This is why intellectual life, the very production of books and the circulation of ideas and styles, has become drearily predictable in our times, presented by men and women who are engaged in the incarnation and the representation and the projection of ideas that are (or, rather, that seem to be) already current, since they think that this is what their minds are for, this is what intellectual creativity is all about.

Well before that conference I had met scholars whose private opinions about teaching were either cynical or despairing or both. I also met professors, and well-known ones at that, who had an impressive office, the walls padded with all kinds of interesting volumes, including recondite and expensive ones that I longed to borrow and look at, while in their neat suburban houses there were alarmingly few books lying around. In one instance I counted them: there were less than fifty. (Perhaps he had a few more in his bedroom, though I doubt it.) Was this man really interested in history? I thought, driving home. Well he was, but what really interested him was his historianship. But perhaps I am too harsh. Was this man cynical? I do not really think so. What limited him were his aspirations: a cause, perhaps even more than a consequence, of the limita-

---

*Most, but not all. It was there that I met a Norwegian physicist, Professor Torger Holtsmark, whose truly exceptional integrity and scientific purpose were, and remained, a starry event in my life, maturing to an enduring friendship. So my going there was worthwhile after all.

tions of his imagination. Conversely, my best friends among intellectuals, the lovable men and women I know, are people whose aspirations may be limited but whose imaginations and attentiveness—a rare combination nowadays—are not. They enlighten my life, because in their company I am lighthearted and happy. What saddens me sometimes is the unhappiness among teachers: their unhappiness in a profession where, after all, one is doing what one can do best, one does what one wants to do, and where the work, if not the living, is easy.

Well I know that I have been making a virtue of necessity: an explication, if not altogether an apology, of my teaching in a little-known college for more than forty years. Yet "virtue" is not really the right word; choice would be a better one. I had my moments, and even periods, of unhappiness—at worst, recurrent moments, rather than lasting periods, because of my fortunately volatile temperament. I have taught much; and I have learned a few things, not unimportant ones. That teachers learn from their students is a bromide, though not a euphemism; at any rate, learning is to a great extent osmotic, and in the case of learning from students probably as much as the other way around. In any event, I have learned less about them than about myself: for example, where my teaching was without much effect, where it went wrong. I had, and have, my disappointments with the students: with their wanting imagination and curiosity, with their alarmingly feeble sense of humor, with their inexperience with books, with their execrable and habitual errors in writing—the latter flowing from their crampedly self-conscious inclination to the effect that in their writing they must employ a different language from speaking: different words, and phrases, sentences and tenses (especially the dreary and dreadful passive tense) that they never use when they speak. Yes, there is a difference between the written and the spoken word, but on a higher and subtler level than what appears in students' papers: if they only wrote the way they speak! And I knew, very soon after my first book, that my profession as a writer has nothing to do with my profession as a teacher, because my books in most instances have not been really applicable to my courses and to my reading lists, and not because of excessive modesty on my part. One of the purposes of my reading lists has been to introduce my students to good historical books, perhaps even more than to acquaint them with the principal histories relevant to this or that course. And even when, at the risk of being immodest, I know that this or that book of mine was fairly well written, I think that they ought to read something else. All through my years of teaching I have seldom felt any compunction about taking short excursions from my scheduled lecture topics when the spirit, rightly or wrongly, so moves me, taking the opportunity of a captive audience to discourse on a subtle matter that sputters or sparkles in my mind at a given moment. Yet I have very seldom directed them to something I have written. I think I know why; and yet somehow I don't.

All of this shows a definite divorce between my two careers of teacher and writer. Perhaps things would have been better if, say, I had been a professor of graduate students at Harvard, but I am inclined to think not very much. I am sure that I would be as loath to foist my published writings on them as I am at Chestnut Hill, and I am not sure whether I would like to discuss my actual work with them, or read them portions of my manuscripts in progress—a dreadfully boring seminar practice, I think. There has been, however, one tremendously profitable result of my teaching these young girls: a veritable golden bridge between my twin crafts of teaching and writing. It took me years to recognize its existence: I may exaggerate its importance, but I honestly don't think so. This golden bridge consists of the fact—and, for once, it is a fact—that my writing has profited from my teaching. Whatever clarity and economy my writing possesses has often been the result of my teaching uninstructed undergraduates. I am not referring to the condition that a college teacher's life, with his many free hours and vacations, enables him to write. I am referring to the necessity—a gradually more and more self-imposed necessity—of speaking about large and complex topics briefly and clearly, and yet without superficiality. This necessity of a verbal economy helped my mind and my practice of writing so much that perhaps in this instance virtue *has* grown out of necessity—if virtue it still is (something that readers of this book may indeed question). I am not alone in this, for I received sustenance, an electric spark of recognition, only a few weeks ago when, picking up a book in the college library, I ran across these splendidly unassuming words in the gracefully short acknowledgments of a very fine scholar, in Professor David Buisseret's *Henry IV,* a splendid (and short) book about that great and complex monarch, the *Vert Galant:* "Much of this work was written while I was teaching at the University of the West Indies, where my students forced me to explain myself carefully about a period and place so foreign to most of them."

CHAPTER 7

Writing

*T*HE RELATIONSHIP BETWEEN the spoken and the written word is not simple. Speech, contrary to Freud's doctrine (and perhaps also to Joyce's idea), is not the transcription of thought; it is the realization of it. Hitler realized that the spoken word counted with the masses: *Mein Kampf,* which he had dictated, was a book to be spoken, he said. Churchill, who, contrary to the accepted notion, was a better writer than speaker, wrote about Balfour in *Great Contemporaries:* "This most easy, sure, fluent of speakers was the most timid, laborious of writers. . . . The spoken word, uttered from the summit of power, gone beyond recall, had no terrors for him; but he entered the tabernacles of literature under a double dose of humility and awe which are proper. He was sure of the movement of his thought; he was shy in the movement of his pen. The history of every country abounds with brilliant and ready writers who have quailed and faltered when called upon to compose in public, or who have shrunk altogether from the ordeal. Balfour was the reverse example, and in this lies a considerable revelation of his character." I am the reverse of Balfour, wherein lies a considerable revelation, if not of my character, then of my mind.

I can hardly remember a time in my life when I did not want to write, surely not after the age of five when I had learned to read. The relationship between reading and writing is even more complicated than that between the spoken and written word. The mental connections and disconnections between them are odd. There are millions of readers who do not like to write. A devoted reader would like to talk about what he or she had read: but that is different from the desire to write. As any writer knows, reading often serves as an escape from the duty of writing. Yet there have been writers, sometimes very good ones, who read very little. Reading is easier than writing: but the impulse to write is deeper than the impulse to read. Somerset Maugham said that when a young author "discovers that he has a creative urge to write . . . [this] is a mystery as impenetrable as the origin of sex." I do not believe this is so. Writing, after all, is yet another form of self-expression. The motive to write is the desire to vanquish a mental preoccupation by expressing it consciously and clearly. The purposes of writing almost always contain at least a minimum of self-love, that is, of vanity.

All my life I have felt and recognized the presence of history within descriptive prose. This happened long before I began to realize that the novel, unlike the epic, has been part and parcel of the evolution of our historical consciousness; and long before I concluded and dared to say that in the near future history may absorb all narrative prose—a process that is well on its way. But this is not the place to repeat or even to sum up matters, however important, about which I have written elsewhere. Earlier I wrote that I was a devoted reader of novels at an early age. Even now I often get more pleasure—and instruction—from reading a fine novel or a biography than from a mediocre history. I do not mean historical novels: I find *War and Peace* interminable, false and boring. I think that *Madame Bovary* and *Sentimental Education* are more historical than Tolstoy. What attracts and inspires my mind are the details and the poignant impressions of how people and things seemed, how they behaved, how they spoke, thought and presumably even felt in a certain place and at a certain time. By the end of the second decade of my life an impulse was beginning to form in my mind. At some time, in some place and in some ways I would attempt a new kind of history.

This impulse has been plaguing me ever since. For a long time, even during my career as a professional historian, it led to the occasional temptation of trying my hand not at a new kind of history but at a new kind of novel. I have a few fragments, usually not more than a few pages, of such attempts somewhere in my files. It took me many years to recognize what should have been obvious. Such attempts were not going to succeed, for a simple reason. This is that while I can be fairly good at describing characters and places, I cannot invent a plot. There is this plain shortcoming in the very functions of my mind. Strings and knots hopelessly discombobulate my brain and my hands. I am very poor at checkers, let alone chess; I can play poker, but I am incompetent at bridge. Probably consequent to this I find descriptions of complicated characters and scenes and places and developing conditions infinitely more interesting than the development of plots. When I read a detective story I am instantly lost. In following the thread my mind is all thumbs. The other element is my acute interest in what really happened, rather than even the most imaginative plot (not to speak of science fiction, which immediately puts me to sleep). I love Dickens and I could speak (or write) at length about his characters and even about his philosophy, but ask me to reconstruct the plot of, say, *Great Expectations:* I can tell only the roughest sum of it. I have a great admiration for what Chesterton and C. S. Lewis wrote, for the philosophical cast and strength of their minds; but I find the Father Brown stories distasteful, and the "Narnia" kind of book painfully difficult to read.

The research and the description of what really happened—*wie es eigentlich gewesen*—this separation of "fact" from "fiction" is, of course, the central statement of purpose and the standard desideratum of professional history, with its canons established by Leopold von Ranke and mostly German historians during the nineteenth century, with many solid and enduring results. Ranke's famous phrase, *wie es eigentlich gewesen,* has been dissected, interpreted and misinterpreted often since his time. But more important than the most precise translation and exact rendering of that phrase, apposite and proper for his time, must be our later realization that history is not a science. (Again the context is important: the German word *Wissenschaft*, especially a century ago, included the more spacious meaning of science *and* knowledge.) What "really happened," to my mind, inevitably includes not only what happened but also what could have happened: actuality mixed up with potentiality. This is why history differs from the Newtonian or Cartesian categories of science. More obviously, history is less than a science but also more than a science, because everything has its history, including science. It took me more than a decade of professional historianship to recognize this and put it in something like this way. Long before that I felt, and thought, that history was closer to art than to science, that indeed history-writing *was* an art. But I outgrew that, too. Around 1958 the final crystallization formed in my mind, to the effect that the entire objective/subjective, science/art (and even fact/fiction) antitheses were inadequate and outdated; that we have outgrown them; that knowledge, very much including historical knowledge, is neither objective nor subjective but personal and participant; that history is not only "an art, like all the other sciences" (Veronica Wedgwood's fine formulation) but a way of thinking, a now inescapable form of thought; and that the awareness and description of this may be my most important task.

Before that, I knew something more directly related to my writing. This was that the historian, like the novelist, is plagued by the elusive nature of truth. Very early in life I learned in Hungary that it is possible to write a history in which every "fact" may be precise and yet the general impression of which may be—often deliberately—false. This happens because a "fact" does not exist in our minds except through its associations; because it has no meaning except through its statement; and because the statement of every fact depends on its purpose. History consists of words, not of "facts"—or, more precisely, of "facts" that are inseparable from (and even unimaginable without) words. Therefore, too, the purpose of writing a piece of history could not be really the final, fixed, finite establishment of "factual truth" or "solution of a problem" (i.e., "The *definitive* history of the origins of the Civil War"), but—as Thucydides, the first critical historical writer, intimated—

the reduction of untruth. And what is the purpose of that purpose itself, of the reduction of untruth? It is not only that of enlightenment or correction or even instruction; it is one of *reminder.* We have to remind people of some things that they, in one way or another, already know.

This brings me to an avowal of a democratic impulse that may surprise some of my readers. I am reactionary enough to admit my thoughts about the dangers of democracy. These exist because of the democratic tendency to interpret equality and freedom in ephemeral, superficial and abstract ways, and of institutionalizing them in deadening and impersonal forms; in sum, because of the deadly inclination of democracy to inflation and to bureaucracy. I am, moreover, aware that the writing and teaching of history have their special dangers in democratic times, something that Tocqueville summed up in forty-eight sentences, in a short chapter entitled "Some Characteristics of Historians in Democratic Times," in the second volume of *Democracy in America.* It may even be argued that writing fine history is an aristocratic art. There are many reasons why it is easier to write a mediocre history than a mediocre novel, and why it is more difficult to write a great history than a great novel—foremost among them the inevitable restrictions of the historian, who cannot invent people who did not exist, statements that were not made, things that were not about to happen and that did not happen. These conditions are true enough. But even their importance pales before the overall commonsense and democratic truism, which is that history does not have a language of its own. It is thought, imagined, taught, spoken and written in our everyday languages (which is, too, why history is a form of thought). This is why there is no difference between a document and a historical document, between a source and a historical source, between a person and a historical person, between an event and a historical event. Any attempt, especially in the twentieth century, to insist on (or even to proceed from) such differences is self-serving, false and, at least potentially, corrupt; and it only helps to diminish further the sense of our connection to the past.

History is not only the study of the recorded past; it is also that of the remembered past.* I was twenty when I chose to work for a history degree; but even then I was aware of two matters from which I have not departed since and never will. One is that there is no categorical division between professional and non-professional history-writing. Yes, there is a difference in some of the training (and in the aspirations) of a Ph.D. in History and in that of an amateur historian. But—unlike, say, in the cases of a professional surgeon and a paramedic—there is no difference in the instruments of their craft, which is everyday language. Nor is there any difference in the character of their knowledge, that is, in the process whereby the reconstruction of history occurs in their minds. There ought not be any difference in the extent of their research and reading. But amateur historians sometimes write better prose than professional historians. The reason for this is simple, even though its consequences are complicated. Many professional historians are writing principally for other professional historians. That limitation of purpose may reduce their range of vision, including their very understanding of human nature. Of course that happens during the bureaucratization of every intellectual profession. The greatest historians (for example, Burckhardt) were aware of this.

There are countless examples of this amateur-professional problem, if problem it is. One example is that of Churchill. I have thought for many years that he was a great historian (for once the Nobel people were right when they awarded him the prize in literature because of his history-writing). Yet I have been amazed how professional historians have paid little or no attention to his histories.† I am not uncritical of Churchill's historianship, not even

---

*"Dreams are the outcomes of memories, not of the subconscious. This separation of memory from the subconscious is the task for a genius of the future." (Diary, July 28, 1983)

†In 1933 A. L. Rowse wrote in *The End of an Epoch* that Churchill, "unlike Trotsky," had "no philosophy of history." This was cited and repeated in 1961 by W. H. Carr in *What Is History?* It is absolute nonsense. What these celebrated British panjandrums failed to see was that Churchill possessed something far more important than a systematic philosophy of history (about which Burckhardt had written that a philosophy of history is a contradiction per se); Churchill had a profound sense of history, that is, a historical philosophy. The

about his monumental volumes of the history of the Second World War, which have their share of errors; still, more than forty years after he wrote those volumes, they have stood the test of time extraordinarily well. They withstood the inevitable changes of our perspectives, and also the inevitable revelations in the immense mass of publications and documents that have accumulated through four decades. I am particularly impressed by a passage in Churchill's first volume of that work *(The Gathering Storm)*. This is Churchill's brief description of the young Hitler; three long paragraphs. I do not recall that this made an especial impact on me when I first read it more than forty years ago. Since that time I must have read one hundred books, a dozen biographies, tens of thousands of pages about Hitler, whose character and mind still interest me and about whom I believe I have made a few serious contributions. But when I recently reread these passages my heart beat faster; for I found that Churchill was absolutely right. What he must have dictated circa 1948, pacing up and down in Chartwell, in perhaps less than twenty minutes, sums up just about everything that scholars have learned to know (and one important thing that they have not yet learned to know) not only about Hitler's early life but about the crystallization of his political mind.* What I am saying is not only that

---

Trotsky example is very telling. Trotsky *did* have a philosophy of history; but that did him no good, and I do not mean only his political career. His writings in exile show that his understanding of the historical realities of his time was woefully cramped and wrong. Also, there exists a portrait that Churchill limned of Trotsky in *Great Contemporaries,* where in a few sentences he sketched the conflict between Trotsky and Stalin: the essential elements in the fall of Trotsky and the rise of Stalin (including suggestive statements of what Stalin's rule meant and where it was to lead). The statements are astonishingly acute and even prophetic, especially when we consider that Churchill wrote this in the early 1930s. They are also more correct and insightful than the gist of Carr's many volumes dealing with the same problem and topic and period—of the Carr who was not an inconsiderable but a very knowledgeable historian, devoting decades of his life to the study and writing of the history of Soviet Russia. *That important thing is Churchill's recognition that the decisive turning point in Hitler's life came in 1918–19 and not before 1914, in Munich and not in Vienna. This is contrary to the even now accepted opinion; and contrary, too, to Hitler's own self-serving argument in *Mein Kampf,* according to which the crystalliza-

Churchill was a great writer-artist, capable of summing up, in his own kind of masterful prose, something that would take another historian at least a chapter. What this involved is not only manner but matter, not only style but substance. What these paragraphs reveal is that Churchill possessed the rare insight that is the fruit of genius. His portrait of the young Hitler is a high achievement of genius whose essence is an understanding of human nature that is profoundly and unavoidably historical. He knew because he understood; and he could employ his understanding to the best of his knowledge—all of it on the acutely conscious level of his mind.

This issue of the flexible boundary between professional and non-professional history has affected the purpose of my writing for more than forty years. My perennial desire to write a new kind of history sprang not from the desire for novelty but from the impulse to demonstrate how history—perhaps especially now, in the democratic age—must include what and how many people thought and acted and hoped for in their everyday lives: in short, the design, the limning and the coloring of the sensitivities of a certain place and period. I shall presently sum up the history of my books, the very structures and the materials of which ought to—necessarily inadequately—illustrate this; but I must insist on something else at this point. This is that this recurrent, and perhaps chronic, aspiration of mine has been involved with my interest in the inevitable overlapping of "fact" and "fiction" (in the sense, too, of the original Latin meaning of the word *fictio,* that is, mental construction), in a kind of prose that may be found in the best of histories and in the best of novels. It will thus be evident that my own attempts toward this kind of history have had certain similarities in scope—but none at all in method, approach or perspective—with the kind of "total" history that people such as the celebrated Fernand Braudel have been composing in our times. Yes: we have come to the unavoidable (and by no means very brilliant or profound) recognition that the lives and the minds of great numbers of people do matter, and that

---

tion of his political ideology happened during his Vienna years, and not in Munich later.

in describing a place and a time and a people we must attempt to reconstruct and to understand many things, including the material conditions of their lives and the formative influences of their minds. But this must be achieved through the *esprit de finesse* rather than through that of *géometrie;* through a sympathetic and evocative attempt of comprehension and not through a kind of retrospective sociology, cobbled together with fragmentary (and sometimes even fraudulent) statistics—and through the recognition of the intrusion of mind in the structure of events, indeed, of matter itself.

If I had any great masters before my eyes they were Burckhardt, Tocqueville, Huizinga. *If* I had any Great Masters . . . I have been blessed (and sometimes cursed) with a fairly independent mind. But I also know that my mind is not really very original. I am only good (and sometimes original) in seeing (and perhaps describing) kinds of connections.*

There is something more important. It involves that particular kind of imagination which is historical. I must leave aside the important argument that *all* imagination is, to a great extent, historical; as C. S. Lewis wrote, no one can imagine a wholly new color or a wholly new monster or a third sex, only a new combination of colors or monsters or of the two sexes that we already know. I must also leave aside the fascinating possibility—and some of its evidences—that in some cases human perception actually *precedes* sensation. In any event, imagination, like perspective, is not only a consequence but an inevitable component of the act of seeing. But here I am writing not about imagination itself but about certain odd elements that stimulate or vitalize or even inspire the imagination of a writer such as myself.

Names, for example. When Peter Quennell in his autobiography

---

*One result of this obsession with connections is my habit of writing long footnotes on the bottom of too many pages in my books. These footnotes are illustrative and explanatory, not only referential. They are the results of my compulsion to tell something significant, or at least interesting, to my readers that would otherwise disturb and unduly crowd a paragraph of the main text. (They surely disturb and unduly crowd the appearance of the printed page.)

writes about "the fashionable dandy Napier Alington," this, to me, is instantly evocative of a place and of a period. I find a slip of paper among my notes: "A British officer, Vivian Usborne, a wonderful 1918 name." In *Heart of Darkness* Conrad wrote of "all the ships whose names are jewels flashing in the night of time." In March 1940 Churchill, visiting Scapa Flow, remembered Kipling's

Mines reported in the fairway, warn all traffic and detain.
Send up *Unity, Claribel, Assyrian, Stormcock* and *Golden Gain.*

There is a sublime music in such things,* as there is a mysterious connection of the very sound and the shape of certain names with the character of their bearers: Bismarck: the strong mark of a fist; Mussolini: the Italian muscleman; Goebbels: the bouncing, compressed energy of a small rubber ball; Stalin; Nixon.

Another example: the evocative power of certain dates. I remember when, before coming to America, I saw a picture of a railroad station in Montana in 1915. It showed a great powerful Great Northern steam locomotive, with white-rimmed driving wheels and a plume of smoke rising from its flat, modern funnel; two or three tall Americans in uniform, standing on the narrow wooden-slatted platform of the station; and behind them mountains, dark and un-Alpine because there was no sign of any kind of habitation on them. I kept gazing at that picture for a long time. What excited my interest was the combination of that place and the year: the year, more than the place. I had had mental pictures of *1915*: of Flanders fields, of the Western front, of the Eastern front, of the Dardanelles, of wartime London or Berlin and the cobblestoned main streets of Budapest and perhaps even of a teeming New York in 1915; but that picture evoked the mysterious vastness and the momentous modern

*And, perhaps, moving from the sublime to the ridiculous, as when Nathanael West named his protagonist Lemuel Pitkin in *A Cool Million.* Within that name are condensed the Late Twenties in a Far Western Civilization, with their compound of arid biblical leftovers *and* Hollywood, the era of Coolidge and of Louis B. Mayer, by now embedded in the historical evolution of the United States.

power of America in a certain year, *at a certain historical time,* instantly filling my mind with an avid, palpable curiosity whereof the only crude approximation would be a new dish on a buffet table of delicacies whose very sight incites one's appetite. Another occasion: I remember that when I read that Greta Garbo had begun her acting career in Stockholm in 1916, an entire slew of associations and images flew into my mind. Stockholm *in 1916:* how must it have been in that neutral hyperborean city then, with its dark three-storied houses, white islands, pearly sky, a foggy bath of pale electric lights, high-wheeled box-like Adler automobiles crunching forward in the snowy streets, Germanophile patricians in their high-crowned felt hats and fur-collared coats; how did those Swedish people live then, what did they think?

Summering in Spain in 1962 I was reading a history of that country in the early twentieth century, including a footnote about an agricultural strike in the Spanish Levant in 1917. And then, walking through the dusty botanical gardens of Valencia I was suddenly overwhelmed by an acute wave of curiosity, by the wish to know more about that sunbaked, semi-African scene, litigious, thin, black-clothed men and women behind and outside of a Europe at war and yet at the same time: Valencia *in 1917.*

Not so long ago I spent two weeks on the French Caribbean island of St.-Barthélemy (mostly to please my wife, since I am not attracted to the tropics; I have, instead, *la nostalgie du Nord*). Walking down to the harbor one day I passed a monument engraved with the names of those French islanders who had served in the 1939–45 war. I recognized the names of the prominent families of that island. I also knew that in 1940 the French Antilles had opted for Pétain, that they were governed by a Vichyite admiral, and that it was not until 1943 that these sun-scorched, somnolent islands joined the Allied ranks and the Allied cause. But how did St. Barts look *in 1940?* Now, in 1982, it was full of sails and yachts and cruise boats. Then it must have been empty, perhaps with a gray-painted American destroyer standing offshore on certain days, watching lest a German submarine come to a short rest in its territorial waters. But what must have been more interesting were the lives and the thoughts of the French families. What did they think and feel when France fell in June 1940? How were they divided, between pétainistes and gaullistes, gradually adjusting their minds in the gathering course of the war and to the gathering presence of American power? How interesting it would be, I thought, to spend a year here and in Paris among the archives of the *département* or perusing the files of the local newspaper; but I also knew that many of the scenes and the evidences of the kind of historical truth I would pursue were not to be found in those archives that would be, at best, their reflections.

A few months earlier I had traveled in Transylvania, spending a few days in those towns that had been inhabited by Lutheran Saxons for centuries, in houses that still had their German look. The Rumanians executed a very successful coup d'état in August 1944, passing instantly from the German to the anti-German camp; but I knew that it took a few weeks, until in the wake of the retreating Germans, the Russian and Rumanian armies arrived in that portion of Transylvania. And what happened during that tense time in these towns when the Russians were approaching, where but a few weeks or even days before a persecuted and cowed community of Jews and an arrogant and stolid community of Nazified Germans lived side by side? Some of the Germans were packing up and leaving, but most of them stayed. How did they behave? Did they and the Jews talk to each other? Would a Saxon lawyer lift his hat when passing a former Jewish colleague in the street? *In late August, in 1944.*

I wished, and still wish, to know more about such matters, a wish that has all the attributes of appetite. Like appetite, this kind of mental interest is neither aseptical nor objective. Yet this kind of interest (and its mental absorption) goes counter to the "laws" of the physical world. When we are truly interested in something we want to know more and more about it; and the more we know about something, the easier we include more knowledge about it in our minds. Yet here is, I think, a difference between the functions of my mental appetite when reading a novel and when reading or researching history. In the former my imagination is principally vitalized by the atmosphere. In the latter case my principal curiosity is directed to events, facts, details—adding to a plot the main course of which I already know. I often cannot remember the subplots (and sometimes not even the main plot) of some of my favorite novels; but I remember not only the plot but also the subplot of the histories I read. This is partly due to the earlier-mentioned weakness of my mind in following plots; but it is also because the concreteness of history in our minds solidly attaches our imagination and memory, to certain unique places and times.

I must now sum up the story of my thirteen books: not their contents but their histories; their conceptions and their purposes. My first book, *The Great Powers and Eastern Europe,* was an ambitious attempt at contemporary or near-contemporary history, mostly because of the unusual availability at that time of diplomatic and other international documents of a recent past. The largest mass of German diplomatic documents had been captured by the Allies in 1945 and was beginning to be published. Other governments had published particular volumes during or before the war. Yet other governments (the British, the Italians, the Americans, the Swedish) were publishing other documentary collections about those years. Without this new mass of materials I would surely not have undertaken that book. But the impulse to write it may have been deeper than that. I was very much interested in many of the obscure episodes and still unresolved questions of the last war, through which I had lived during my formative years. I was not ashamed of this interest in so contemporary a history; I thought (after all, so had Thucydides) that my book would perform a service in correcting or reducing untruths still current. This work took me about five years with the usual ups and downs. Among the ups, the wintry evenings in the old Furness Library of the University of Pennsylvania stand out in my memory. The downs were my troubles with my first American publisher. The American Book Company was a textbook house that had chosen to go into the "trade" field shortly before my manuscript had come to their attention by way of their chief history reader. He was a saturnine, strong-minded, well-prejudiced and extremely intelligent scholar, Professor Gaudens Megaro, who became one of my close friends, until his strange disappearance and sudden death a few years later. The trouble came because sometime before the completion of my book the managers of the American Book Company had changed their minds about going into the trade field. Consequently, they regretted their contractual commitment to such a large work—not a textbook—such as mine, which they now could not let go. In short, they had something like a muskrat—not a tiger but nevertheless a sizable and difficult animal—by the tail. The book sank without a trace; but not only because of the, by then, drastically reduced marketing budget of its publisher. The ideological climate of the American professorate was still governed by the orthodox liberal ideology of the 1940s and before.

Before I finished my work on *The Great Powers and Eastern Europe* my mind had begun to wander to different fields. My interests, at that time, were even more undisciplined than ever before or since; they were perhaps especially inchoate. Intellectually speaking this was an unhappy phase of my life—while at the same time that life was lightened and merrified by my engagement and marriage. The page proofs arrived at my apartment on the day of our wedding. I had to do the index during our honeymoon. I was, of course, unhappy with the lack of recognition of this first book of mine, something that I immediately attributed—perhaps exaggeratedly— to the ideological (and also methodological) narrow-mindedness of so many intellectuals, including, alas, historians. Meanwhile I went on reading indiscriminately and voraciously, including the works of some of the great historians of the nineteenth and early twentieth centuries, filling in large gaps left over from my Hungarian university education. In an earlier chapter I wrote of the condition, unknown to Americans, whereby the blessings of America made it possible for refugees from Europe to travel and discover a Europe that they might otherwise not have known. Here I must record my indebtedness to another blessing of this country whereby a refugee from Europe might learn here more about European history or literature or art than almost anywhere else in the world, because of

the freedom and richness of the large American libraries and because of the relative leisure of the life of an American college
teacher. In 1955 I began to write the first portions of what eventually
became *Historical Consciousness,* my most important book.

This was not completed for many years, and was published more
than thirteen years after I had begun it. I had to interrupt its writing
several times, often because of my doubts about its form. On more
fortunate occasions I stopped because of commitments to other,
smaller books. One of my articles in *Commonweal* was read by
Dwight Macdonald, who praised it in a letter to their editors that
they then sent to me. I was pleased because I liked Macdonald's
writing; I called on him in New York, and soon we became the
closest of friends. He mentioned me to Jason Epstein and Nathan
Glazer, who were then in charge of what was becoming the paperback revolution, having convinced Doubleday of the existence of a
large tappable reservoir of potential buyers of quality books in
paperback reprints, especially in colleges and universities but also
among intellectuals of all kinds, somewhat similar to the Penguin
series in England. Epstein published one of the subchapters of what
was to become *Historical Consciousness* in his *Anchor Review.* Was
there anything I'd care to write for them? he asked. Well, there was,
I said. There existed parts of Tocqueville's second, unfinished book
on the French Revolution and his correspondence with Gobineau,
too, that had not been published in English. I would translate them
and write an introduction. We agreed.

This work took me about a year—1956, the year when my son
was born. Translating long texts is something that does not really
accord with my temperament; and I remember a few beastly summer days when I was forced to descend to the cool damp cavern
of the cellar of our rebuilt old house, with drops of dirty water
plopping periodically onto the pages of the Tocqueville *Oeuvres
Complètes* at my right hand. Yet I was fairly enthusiastic about this
work because of my tremendous respect for Tocqueville. *Monsieur
le Comte, mon semblable, sinon mon frère.* Alexis de Tocqueville died
in the year when the oldest of my grandparents, my paternal grandfather, was born. Is he a Great Contemporary of mine? Yes he is:

because he is the Aristotle (and perhaps the Plato, too) of the democratic age, the greatest of its political and social thinkers and writers and one of the greatest of its historians. He will be our Great Contemporary for many generations to come, until the age of political democracy (and the bureaucratic morass into which it now devolves) will disappear and a new kind of society will form. Like other European intellectuals in America, I had found *Democracy in America* the most profound and the most telling book ever written about the United States. From there I went on to realize that its second volume is even more important than the first, since it is more about democracy than about America in the 1830s. Then I began to read everything that Tocqueville wrote about the history of France, and also about himself: the incomparable *Souvenirs,* his history of the Old Regime, his unfinished book about the French Revolution and the extant collections of his letters, some of which contain the most startling illustrations of his extraordinary vision and mind. I was also critical of and impatient with the standard liberal American commentaries of Tocqueville. In the Introduction to my translation I tried to suggest the main Tocqueville questions. Was he a liberal or a conservative? Was he a sociologist or a historian? Was he an aristocratic agnostic or a believing Catholic?—indicating that, even as he transcended customary categories, the second halves of these pairs were truer than the first.

In 1959, when my *Tocqueville: The European Revolution and Correspondence with Gobineau* was published, Tocqueville had become a subindustry in academia. Thereby, rather expectably, my work and my interpretation were either studiously ignored or dismissed as "special pleading" (the words of one commentator). Because of an odd compound of sloth and pride (as Christopher Sykes once wrote, "Scruples and sloth make happy bedfellows") but for other reasons, too, among them the undisciplined ranging of my interests, I often have been inclined to abandon my scholarly efforts in fields where they are treated as unwelcome intrusions by most scholars. This was surely true about my Tocqueville work. I knew, however, that there was evidence somewhere about Tocqueville's religion in the last phase of his life, something that I could prove beyond (or, perhaps, beneath) "special pleading." Well, if they wanted documents, I will find documents. (Re-search: we find what we are looking for—at least most of the time). And indeed, in August 1962, on a long day trip from Paris to the very modest convent of the Sisters of the Notre-Dame de Secours in Troyes, I found three overlapping, separate and contemporary manuscript accounts by the nuns who had cared for Tocqueville in 1859. The Superior of the house allowed me to take these handwritten documents to America—a rare generosity, especially in France. I returned them a few months later. I published these accounts, in a long article, in the July 1964 issue of the *Catholic Historical Review.* They made no difference: none of the Tocqueville scholars in America has referred to them ever since (though the leading French Tocqueville scholars have).

Directly upon completing my Tocqueville manuscript in 1957, I returned to my book about historical thinking. I took advantage of my first sabbatical and of a small but very useful grant from RELM Foundation, a conservative institution whose director was brought into contact with me by Russell Kirk. The history of my writing of *Historical Consciousness,* 1955 to 1968, is summed up briefly in its Appendix, wherefore I am loath to recount this story again. Instead, I am compelled to say something about its gestation and structure because these matters relate to the history of my writing. *Historical Consciousness* is not a philosophy of history but its opposite: a multi-faceted statement and exposition of a historical philosophy. Its purpose is not the demonstration of a systematic knowledgeability of history; to the contrary, it wishes to demonstrate the profound, yet considerably unsystematic, historicity of our knowledge. It deals with many things: with the evolution of our consciousness of history since the seventeenth century; with the emergence of the now widespread historical form of thought; with the necessary rethinking of the essential problem of causes, and of more mundane matters such as public opinion and popular sentiment; with what "fact" and "fiction" really mean; with a reasonable hierarchy of historical forces in our times, ascending from what is least significant (economics) to what is most significant (thinking); with the difference between categories and tendencies, leading to the question of human characteristics and including the persistence of national characteristics; with the relationship of imagination and memory, indeed, with that of "evolution" and history; with the necessity to recognize the inevitable involvement of the historian and his subject, that is, of the "observer" with what is "observed," leading, in the end, to the correspondences between this view of historical knowledge and the proven recognitions of quantum physics, whereby near the end of the so-called Modern Age the Cartesian and Newtonian views of man and of the universe must be rethought. It is a great mistake to write about more than one thing. The best parts of one's book become invariably lost. It befuddles a few readers and most reviewers. It is a great mistake, too, as Stendhal once wrote, to be more than one or two steps ahead of the public mind: if an idea is "five or six degrees ahead, it gives them an intolerable headache." A century and a half later even two steps are bad enough. What Stendhal wrote about the public mind is true of the professorate only in the sense of a metaphor, since professional intellectuals are good at avoiding headaches. It is the author whom they will treat as intolerable, whereby his ideas and his books won't count.

In 1958 I had no publisher for this book. This did not matter; the manuscript was far from complete. What mattered that year was the great event of my discovery and reading and comprehension (in that order) of Werner Heisenberg's 1955 Gifford Lectures. I knew that some of my views about the nature and the limits of our historical knowledge corresponded with what certain contemporary or near-contemporary writers and philosophers—say, Ortega and Unamuno; Bernanos and Péguy; Pieper and Wittgenstein; Guardini and Frankl; Camus and Simone Weil; William James and Santayana, and, of course, Tocqueville and Burckhardt—had at least suggested in some of their writings. I suspected that there might be a few correspondences between the discoveries of modern physics and my own convictions of the indeterminacy of historical—that is, human—thinking. Yet I had not imagined that so many of these correspondences would appear, in startling and concrete ways, until I read those Heisenberg lectures (after which came my reading of his other writings). I can recall those sunny mornings in the sea-grape arbored booth of a restaurant in Siasconset, where I had to work after the college girl waitresses—as was their habit, disdainfully—had cleared the breakfast dishes and cutlery away. (With my wife and baby we were poor relations on the already then trendy and expensive Nantucket Island; our room was small and cramped, which was why I would work best in that restaurant after an ample breakfast, scribbling furiously while my wife and child were on their way to the beach.) It was then that I found how not only the philosophical recognitions but sometimes the very phrases of that great German physicist corresponded uncannily, and at times literally, with what I had written about the structure of events, about how things happen and how their "happening" is inevitably involved with our own "observation"—that is, with our own participation, *and* with our knowledge of its limits—in the very world of matter. I worked up a large two-page chart of these correspondences for my book. (Eventually I left that chart out of it; it is still somewhere among my leftover papers.) I knew then what this meant. It meant a new, anthropocentric recognition of the universe: the end of the Cartesian division and separation of "object" from "subject," of observer from the observed, of matter from mind. It would lead to a new anthropocentrism that is complex and not primitive, chastened and not arrogant, issuing from our recognitions of the inevitable limitations of human knowledge, of every kind. Later that year—it was a beautiful Friday in September—my wife and I were driving out to dine with another couple. On our way I told my wife that I may have arrived at an intellectual discovery of great magnitude.

She did not understand this at the time. She was a very intelligent and deeply honest woman; we had many intellectual interests and preferences in common, and the kind of mutual respect that is the foundation and the refuge of every enduring marriage. She was, however, influenced by her earlier reading of the first drafts of the putative chapters of my developing book, which she had found verbose, opaque and sometimes difficult to follow—rightly so. That natural and pragmatic experience carried over to her reaction to my excited declaration on that melancholy evening. She would understand the essence of my historical philosophy later. It was, after all, a commonsense one, she would say—and she was, I dare say, right. But her first reaction depressed me because of my isolation. I needed her to talk about this matter and, at least for a while, I couldn't. Less disheartening—because they were more expectable—were my subsequent experiences with physicists. I had been, after all, interpreting paragraphs and passages from the texts of a physicist whose *meaning* I thought I wholly understood; but was I correct in my understanding of *what* he was writing about? My knowledge of standard physics was, after all, close to being nonexistent. During the next two or three years I wrote, and attempted to talk, to a number of physics professors, local as well as eminent ones. I got nowhere. With one exception (Henry Margenau, of Yale) their answers to my written or spoken queries were a compound of tut-tutting and disinterest. Yes, they knew all about Heisenberg; yes, the indeterminacy principle was obviously proved; yet what it meant, and even what it encompassed, interested them not at all. About that *meaning*—well, Heisenberg might be right, he might be wrong. Their answers and their lack of interest suggested that the matter was not much worth thinking about. In sum, their reactions (or, rather, the lack of their reactions) reminded me of so many of our professional historians who, in the second half of the twentieth century, would admit that, yes, historical determinism is outdated, and then go on teaching and writing as if history *were* determined. However, I got over this through the simple expedient of writing and then calling on Heisenberg himself, in 1962 and 1968. I was relieved to hear and read (in some of his letters to me) that I had not been mistaken in attributing certain observations or ideas to him. He wholly agreed with what I had written in my History and Physics chapter, which was all that I wanted to know.

But I am running too far ahead. In 1959 none of my book was in near-finished form. During that fall I suffered a letdown. There was the recurrent illness of my wife. Among other matters, I was disheartened, too, by the enduring and dangerous unwillingness of American public figures (and of many intellectuals) to understand the conditions of the American relationship to the world and to Soviet Russia. Khrushchev had come to the United States that September. There was something pathetic in this Russian peasant tsar's hardly suppressed admiration for everything American at the same time that his hosts, including President Eisenhower, walked beside Khrushchev with their noses in the air and with suspicion and distrust written all over their faces. More important: I was getting a bit tired of writing my historical philosophy book. There I have been exhorting historians to write history rather than write about history. But wasn't this exactly what I was doing now? What was the use of all these theses and theories and arguments? As Santayana said, "In the great ages of art nobody talked of aesthetics." Wouldn't it be a more reasonable thing to take a piece of recent history and write it—and demonstrate there the validity of my arguments about the hierarchy of certain historical forces? On a yellow legal pad (another small American blessing) I wrote out a table of contents for two books. One of these potential histories would deal with the history of the world conflict of the United States and Russia. I sent it to the new editor of Doubleday Anchor. A few days before Christmas late in the evening the telephone rang. This editor offered me a contract. Directly next morning my writing of *A History of the Cold War* began.

There followed the happiest six months of writing in my life. Immediately I went out to buy typing paper, a new ribbon, a box of good cigars and a case of Bass Ale. I wrote this book—a not insubstantial one, either in size or in its composition—during fourteen or fifteen weekends, a draft of each chapter (thirteen overall) each weekend, closeted in my little fruitwood-paneled library, enveloped in a cloud of tobacco. The entire book had been wonderfully clear in my mind. Except for the penultimate chapter, I hardly stopped at all. I set a very wide left margin on my typewriter and wrote the entire book in one full sweep, in one draft, making my corrections and emendations on that wide, pristine, snow-white expanse on the left side of the paper. I especially remember a Saturday in late March 1960 when I had finally wrestled down the first draft of that long, difficult and fairly verbose penultimate chapter.

Having worked without stopping from eight in the morning to six in the afternoon, I took a deliciously hot bath, dressed and drove with my wife a mere half-mile away to a dinner party of my favorite friends, the Drakes, where, to Larry's dismay, as I later found out, I was sufficiently ebullient to consume half a bottle of brandy after dinner. On the way back from dropping off the babysitter I drove our car into the side of a telephone pole. My wife was already safe at home. I didn't care. I was happy.

The next Christmas was dark. My wife was in the local hospital, very ill with an undiagnosed high fever. Yet the year 1961 opened as *annus mirabilis,* for many reasons in my private life. A few days after New Year my wife's condition turned around; she was recovering beautifully, coming home on the Sunday morning when *A History of the Cold War* had a splendid congratulatory review by Cyrus Sulzberger in *The New York Times Book Review.* I also received a much cherished long letter from George Kennan, who wrote that, among other things, my book was "a really great work of philosophical-historical analysis . . . the deepest and most important effort of this sort that has been made anywhere to date. It abounds with things which to my mind need saying; many of them things that I have tried to say myself, but never so comprehensively; others—ones that I have dimly realized but never pushed to the point of formulation; still others—insights that had never occurred to me, but the validity of which I instantly recognize." How I have been pleased with that. A paperback and German and French editions were to follow. Jason Epstein, who had left Doubleday for Random House, took notice. He offered me a contract for *Historical Thinking.* So I was on my way—or so I thought. I had enough money to send my wife to Florida for the coming winter, for her to escape her recurrent pulmonary illnesses in the cold months. (In the end that cost me little money, since she took it upon herself to work at two jobs and came home in April shining, tanned and with an unexpected saving of $1,500.) We traveled in Europe next summer. On my return I found that Epstein had sent my manuscript back, with such editorial suggestions that I could not in conscience consider, let alone follow. I returned my contract and put *Historical*

Thinking away. I wrote *Decline and Rise of Europe* (a long historical essay) for Doubleday in 1963–64. I went off to teach in France for a year. I added two chapters to the paperback cold war history in 1966. Then I met (in the same house where I had drunk that unconscionable amount of brandy six years before) Cass Canfield, Jr., who gave me a contract for *Historical Thinking.* I rewrote the entire manuscript, boiling some of it away, making it a better book. Two months before its publication another department of Harper & Row, unbeknownst to Cass, published a textbook with that very title. Then and there I had to change my title to *Historical Consciousness.* I did not really mind. After thirteen years my book was in print. It sank without much of a trace, faster than any other book of mine. That did not surprise me—I was inured to it, it had happened before. I now had a double contract. One was for *The Passing of the Modern Age*—the title echoing Huizinga's *The Waning of the Middle Ages,* but otherwise a very different book, a historical essay, not much more than a summation of the devolution of institutions and standards at the end of our age. It was published on the day my wife died, November 15, 1970.

The other book was to be *The Last European War, 1939–1941,* which I consider my second most important work. I had lived through the Second World War in my youth. I kept up an interest in it. It was not only a great, searing and at times mentally inspiring experience. I sensed then, as I knew later, that this world war was not only enormous in its extent but also more complex than its predecessor, because it involved much more than the movements of armies and of states; it involved the movable sentiments of entire peoples. In many ways the mental earthquake of that war was bigger than the physical one. And this was especially true of its first part, of the twenty-seven months 1939–41, before Pearl Harbor. After December 1941 Hitler could no longer win his war because the British and the Russians had held out against him until finally the Americans joined them with full force. But before Pearl Harbor he could have won it. At times he came close to winning it, which is what so many people either forgot or did not wish to think about. So my book would include the movements not only of the armies

and of governments, but of public opinion and of popular sentiments and perhaps even beliefs during those years. The reactions
of peoples to the stupendous German triumphs were one thing.
Others were the beginnings of the end of bourgeois politics, of the
British Empire, the beginnings of the Americanization of Europe
and of the extermination of masses of Jews. I wanted to write a large
and profound book about those years, a newly designed and crafted
vessel whose structure would naturally incarnate my own ideas
about how history ought to be seen and therefore written, a representation of some of the governing ideas of *Historical Consciousness.*
I divided *The Last European War* into two parts: a "narrative" and
an "analytical" portion ("The Main Events" and "The Main Movements")—in other words, a description of *what* happened, followed
by a description of *how* and *why* events, tendencies and developments came about. In the second, longer part I moved from the lives
of the peoples to the march of the armies to the movements of
politics to the relations of states to the sentiments of nations to the
convergences of thought and of belief, in that order (these were the
titles of successive chapters), in accord with the hierarchy already
suggested in *Historical Consciousness,* along an ascending order. I
had done this earlier, in *A History of the Cold War,* and would do
this later, too, in my *Outgrowing Democracy: A History of the United
States in the Twentieth Century.* I knew that the first portion—as
important and in many of its details as new as the second—would
be overlooked, even by sympathetic reviewers. But because this
book was much more than a historical essay, because it filled many
gaps in our knowledge, because it was the only near-encyclopedic
work on the years 1939–41, because its materials had come from my
research and reading of many thousands of books and articles and
documents in many languages, I hoped that the very structure and
the method of the book would be noticed and perhaps discussed by
other professionals. It wasn't. The very writing and the publishing
of the book went through years of vicissitudes. I began it in 1967 but
interrupted it twice, once for the writing of *The Passing of the
Modern Age* and again during the tragic year of my wife's fatal
illness and death. I finished it in 1973, but it was not published until

March 1976. In one instance, the book was delayed when the secretary who was supposed to retype the manuscript (the ephemeral paramour of the chief editor) forgot it in the broom closet of her summer rental apartment on Fire Island. Another torpedo befell it around the time of the book's launching: the excellent and sympathetic editor newly assigned to it was fired. But never mind: the book was published, and I am pleased with it still. Before it sank out of sight it had received a few respectful salvos of star shells; and a few foreign lifeboats hauled around to salvage it, whence its German, French, British and Brazilian editions. Thus, unlike many other books of mine, it did not quite sink without a trace. There were a few bubbles on the surface, including, alas, the ugly oily slick exuding from one of its reviewers, who suggested that my treatment of the Jewish tragedy could be exploited by anti-Semites. This, of course, was not only wrong but the very opposite of what I had intended and written; but it surely accelerated the disappearance of this, I believe, well-wrought vessel, to the extent that its remains on the bottom are unmarked in many of the maritime charts of its region. Enough of this figure of speech: what I mean is that *The Last European War, 1939–1941* is often omitted from the very bibliographies of works dealing with its subject.

Often during the last phase of writing a book I grow tired of it—less tired of the work itself than of the place it preoccupies in my mind. Then I begin to think what I should write next; and, to use Jean Dutourd's fine phrase, the *petite musique* of certain ideas and phrases is beginning to form in my mind. The idea of a book about Philadelphia was already crystallizing when I finished *The Last European War*. However, I had no other publisher than Doubleday at that time; and I loathed the effort of addressing unsolicited letters to publishers and editors who presumably knew nothing of me. Thus Doubleday and I agreed on my writing a short book about the year 1945. *1945: Year Zero* was smaller and different from the structure of my other books; its writing took me a year and a half. It was a good little book, a destroyer compared to the aircraft carrier of *The Last European War*. Long before its proof stage I returned to my Philadelphia project, which was perhaps the second of my most delightful book-writing experiences. I was longing to get away from large canvases, from portraying great wars and civilizations. I wanted to try my hand at a miniature. But the crucial inspiration was, of course, not the size of the canvas but the scene. I had an amateur and secondary interest in the history of my adopted city (I live nearly forty miles west of it, but in Philadelphia it is not geography that matters) for many years. In 1958 *Encounter* had printed my short and impressionistic article about Philadelphia and Philadelphians, which led to the agreeable result of its inclusion in the University of Chicago's manual, *Selected Writings in English,* among samples of fine English writing. In my private library alone there were hundreds of the oddest books about Philadelphia. So I began this book in 1976, leading to its eventual title, *Philadelphia: Patricians and Philistines, 1900–1950.* The first chapter was a detailed description of the city in 1900, the last in 1950; the rest were biographical portraits of seven famous or not so famous Philadelphians, *qui floreabant* during the first half of this century, with odd dualities in their character.

There were particular pleasures attendant to the writing of this book. One of them was the search and the finding of material (including photographs) in various Philadelphia libraries, where my discovery of material oddities was enhanced by the atmosphere; and at the end of the darkening afternoons stood the prospect of a short walk in the cold wintry air and a good dinner downtown with one of my friends.* Another pleasure was talking about this book and its characters with my second wife on warm summer evenings over dinner on our screened porch in the country, high above the bushes but secluded under trees, with the sounds of bullfrogs and cicadas

---

*There was, too, my call at the house of a charming and harebrained descendant of one of my subjects, who produced, without a moment of hesitation, a very large black leather chest containing her illustrious forebear's remnant papers. The chest served as a wondrous footrest in my library for a number of years—I had some difficulty in returning it to its elusive proprietress. The papers, alas, were not especially valuable; they were the papers of a man who had written, among other things: "I never wrote a letter to a woman you couldn't chill beer on."

lightening the heavy green stillness from the dark pond and the creek. I had plenty of trouble getting a publisher for this Philadelphia book. Eventually, through a rare stroke of fortune, the manuscript landed on the desk of Robert Giroux who, *rara avis,* actually *read* those hundreds of pages of an unfinished manuscript by an unknown writer. I was delighted to meet him, this last old-fashioned gentleman in what once had been an occupation for gentlemen. He convinced me to add a chapter on Albert C. Barnes, the collector of art, something that my wife, too, had urged and that previously I had refused to do. This took another summer's work, but it was worth it. My Philadelphia book was published in March 1981; Farrar, Straus & Giroux printed a physically very attractive book. It may be one of my best written ones. It was a book whose publication was followed by a series of agreeable events. By this I do not only mean that it had a few very respectful reviews but that I had the occasion, too, to do a few lighthearted causeries (relating, among other things, a fair number of anecdotes that I left out of the book) in two or three of the small Philadelphia clubs, to audiences consisting of many men and women whom I knew, in pleasant little clubhouses built in the Twenties, including the ineffable Philadelphian climate of civility, that urbane atmosphere further enhanced by the great trees swaying outside the windows and the yellow lights bathing the small alleys and squares of the city in the windy autumn evenings.

It will now be seen that the topics of my books have been different ones; and that I have been moving from European to American history through the years. And why not? I have lived in this country for a long time. Whether I was becoming a part of it I cannot say; what I can say is that it was becoming a part of me. In 1981 I began an attempt to write a history of the United States of the last one hundred years, along a structure again in accord with those of some of my previous works and *Historical Consciousness.* I was assisted and inspired by a great and good friend, Nick Rizopoulos (then of the Lehrman Institute), whom I gained during this work. *Outgrowing Democracy: A History of the United States in the Twentieth Cen-*

tury was published by Doubleday in March 1984. A year later a new, enlarged edition (by two important chapters) of *Historical Consciousness* was published by Schocken Books.

That year William Shawn, the editor of *The New Yorker*, took notice of my writing. During the next eighteen months I was a grateful beneficiary of his sympathetic appreciation of my work. He printed six articles of mine in *The New Yorker*, carefully wrought pieces on very different topics,* encouraged by his interest and polished with the aid of the unusual and old-fashioned editorial scrupulousness of his magazine. When Shawn left *The New Yorker* in January 1987, I was saddened. I also thought how odd the tides of American development have been. When *The New Yorker* had started out in 1925, at the high tide of modern American urbane sophistication, someone said, or wrote, that *The New Yorker* was not meant for "the old lady in Dubuque." Sixty years later many of the readers of *The New Yorker* were old ladies in Dubuque and other traditional readers of literature tucked away in the oddest of places.

So my interests were not only moving in the direction of American history, but simultaneously in the opposite direction as well. In 1985 I began to think about a book dealing with the cultural history of my native country; more precisely, about life in its capital city around 1900. So many books had been recently addressed to intellectual life in Vienna around 1900; I thought that the time had come to direct English-speaking readers to the, in many ways, no less interesting culture of Budapest, the other capital city of the Dual Monarchy, in 1900, which was unknown to them. Materials about that subject had become available, and were accumulating; and the libraries in Budapest were now open for research.

---

*They were an essay-review of James Lees-Milne's two-volume biography of Harold Nicolson; of the three-volume edition of the complete Churchill-Roosevelt correspondence; of Witold Rybczynski's beautiful book *Home;* my three articles were an account of the Gotthard Walk, a thirteen-day trek across Switzerland with my daughter; of a visit to the ruins of Dresden and its rebuilt Opera; and a profile of Gyula Krúdy.

* * *

Looking back at my books I can see certain similarities that I had not recognized before. I have written thirteen books in four decades, so the average time for my writing a book has been about three years. This is the case of my last three books, so perhaps I am only now hitting my stride, though I doubt this. Another curious coincidence that I found only lately is that most of my books, including this one, consist of nine chapters—something that has never been a conscious decision at the time of their planning. All my books have been published by trade publishers. This has been my definite preference, for two reasons. One is my conviction that historians should not write only for other historians—even though there are important occasions when they must, and should. The other is money. Well these preferences have not really worked. When a professor succeeds in having a book printed by a reputable commercial publisher some of his colleagues will profess a kind of pristine disdain that often cloaks their less pristine sentiment of envy. They are wrong to be envious. There is little money in this kind of writing. (There is more in the grants and appointments that may be accumulated due to one's academic publications, affiliations and connections.) They are wrong, too, in being disdainful. To write for more people than academics does not necessarily connote superficiality. Often the very contrary is true. I may have been a prolific writer; but I have not been superficial.* I have, I think, profited from the self-imposed condition of living apart from the

---

*Of course I am not alone in this predicament. David McCullough, who is a very good American historian, wrote the finest history of the building of the Panama Canal: *The Path Between the Seas*. In a widely adopted and most remunerative American history textbook by Harvard Professors Freidel and Brinkley, this work appears in the Bibliography in these words: "A lucid popular history of the building of the canal." What do they mean by "popular"? Here is an example of the, perhaps unwitting, petty snobbery of the professorial guild. McCullough's references and his bibliography alone show that he did all of the research and the homework of a first-rate professional historian—and then some.

sometimes airless circles of academics. This explains, too, why among my many articles I sent relatively few to academic journals. The exceptions to this are my scholarly book reviews. While my books and essays often contain—sometimes inordinately—more than a single topic and a single argument, my book reviews do not, for then a single topic is given: a single book. The intellectual commerce of our times has led to the habit of book reviews that serve as instruments for displaying the reviewer's opinions and prejudices, and his scholarship at its feeble best. My practice of reviewing is the old-fashioned one: telling what the book contains and trying to include a mention or at least a summary of anything that I find new or significant in its details.

I have been a prolific writer, for all kinds of reasons. I think I can express certain thoughts and matters better in writing than in speaking. My impulse is to the expression and not really to its reverberation (as Eliot said of literature: it is "the impulse to transcribe one's thoughts correctly")—which is not the case with speaking, nor that of writers whose aspirations are celebrity and money. I am not indifferent to these things, and only imperfectly immune to their temptations. (Gibbon in 1763: "I do not wish that the writer make the Gentleman wholly disappear.") Yet I also feel that we have fallen to a level of intellectual commerce where the instant academic and/or commercial success of a book of mine may mean that there must be something wrong with it. (It would give me great pleasure to have to revise this sentence.)

In any event, there are in this vast country a few hundred men and women, mostly unknown to me, who will read anything I write—if and when they become aware of its availability. Still I have failed in my self-designed task. I have not been able to create that new genre, that new kind of history whereof I have been the occasional John the Baptist, at best. Yes, I have, here and there, attempted the great task for a historian, the tale of some subjects of the last one hundred years, not a retelling of the Decline of the West, surely not a Spenglerian speculative systematization of it, but the *conscious* historical recognition of the opening of a new phase in the evolution of our consciousness. Or, in other terms: the great, the profound difference between evolution and history.

But how I desired to paint some of this in a microcosm! I would paint a clear and beautiful slice of the sad music of humanity, on the surface canvas of which people, their characters and their episodes, their words and thoughts and actions and reactions, would reflect the conditions and the tendencies of a certain historical time—and suggest, at the same time, the potentialities of what lay before them. For example, the rise and fall of Anglomania in Europe, 1815–1955, and not only from its political and literary evidences. Or the fading of the Anglo-Saxon Eastern patriciandom in the United States: the fading of their strength and of their presence; of their convictions rather than of their optimism, out of evidences that are implicit rather than explicit, describing their reactions and their actions, of what they came to understand rather than what they knew, their sometime despair of life rather than their fear of death, the stiff bravery of their race still in their brittle bones but with the sense that the instinct of their courage had become solitary, it would no longer be national or communal. Edith Wharton once wrote about the society of Old New York more than a century ago that it was a bottle now empty but at the bottom of it there still remained a fine kind of lees, an essence of rarefied, and often unspoken, sentiments. I should not only describe the lees but its components and, of course, its devolution: the evaporation of the wine, a description in which, again, the *why* would be implicit in the *how*. Yes, somewhere I could write about a party, say, in one of the Philadelphia suburbs, of young handsome couples recognizable to me and therefore describable: people thinking, without much feeling, that they and their country were at the top of the world, drinking and dancing under the roofs of large trees, to the music that their kind liked, tunes such as "Dancing on the Ceiling" or "What's New?" without knowing that while their ears were attuned to the rhythm of that music, its essential harmonies were melancholy—this around the time, say, 1947, when Washington had become The Capital of the World and when someone like Dean

Acheson thought that he was Present at the Creation. For there had been a connection between these things—and well before what was going on in the Sixties in the lives of decent middle-aged people, when their sons and daughters chose to go barefoot and filled the inadequacy of their resistless freedom with drugs and an unceasing, battering, primitive music—and also of many other things besides. Here and there in some of my books I related and connected such materials, fragments of evidence and life whose connections were clear, at least to me, no matter how unusual and perhaps even startling their correlations were. But not enough for a book: a few coherent vignettes do not amount to a creation. History is a seamless web and not a collage. And a description of any portion of that web is neither the business of an arachnologist (*vide* a social scientist or a quantificationist historian), nor of a modernist painter (*vide* a "nonfiction" novelist) who cannot see, and therefore cannot paint, beyond a collage of colorful shapes. It requires a new, a stunning conjunction of an old-fashioned master draftsman and a visionary master painter.

I have now written about painting with words. Yet I am a writer, not a painter. I think that my travails in writing a book have more in common with the work of a sculptor than with that of a painter, the first draft especially corresponding to the heavy labor of someone striking and hammering and beating and carving something recognizable out of a large lump of stone, before the chiseling can begin: recognizable, that is, only to him at that stage. (My first drafts are not only crude; they are undecipherable for anyone except myself.) But because I chose to be a writer, not content with being not much more than a competent researcher and archivist, I must say something about the awesome handicap of having to write in English, which is not my native language.

This has been a handicap, not a dilemma, because this was my choice. In 1946 I left Hungary behind when Hungary was left behind the iron curtain. Whether I would leave now I doubt; but had I lived in my native country till now, I would surely be a different man. Since this book is written in English, for English-speaking readers, I will not say much about my relationship to my native language, except to state that I speak it accurately—at times with a few old-fashioned mannerisms and words that people on occasion notice when I visit my native country: when they remark that, this gives me pleasure. While I still *feel* Hungarian (an inadequate shorthand statement for something complex and important), during the last forty years I have come to think in English. Almost always I dream and count in English. (Counting in a language is significant. I was once told by a French police officer that when they are not sure about the nationality of a suspect, experienced detectives will attempt to listen to him when he is counting.) Because of my lack of practice I sometimes find it more difficult to write Magyar than English, and I am unwilling to speak Magyar in public without a prepared text. In 1983 the Historical Institute in Budapest invited me for a talk. I wrote my lecture with care, polishing it with greater concentration than if I had been asked to speak anywhere else in the world. Afterward the chairman said: "We haven't heard such language in this room for a long time." This compliment touched the depths of my soul.*

I wrote about my lifelong love affair with the English language earlier. I have been married to it now, and there can be no question of divorce, or even of a long separation. When I am away from an English-speaking country I begin to worry about the dangers of absence, of the unfaithfulness of the dear thing in my mind. It is a dear thing, like my wife—also, as Cyril Connolly once wrote, "Our language is a sulky and inconstant beauty and at any moment it is important to know what liberties she will permit" (again, like my present wife). But my marriage to English is a prosaic marriage,

---

*This first public speech of mine in my native city after thirty-seven years was a sentimental occasion. It also happened on the one hundredth birthday of my father; and in a district of the city that my father had loved, studied and once filmed with amateur dedication. It was a fine sunny morning; but my appearance was not sufficiently elegant. Having misplaced my glasses, I was dependent on the glasses borrowed from a friend, which in turn depended dejectedly from my nose.

meaning that it involves mostly prose, not verse—especially not free verse.* Yes, good prose, like a good prosaic marriage, may *contain* told and untold depths of poetry within it; but it does not *consist* of poetry. While I enjoy and, I think, comprehend modern and classical English and American prose as well as I enjoy and comprehend the prose of my native country, this is not true of poetry. I comprehend poetry, good and bad, in Magyar better than in English. I think that the reason for this is simple. It includes not only my education in Hungary but the fact that all genuine poetry is tribal, like a family joke.†

Such reflections have led me to wonder what would have become of me as a Magyar writer. I was overwhelmed by such sentiments in 1981 when I read Jean Dutourd's breathtakingly scintillant, witty, proud and supremely elegant speech as he took his chair at the Académie Française. I envy Jean for many things. How fortunate he is to write in his native language! As I read his prose in a language that, at best, is my third or fourth one, I knew how my fortune and my abilities were hopelessly (and I mean hopelessly) remote from his. He was able to summon his highest talent and produce a masterpiece of a traditional address in his living, shining native language, one of the finest addresses that must have been delivered in three hundred years under that cavernous dome on the banks of the Seine. I wrote him about this; and he answered with his usual brevity, generosity and wit. He soothed me with a phrase by Rivarol: "My country is the language in which I write." Yes, or rather, of course: my country is America now; but in Rivarol's

---

*There is, too, a fortunate conjunction. English and Magyar, no matter how different, have certain salutary tendencies in common. The rhythm, the grammar, the syntax, the very rhetoric of the Magyar language are very different from English; but both Magyar and English have the great virtue of directness. Magyar, like English, is a very descriptive and at times surprisingly onomatopoeic language. It is uncomfortable with anything abstract, and it eschews the passive tense, like English and unlike German.

†But even in prose I run across English sentences that make me fully aware of my foreignness. "His smile, he saw, would have been pleasant if it had ever got up into his eyes as well." I could not have written this.

French "my country" is *"ma patrie"*; and in spite of my American loyalties and my marriage to English my fatherland remains Hungary, after all is said.

Every careful writer possesses certain cherished examples of prose that stimulate his imagination: in my case, a historical rather than a literary imagination. I have a folder in which I occasionally stuff small slips of paper copied out after I have run across a passage that I find very good. That folder (it is, alas, not a thick one; it is disorderly, and desultorily kept), marked Fine Writing, contains a bunch of such slips. I read through them as I was preparing this chapter on my writing. Now I think I ought to reproduce some of them, for the sake of illustrating myself.

Here is a description that has the material smell of historical truths and is, at the same time, a wonderfully economical summary of complicated facts:

> The royal household was a gigantic nest of costly jobbery and purposeless profusion. It retained all "the cumbrous charges of a Gothic establishment," though all its usage and accommodation had "shrunk into the polished littleness of modern elegance." The outlay was enormous. The expenditure on the court tables only was a thing unfathomable. Waste was the rule in every branch of it. There was an office for the Great Wardrobe, another office of the Robes, a third of the Groom of the Stole. For these three useless offices there were three useless treasurers.
>
> (John Morley, *Burke*)

Here is a very different sample of prose, which is autobiographical. It is a rich evocation of a vanished decade—masterly, with its mixture of scherzo and adagio, because its author's style, probably unconsciously, breathes the atmosphere of an impressionism that was not merely a retrospectively regnant style but that is so suited to depictions of the 1890s:

Then came a summer term at Scoones, distracted and dislocated by many amusements. I went to the Derby that year and backed Persimmon; to the first performance of Mrs. Campbell's *Magda* the same night; I saw Duse at Drury Lane and Sarah Bernhardt at Daly's; I went to Ascot; I went to balls; I stayed at Panshanger; and at Wrest, at the end of the summer, where a constellation of beauty moved in muslin and straw hats and yellow roses on the lawns of gardens designed by Lenôtre, delicious with ripe peaches on old brick walls, with the smell of verbena and sweet geranium; and stately with large avenues, artificial lakes and white temples; and we bicycled in the warm night past ghostly cornfields by the light of a large full moon.

(Maurice Baring, *The Puppet Show of Memory*)

Here is Joseph Conrad, a foreigner who never learned to speak English faultlessly but who was not only a great master of English prose: these lines, to me, amount to a historical and pictorial—not epic or poetic—written apotheosis of an England, evoking, to me, England circa 1888 (though this passage comes from *The Nigger of the Narcissus,* published in 1898):

A week afterwards the *Narcissus* entered the chops of the Channel. . . . Under white wings she skimmed low over the blue sea like a great tired bird speeding to its nest. The clouds raced with her mastheads; they rose astern enormous and white, soared to the zenith, flew past, and falling down the wide curve of the sky, seemed to dash headlong into the sea—the clouds swifter than the ship, more free, but without a home. The coast, to welcome her, stepped out of space into the sunshine. The lofty headlands trod masterfully into the sea; the wide bays smiled in the light; the shadows of homeless clouds ran along the sunny plains, leaped over valleys, without a check darted up the hills, rolled down the slopes; and the sunshine pursued them with patches of running brightness. On the brows of dark cliffs white lighthouses shone in pillars of light. The Channel glittered like a blue mantle shot with gold and starred by the silver of the capping seas. The *Narcissus* rushed past the headlands and the bays. Outward-bound vessels crossed her track, lying over, and with their masts stripped for a slogging fight with the hard sou'wester. And, inshore, a string of smoking steamboats waddled, hugging the coast, like migrating and amphibious monsters, distrustful of the restless waves. . . .

At night the headlands retreated, the bays advanced into one unbroken line of gloom. The lights of the earth mingled with the lights of heaven; and above the tossing lanterns of a trawling fleet a great lighthouse shone steadily, like an enormous riding light burning above a vessel of fabulous dimensions. Below its steady glow, the coast, stretching away straight and black, resembled the high side of an indestructible craft riding motionless upon the immortal and unresting sea. The dark land lay alone in the midst of waters, like a mighty ship bestarred with vigilant lights—a ship carrying the burden of millions of lives—a ship freighted with dross and with jewels, with gold and with steel. She towered up immense and strong, guarding priceless traditions and untold suffering, sheltering glorious memories and base forgetfulness, ignoble virtues and splendid transgressions. A great ship! For ages had the ocean battered in vain her enduring sides; she was there when the world was vaster and darker, when the sea was great and mysterious, and ready to surrender the prize of fame to audacious men. A ship mother of fleets and nations! The great flagship of the race; stronger than the storms! and anchored in the open sea.

Here now the same period, though a different place, recalled with the spare romanticism hidden underneath the narrow shoulders of an austere (though not unambitious) Scotsman:

There was the bridge with the river starred with strange lights, the lit shipping at the Broomielaw, and odours which even at their worst spoke of the sea. (John Buchan about Glasgow, circa 1890, in *Pilgrim's Way*)

Jan Morris is not a historian; but her sense of a place and of a time, flowing from a historical imagination dependent on solid knowledge, suffuses her prose at times with images whose appearance is not only evocative but tangible:

> Victoria returned to her palace in the evening, exhausted but marvelously pleased, through the blackened buildings of her ancient capital, whose smoke swirled and hovered over the grey river, and whose gas-lamps flickered into tribute with the dusk. (About the Diamond Jubilee, 1897)

One more sophisticated appreciation of that decade:

> To appreciate the gulf between that period and now, one may recall that when the brilliant man-about-town Harry Cust, editing the "Pall Mall Gazette" in the 90's, wrote a leader on the downfall of the Casimir-Perier cabinet he gaily headlined it: "Perier Joué."
>
> (D. B. Wyndham Lewis, *English Wits*)

There is nothing fancy, or even artistic, in this description. But I can think of no better summary of the Dual Monarchy before 1914:

> Only those who knew what life was like in old Austria-Hungary can judge the country fairly. To sit in the Mirabell Gardens and look up at the castle of Salzburg, to saunter down the Stradone in Ragusa, to see the Goldmacherhäusl, the alchemist's cottage, gleaming on the Hradschin in Prague, to hear the tolling of the bells of the Stefansdom in Vienna, to admire the frowning castle in Budapest, the mosque in Mostar, the Mickiewicz memorial in Cracow, and the Dante memorial in Trient—is to realize that tradition and selfishness, geographical necessity and the play of chance, had collaborated here to build a structure supremely individual, of which three men so different in outlook as Palacky, Bismarck, and Disraeli remarked that if it did not exist, for the sake of European peace it would have had to be invented.
>
> (G. Reiners, *The Lamps Went Out Over Europe*)

Again 1914. From the diary of an ordinary Englishman. I do not think that even Sir Edward Grey's famous phrase of that night ("The lamps are going out all over Europe") strikes a note comparable to this singular, deep tone:

> *Rake. Night of 4 August, 1914.* Out in the garden of my house at 11 P.M., listening to what I imagined to be a War signal: a gun fired at Portsmouth, very faint in the distance, this whole thing a climax to my various private troubles. . . . [Train ride to London]. Wind, hot sun and coal dust, and over all the great shadow of the War.
>
> *(The Ordeal of Alfred M. Hale,* Paul Fussell, ed.)

Here is the frozen Petrograd of 1920, described by someone more sensitive (and perhaps even more knowledgeable) than political historians of that period:

> *(1920. Petrograd.)* That was the time to see the Palmyra of the North in the majestic misery that endowed it with a new beauty: its suddenly yawning squares, its distances subtly merging into haze; its main streets all silent after the noisy tumults of war and insurrection, forgetful of the familiar sounds of the time gone by when the city was still alive; its stations now without trains, its port without ships, the palaces along the quays all staring blindly; the Stock Exchange, on the other side of the river, again a temple, and there was the Smolny convent, all whirls and spirals, entablatures and rock work, Rastrelli's astonishing currant-and-cream cake, royally served on a vast platter of snow, which in the days of October had been the revolutionary headquarters. During the yellow thaw, at the end of 1920, there were few people to be met in the center of the city; these walked in the middle of the street, the houses on either side being riddled with bullets, revealing their nudity through crumbling plaster and the planks that served as a dressing for their wounded windows and plate glass. People passed under the triumphal

arch and then seemed to lose themselves, adrift in the great square; at the far side of it the Winter Palace, in that livid light in which the city slept, seemed merely its own shadow, haunted by the ghosts of those who had once dwelled in it. But far into the night, and into the fate there was no escaping, the city preserved her own spectral beauty, looking fairer than ever in the washed air of spring, untarnished by smoke from the now silent factories, her porticos and colonnades displaying once again the graces no longer enjoyed, no longer of this world.

(Wladimir Weidlé, *Russia: Absent and Present*)

(1920. Kolchak's Siberian army.) Men with axes were busy freeing the trains of their colleagues which, as always after a prolonged halt, were anchored to the permanent way by great stalactites of discoloured ice depending from lavatories and kitchens. The half-battalion of Japanese infantry who had arrived on Skipetrow's heels were enigmatically ensconced in a siding; it was given out that they had come to supervise the evacuation of their nationals.

(Peter Fleming, *Kolchak*. The question arises whether the second sentence is unintentionally funny.)

The evocative power of certain place-names: because such names are not only inseparable from their places but from a certain time:

(1923.) My mother's favourite sister had married a rich man. Aunt Mab was very beautiful but she also had special smells, smells of furs and Edwardian lure. Uncle Walter gave me a steam train and a watch for Christmas. Wherever we went with Aunt Mab there were presents and large houses and the appeal her wealth made for an imaginative child was irresistible. Bishopscourt, Loughananna, Rochestown, Marlay, the names of her houses (for she moved every six months) held a poetry for me . . .

(Cyril Connolly)

And to me Compton Wynyates sounds and spells more elegant than Choisy-le-Roi. . . .

I have included these samples of prose for two reasons. They will illustrate some of my own inspirations and aspirations: if *le style, c'est l'homme,* so is *le goût.* More important is my conviction that these excerpts are deeply historical. They are "material" that I like to use and that historians ought to use. By "use" I do not necessarily mean their inclusion or precise citation. What I mean is that they are wondrous instruments for a deeper and more satisfying comprehension of certain places and certain periods, which is exactly what historians must achieve. History is a descriptive business, not a defining one. This business of description versus definition is the essence of the difference between history and "science"; between words and numbers; between Pascal and Descartes; between two views of the world. Without description history cannot live in our minds because history, I repeat, is not only expressed but *thought* in words.

These samples, picked at random, are not necessarily samples of the best kind of historical-atmosphere descriptions that I know exist. I have not included anything from my favorite writer, the Magyar Krúdy. Nor are there American writers in the previous sample, even though I have many slips from them in that Fine Writing folder of mine. That file, as I said, is a desultorily kept and disorderly one. Yet I must still add some things from it, in order to illustrate the inspiration that certain kinds of writing give me. "Silence. The subdued hum of London was like the bourdon note of a distant organ." (William Gerhardie. The music of a period.) Somerville and Ross describe (in *The Real Charlotte*) the landing of the Irish Mail at Kingston: "The paddles dropped their blades more and more languidly into the water, then they ceased, and the vessel slid silently alongside the jetty, with the sentient ease of a living thing"—well, I have not seen a paddleboat coming in from the sea, but I have seen the Irish Sea when it was flat and calm and that is how it must have been. When Charlotte "had the unusual gift of thinking out in advance her line of conversation in an interview, and, which is even less usual, she had the power of keeping to it"—useful to keep in mind for describing an able diplomat.

So are some of the philosophical aphorisms tacked up above my desk. And so are the very histories of words—how, for example, *spiritual* in the Middle Ages meant the opposite of what it means now; how *melancholy* meant a bodily function four hundred years ago; how the word *anachronism* three hundred years ago did not exist; how *old-fashioned* was a pejorative adjective two centuries ago in England and less than a century ago in America, and how its reputation is now rising, while that of *modern* declines. When new words appear and endure, when old words disappear or change their meaning, this means that the thinking of a certain people at a certain time changed, which is what history is mostly about—for words are not the symbols of things; they are symbols of meanings.

Does this then mean that history is art, after all, *impur et complex?* No, there is a difference between an art and a form of thought. Yes, every novel is a historical novel; yes, "fact" and "fiction" overlap. But an evolution has occurred. Exactly a century ago Thomas Hardy wrote that "conscientious fiction alone it is which can excite a reflecting and abiding interest in the minds of thoughtful readers of mature age, who are weary of puerile inventions and famishing for accuracy; who consider that in representations of the world, the passions ought to be proportioned as in the world itself. This is the interest which was excited in the minds of the Athenians by their immortal tragedies, and in the minds of Londoners at the first performances of the finer plays of three hundred years ago." I am convinced that *conscientious history* is now replacing that desideratum which Hardy stated as "conscientious fiction." It is history "which can excite a reflecting and abiding interest in the minds of thoughtful readers of mature age" who are "weary" (and how weary we are) of "puerile inventions" while they are "famishing for accuracy"—and for reality and truth in representations of a world.

Jean Dutourd wrote in his *jeu d'esprit, Mary Watson:* "*écrire une histoire, c'est transformer un morceau de temps en un morceau d'éter-*

nité. " To transform a fragment of time into a fragment of eternity—easier said than done. But one must go a bit beyond art. *"En art, comme ailleurs, il faut vivre au-dessus du ses moyens"*—"In art, as elsewhere, one must live beyond one's means." Or Saki: "The art of public life consists to a great extent of knowing exactly where to stop and going a bit farther." Are these aphorisms applicable to history-writing? I know that in my writing and in my life I have had the old Magyar habit of living beyond my means. This includes my fondling of that dear and sulky and inconstant beauty, the English language. (There is a funny repartee in one of Waugh's books: "He probably speaks perfectly good English." "Oh yes . . . but we must not encourage him.")

I chose to write and teach, in that order, even though these priorities became eventually, and not necessarily disagreeably, confused. But chronologically my writing outlasts my teaching. I began to write before I became a teacher; I can foresee the time when I will have to give up my teaching; I can hardly imagine a time when I would no longer write. What I could not foresee, until lately, is the prospect of something somber. This is the end of the Age of the Book. I have known for a long time that the Modern Age, the great chapter of Western civilization that began about five hundred years ago, is passing. The invention of printing was one of its early features. It developed together with the rebirth of learning (which was a term long used in England for the Renaissance. More people in Western Europe knew how to read Greek and Latin in 1520 than in 1320). But it is only during the last twenty years or so that I have begun to see how the now rapidly declining habit of book reading is not a transitory or a superficial phenomenon. Living in the United States I have been well situated to observe this. I am now living among a people, teaching its young, whose imagination is no longer verbal but pictorial. Television and the movies have, of course, contributed to this. Yet this development preceded television. Its evidences are all around us. They involve more than habits. They involve the very functioning of people's minds. Yes: there are fewer book readers. But contrary to accepted ideas—that is, illusions—there were not many American book readers or French book readers (and book buyers) fifty or one hundred years ago, either. Their influence, however, could be considerable on occasion; it is not now. There is another difference. We are now in the increasing presence of people who don't read because they don't want to. They don't want to because they are unused to reading. There are fewer bookstores. Most of these are not really bookstores: they do not store books. They will not stock (or even order) books that are not currently mass-produced. Many American libraries are emptying, too, not yet of books but of people. I am afraid that sooner or later a diminishing number of their visitors will be followed by their diminishing acquisitions of books. Oddly—or perhaps not so oddly—this is happening when "education" has become truly universal, when four out of ten American high school students go on to college, that is, spending at least twenty years of their lives in schools; and at a time when the number of new books published is still increasing.

Again we face a phenomenon when numbers do not matter; or, rather, they matter in an inverse way. The inflation of education and the inflation of printed matter are part and parcel of the general phenomenon of inflation in the age of democracy, especially in the twentieth century. Whether it is money or books or degrees or sex, when there is more and more of something it is worth less and less. The Hungarian poet János Pilinszky wrote: "Just as masses of automobiles paralyze traffic, publishing masses of books impedes reading. When you are getting published, while no one reads you, this is not really publishing. I feel that we are moving back toward a kind of anonymity, somewhat like artisans in the Middle Ages who were great creative artists, having found their own spheres of art within their lives."

This somber perspective is not devoid of a silver lining. I believe that the necessarily small minority of men and women who take pleasure in books will find each other and draw closer together. There are already signs of such a development across the isolated (isolated from books and culture, that is) suburban wastelands of this great country. I also find it probable that the otherwise catastrophic technology that led to the deadly flood of external and impersonal "communications" at the expense of authentic and personal ones may have some interesting consequences. This may include the possibility that in the future writers might not only write but type, print, bind, pack and send out—that is, "publish"— their own books, depending on an existing network of their potential readers and buyers (and on the mails). This would mean a return to the early modern centuries when the printer and the publisher and the bookseller were the same person. It would lead to the breaking of the increasingly cumbrous and entangled chain of middlemen whereby writers and their readers are supposedly brought together but, in reality, more often kept apart. (It would also mean that writers, not publishers, would get most of the profits.) But I am a historian, not a prophet.

Like many contemporary authors I have a string of horror stories about publishers. I shall not dwell on them unduly. Because of the frantic pace of the publishing business, the editors assigned to five or six of my books left their firms between the delivery date of the manuscript and its publication. Another of my books was already printed and bound when its title had to be changed in a frenzy: the same firm had just published a textbook reader with my title, a fact of which my chief editor and his entire department were unaware. Six months after the publication of yet another book of mine the computer of the publishing house twinkled the information to bookstores that no such book existed on their lists. I mentioned earlier how an entire manuscript of mine was lost by the girlfriend of the editor. Despite insistent requests from publishers to submit my corrections for a second printing, sometimes the result was these corrections were left out of that printing, for "technical reasons." One day my telephone rang early in the morning: Tokyo was calling, inviting me to come to Japan, offering a substantial honorarium and the luxury of first-class airfare halfway across the globe. Not until I landed in Tokyo did I learn the reason for this invitation. One of my books had been translated and published in Japan four years before. I had had no information from its New York publishers about this. Such ludicrous happenings (in many cases leading not only to my financial loss but to that of the publishers) are, of course, not particular to the publishing industry. They are typical of the impersonality, of the standardization and of the consequent inefficiency of large corporations, with their computer-thinking (or lack of thinking) in our days. They are not very different from the troubles one might have with his credit-card account or with the Internal Revenue Service. They are the results of impersonality: of inattention, not of ill will.

In our times the fate of books—together with much else in the world of merchandise—is largely, though not entirely, predetermined, even before they are published. This is relatively new. The critic Richard Schickel recently wrote a telling passage about this: "Art," he wrote, "was a classically free market until recently. It was, indeed, one of the last such in our corporate economy. Now, however, with the intervention of marketing . . . it becomes a market organized as a series of self-fulfilling prophecies . . . your work is either a hit or a flop; there is no viable middle ground. And that status is decided beforehand in the marketing meetings, which may well precede production, and assuredly do precede distribution. The chance of the market reacting unpredictably, resisting the massive interventions of promotion and publicity, of consumers revolting against the prophecy that is really a fix, is minimal." This surely applies to the publishing of books. In the past the decision to publish a book was made by the editors; the sales manager was called in afterward. Now the sales manager is a principal in the decision whether to publish a book or not. Of course there are practical reasons for this. One is the large increase in the actual cost of matter: the paper. Another factor is the passing of an urban civilization in the age of suburbs: what matters is what books can be placed on the shelves of the book-supermarkets there. The size of the first printing and the promotion budget are what matter, since because of the decline of book readership and the passing of an urban civilization the reputation of a book can hardly expect to prosper by word of mouth. When Franklin and Emerson said that in this country all someone has to do is to build a better mousetrap they were mouthing nonsense. What he has to do is to *advert* people (often at the cost of frequent and incessant repetition) of the existence of his mousetrap. This is probably even more so in the book business. A manufacturer of an unusually good mousetrap may, after all, acquire a modest reputation among his neighbors in want of dead mice. The writer of an unusually good book does not have such a chance.

However, I have my consolations. The first of these is that I cannot do otherwise. Writing and teaching are my métiers. My writings are being published. They may disappear rapidly, they do not earn much money; but I do not think that the conditions of a writing career are in every way worse than they were in the past. They are surely different; but what Walter Scott wrote more than a hundred and fifty years ago is still apposite, at least to me: "Literature," he said, "is a good staff but a bad crutch." I am fortunate in not having to depend entirely on my writing income. My son, without the slightest pressure from his father, but inspired by his own great intelligence and talent, chose a similar career of teaching and writing. I am fortunate because my writing brought me exceptional friendships. Through my writing I have gained the correspondence and the confidence, and sometimes the close friendship, of great contemporaries: very different men and women, such as Dwight Macdonald, George Kennan, Jacques Barzun, Malcolm Muggeridge, Jean Dutourd, Owen Barfield, Dervla Murphy. To this random and incomplete list of great and honorable men and women I add the existence of people who will read what I write with the kind of acute and abiding interest that fills me with gratitude and does me honor. At times, in a wildly optimistic mood, I hope that I may gain the reputation of someone who is the opposite of a celebrity. A celebrity is famous for being well known. I prefer honor to fame; but I won't mind being famous for not being well known.

We would have more book readers and book buyers if the publishing and book-distributing people did a better job. At the same time they *would* do a better job if more people were interested in books. This reciprocal relationship between the providers of goods and their consumers does not prevail in the world of scholarship. There are more and more people attending schools at the same time when the standards of teaching have fallen. The deterioration of teaching in an age of democracy is, of course, especially deplorable; but this is a relatively new phenomenon, for the estimation of which we have, as yet, little historical perspective, since mass education is hardly more than a century old. The world of scholarship is a different matter. It is of less importance than people and, of course, many scholars believe. In the great ages of culture universities often did not count. Oxford and Cambridge mattered little during the Elizabethan Age; during the Golden Century of Spanish art and literature the universities of Spain were wretched, abysmal places; during the entire French Enlightenment the university of France hardly figured at all. Of course there were many private scholars and artists and scientists in those times, a tradition that has now almost entirely disappeared. Now there is practically no scholarship left outside universities and research institutes. One hundred years ago in England scholars smiled at the idea that a historian ought to have a doctorate. We may yet see a world where every "serious" poet would be required to have a Ph.D. In the long run this would not matter much either. The life and the culture of peoples would go on, more or less independent of their universities. Certified academics would keep on writing for other academics. Consequently their knowledge of the world, and the value of their productions, would be limited. That, too, is nothing new. It is not the unworldliness but the petty worldliness of scholars that such different men as Juvenal and Abelard and Rabelais and Montaigne and Samuel Johnson and Randall Jarrell have described, in different ages, laughing about it rather than deploring it.

What is new is the contemporary inflation of scholarship. There are fewer publishing houses and fewer bookstores than fifty years ago. There are many more professors with the highest professional degrees. In the past scholars knew of each other, but this is no longer so. Four hundred and seventy years ago, at the beginning of the Modern Age, Erasmus's books were read eagerly by the kings of England and France, by the Pope and by many other people of

various ranks, including a customs' collector on the Rhine at Basel
who was delighted to meet that author. Unlike Erasmus, Giambat-
tista Vico two centuries later was an unknown scholar, and not at
all a peripatetic one; yet soon after his first book appeared he received long letters and comments from scholars in France and
Germany. In our times many scholars flit around the world from
conference to conference; they and their books cross the ocean in
a few hours; yet professional scholars specializing in the same
"field" are often ignorant of the existence of colleagues living but
a few miles away. Fifteen years ago, introducing my Bibliographical
Remarks in *The Last European War,* I wrote: "Five hundred years
ago the Modern Age began with the sudden increase of all kinds of
communications, including printing. This age is now ending with
a breakdown of communications, because of their inflation. There
are public idiots who proclaim this flood of communications as the
'knowledge explosion.' " I think I must clarify this statement further. What is still advancing is the technology—the mass and the
speed—of communications. What we must understand is the difference between mechanical transmissions and authentic human
communications; between the speed of communications and the
slowness of the movement of ideas; between the availability of
communications from a distance (i.e., *tele* communications) and the
deteriorating receptivity of minds. The existence of this kind of
ignorance is undeniable, though its sources are complex. They
include the devolution of liberal democracies into bureaucracies. In
a democracy more and more people speak. In a bureaucratic society
fewer and fewer people listen. The result is the increasing institu-
tionalization of ignorance, with fateful consequences well beyond
the world of learning. As Christopher Dawson once wrote, "The
more ignorant men are, the more inevitable their fate."

The insistence, within the academies, of publication, the syndrome of "publish or perish" hardly affects this condition. The
reason for this is seldom acknowledged, though it is obvious. Scholars no longer read much, not even each other's books. They will
read *some* books; more often, articles; even more often, reviews; and
the latter only in certain publications. That reading reviews rather

than reading books is an intellectual shortcut is obvious; also, so much is being printed in so many places that only a few assiduous readers can keep up with it. Yet the sources of this practice (or malpractice) are more complicated than that. We are in the presence of a situation that has had few precedents in the past, surely not in the history of the West. This is that not only have common people lost the time and the inclination for reading; so have many academics. That people who don't read don't write is natural. What is unnatural is that we have now entire slews of professional experts who read little while they write much, for the sake of firming up their professional status. In this respect, too, we may see the devolution of democracy into bureaucracy; or from a largely contractual to an increasingly status-dominated society. It is the affiliation, not the quality of the work, of an academic that matters. It is thus that the estimation of scholarship tends to degenerate into something like a cultural anthropology.

I cannot comprehend why successful, recognized and celebrated writers have been downcast by a single example of adverse criticism. Harold Nicolson was deeply and lengthily depressed by Edmund Wilson's superficial criticism of his writings in *The New Yorker*. A poor review of one of their books would send such different authors as Virginia Woolf and Ernest Hemingway to their particular slough of despond, where they would wallow and thrash for some time. I cannot understand this. I admit that when, during an hour or so between my classes, I repair to the college library and look at some of the recent scholarly periodicals, I am sometimes overcome with furious rage when I see shoddy or dishonest stuff printed—and also, alas, when I find that my own work has been ignored by scholars who ought not have done that. I am compelled to admit such things in what is, after all, a kind of intellectual autobiography. Yet if my story is a story of failure, much of the reason for this has been myself. I chose my profession to be intellectual, which is not identical with the choice to be a professional intellectual. This was a mistake, because the world of professional intellectuals does not wish to know that. I am not slow-witted, but it took me perhaps thirty years to recognize—to recognize, and not merely to sense—that this distinction was fatal to the reputation of my works. The results have been obvious. I did not stoop. But I did not conquer. Many of my books remain and will remain unread by those to whom they have been directed: scholars and students and amateur readers of history. This includes academics who are supposed to be specialists in our "fields." Walter Rathenau was supposed to have said that there are no specialists, there are only vested interests.

I am compelled to illustrate this with what is perhaps the most abysmal experience in my scholarly life. *Historical Consciousness* is, I repeat, my most important work. During the thirteen years of its gestation and writing, interest in historical philosophy grew among American and English academics. One of the results of this was the publication of a new scholarly journal, with the somewhat ungainly title *History and Theory*, dedicated to the detailed discussion of philosophical problems of history. This journal failed to print a review of *Historical Consciousness*. I was not surprised by this, nor was I particularly distressed. But when, a few years after my book's publication, I was browsing in the college library and I ran across the latest issue of *History and Theory*, I was overwhelmed by a black cloud of rage. *History and Theory* had published an entire thick issue, a *Beiheft*, consisting of an extensive bibliography without equal. It listed *everything* that had been published in every retrievable language, relating to topics, themes and problems of historical philosophy, during the four years 1965 to 1969, when my book, too, had been published. This list of more than one hundred pages, included hundreds of works not only in English but, on occasion, in Bulgarian. Its entries listed not only books but articles; not only articles but also reviews; not only reviews but even reviews of reviews. It did not list the book *Historical Consciousness*. I sent a short angry letter to the editors, "to assure you," I wrote, "that by having tried to render my work into an Unbook you have not succeeded in making me an Unperson."

I am asking my readers to stop for a moment to consider what this means. For once, I believe, this has little to do with vanity. When a book is omitted from a bibliography, and from possibly the most complete bibliography of a limited subject, this means that future students of this subject will be, naturally and excusably, unaware of its very existence. Such practices exist in the Soviet Union, for political reasons. But this kind of thing happened, and is happening, in the United States. I have been thinking about this for some time. The omission from a bibliography, in that case, was not the result of malevolence or of conspiracy. I am not important enough for that. But my book (like some of my other ones) was probably uncategorizable. It did not fit. And thereby lies an ominous lesson for the future. My purpose in detailing this episode is not to draw attention to my misfortunes, which, like all human misfortunes, are at least partially the result of my own making. It is to draw attention to what can happen, indeed, of what is already happening, to books during The Knowledge Explosion. Let me insist again that I am interested in the pursuit of truth, not in that of justice. And the instruments and the instrumentators of the pollution of untruths that lie like a cloud cover over our world, a mental pollution whereof the physical pollution of the world is but a consequence (as indeed those candy wrappers and beer cans lie on the roadside because some people had thrown them there), include, alas, many Experts with Degrees from Institutes and Ministries of Truth. They are processing words, answering machines and computing very selective data. The year 1984 is now well behind us. Our world is not, as Orwell wrote it might have become, one of political totalitarianism. Nor is it reactionary (in *1984* Orwell wrote that science and technology would decay under totalitarianism: "science, in the old sense has almost ceased to exist. . . . the fields are cultivated by horse-ploughs . . ."). Just the opposite: Newspeak and Doublethink and untruth are "scientific" and "progressive." They are instruments of a new bureaucratic kind of tyranny that Tocqueville had envisaged though Orwell did not. Their main instrument is the computer, which is not a robot, since it is "programmed" by men. Whatever does not fit in it will remain unrecorded for posterity. It reduces life to a system. A system, by its very definition, is exclusionary. Whatever is not part of it must be discarded, forgotten, destroyed. It was not a historian but a computer scientist, J.

Weizenbaum, who wrote (in *Computer Power and Human Reason*, 1976) that the computer "has begun to be an instrument for the destruction of history. For when society legitimates only those 'data' that are in one 'standard format' and that 'can easily be told to the machine,' then history, memory itself is annihilated. *The New York Times* has already begun to build a 'data bank' of current events . . . how long will it be before what counts as fact is determined by the system, before all knowledge, all memory, is simply declared illegitimate? Soon a supersystem will be built, based on *The New York Times*'s data bank (or one very like it), from which the 'historians' will make inferences about what 'really happened,' about who is connected to whom, and about the 'real' logic of events. There are many people who see nothing wrong in this."*

The measuring and ordering of time is a human invention. But, as St. Augustine said, it is impossible for us to imagine what happened before God created time. In any event, there is another time than clock time—which may be a consolation even for those who do not believe that there is another world than this. Thus every one of us—a father, a mother, a lover, a scholar, an artist, a writer—may take some comfort from hoping, and knowing, that his efforts might be recognized and perhaps even appreciated after he will be gone. This is a thin diet for the minds of most of us, and not much sustenance for our daily lives, but there it is. For a writer, an artist, a scholar it takes strength to find consolation in this kind of lonely and faraway prospect.† Because of what is happening in our world

---

*Simone Weil (1942): "The relation of the sign to the thing signified is being destroyed, the game of exchanges between signs is being multiplied of itself and for itself. And the increasing complication demands that there should be signs for signs. . . . As collective thought cannot exist as thought, it passes into things (signs, machines . . .). Hence the paradox: It is the thing which thinks, and the man who is reduced to the state of a thing." Bernanos (1946): "Between those who think that a civilization is a victory for man in the struggle against the determinism of things . . . and those who want to make of man a thing among things, there is no possible scheme of reconciliation."

†Diary, July 11, 1980: "Suddenly the thought comes to me: no work of art is ever *finished.* I am not only thinking of the fact that the pigment decays, etc. or that a cathedral must be forever cleaned and restored, or that it changes when a city

some of us may now be deprived of that, too. Yet this ultimate deprivation—ultimate, that is, for some people—does not overwhelm me. I think much about the future of those whom I love and whom I shall leave behind, and I am, perhaps deeply, concerned with the prospect of the human world: *avant moi le déluge?* I believe in the existence of another world than this. I believe in the immortality of the human soul. I am even inclined to believe in the immortality of human memory, in some form or another. Yet I am indifferent to the immortality of my writing. Perhaps I am not such a serious writer, after all.

---

grows up around it, etc. I am thinking of the condition that it is not separate from the rest of the universe, and from the human beings who will come into contact with it centuries after its creation."

But (1988): I am not certain that my writing is "art."

CHAPTER 8

Dwelling

J LIVE IN A STILL unfinished house. Sometimes I think that there exists now a silent race between what remains to be completed in and around this house and what remains of my life. Where and how I dwell means unusually much to my bourgeois self. I believe that the foundation of decent life is permanence of residence. A desire for permanence may explain many of the self-imposed circumscriptions of my life, including self-imposed professional handicaps. It is a mark of my character, amounting to loyalty at its best and to weakness at its worst. In the United States I sought not acculturation but permanence. I came to a country where after the Second World War some of the private freedoms inherited from the past still existed. They were a living inheritance, existing less in the changing society and institutions of the country than in the private preferences of some Americans.

For thirty-five years, I have been living in the same place, on the same property. For thirty years I lived in the same house, eighteen hundred feet from my present one. I wrote earlier about Chester County and myself circa 1949, a countryside that I found before I found my first wife. In some ways this was odd. In other ways it was not. I was born in a city; my upbringing was metropolitan and cosmopolitan. Yet I remember my sentimental longing for life in the country at an early age. There was this child's longing for the unvisited copses and spinneys and fields on the horizon, their odoriferous mystery and the silence in finding oneself under the great bell of a sky. (Charles Lamb wrote that "the solitude of childhood is not so much the mother of thought, as it is the feeder of love, and silence, and admiration." "I like solitude, I dislike loneliness," my wife Stephanie once said.) There was an ancient ancestral atmosphere in my days and nights in the Hungarian country, and not only because the very circumstances of life in the country houses of our relatives and friends were behind that of a modern Budapest. There was that contrast between the outer and the inner worlds, between the meadows and the vineyards outside and the interiority of the garden and the house, of the hot noondays and the chilly evenings, including the feel of the clean smell of the linens and the warm comforter in the room where I slept.

Many years later I recognized that, for some people, a fundamental shift of elective affinities had occurred. In the Dark Ages people abandoned the cities of the Roman Empire because they found that it was safer to live in the countryside than in the cities. Then came one thousand years when our great cities were built. Then, by the middle of the twentieth century, I was only one among many men and women, especially in America, who chose to live away from large cities even before the dreadful expenses and the threats to personal safety in these cities became endemic. For sensitive Americans—evident in the ubiquitous reminiscences of American writers and artists—life in an American small town around 1900 was dreadful for many reasons, including the absence of privacy. Two generations later the opposite was happening. Certain small towns began to attract some of them, fearful as they had become of their lives in a city such as New York, where the solid assets of privacy had degenerated into the fluid and desperate dangers of anonymity.

But this is an account of my life, not a lecture in history. Six or seven years after coming to America I found that I had become very lucky. I found a fine wife and an amazing father-in-law. His family estate was in the county and the countryside I loved. That family farm had been theirs for nearly two hundred and fifty years; one of their ancestors may have been one of the first white settlers in this part of the county. My father-in-law, prodded by his aging mistress, a Central European princess (a princess by marriage only, and a woman with a controversial reputation—to whom, however, I shall always be grateful: she had introduced me to my wife), had recently chosen to rebuild the farm, adding buildings and eventually restoring the old main Pennsylvania farmhouse of his ancestors. This was a splendid prospect, not to speak of their attendant promise of turning over one of the houses to my wife and me in the not too distant future. But then catastrophe struck. Two years after our wedding my wife's father died suddenly of a massive heart attack. We found his enormous, bloated body in his bedroom on a hot and horrible Saturday morning of the Fourth of July weekend. Within two weeks his enemies (there were many) found that he had not filed income tax returns (and his income was a large one) for some years. After two hundred and forty-two years Anderson Place had to be auctioned off by the government.

Yet we had our house. Not the house my father-in-law had planned to give us outright—something that my wife, in any event, would not have accepted because of the division of her loyalties between her parents—but another odd building, at the edge of the same property, not very fortunately situated on the side of the road. This was a one-room country schoolhouse that one of my wife's ancestors had donated to the township in 1840, with the old school bell still in the belfry but otherwise in ruins. A few years before our marriage, my wife's father had thought of rebuilding it for his brother, a retired rear admiral who was incapacitated by multiple sclerosis. Then his brother chose to stay in Washington. Except for a new roof the project was abandoned. The year after our wedding my wife and I contracted to rebuild it, along our own designs, dependent on our income. Her father would have paid for all of it; but she did not want that, partly because she knew his imperious addiction to building: this was to be our own. She was right: the fact that the mortgage was in our name enabled us, after much legal wrangling, to be free of the government's lien on whatever was left of her father's tax-indebted estate.

But we had so little money.* We had moved into the house a

---

*Wilde: "Land gives one position and prevents one from keeping it up."

month or so before her father died so suddenly. The house stood in a prairie of high weeds—indifferent, perhaps even hostile, somehow mocking the ideas of this ambitious foreign intruder. There were no steps, as yet, leading to the front door (or to the back one). We were bereft of a driveway, patio, terrace, garden, plantings, hedges, fences, grass—and of the equipment and the appurtenances and the help from the neighboring family estate on which we had counted. What we did have was the heating and plumbing of the house installed, plus some old cherrywood paneling out of an older house of my wife's family, two small Dutch brass chandeliers, and the shape and furniture for a Regency drawing room. Well this ought to illustrate my predilections. In the eighteenth century the ideal of the city house with a garden was *rus in urbe*, a small piece of the country in the midst of the city. But this was the mid-twentieth century. My predilections were the opposite: the English *urbs in ruri*—the comforts and some of the pleasantries of an urbane and perhaps even elegant civilized house in the midst of the country. At times I thought that I came close to achieving it.

But it took blood, toil, sweat and tears—and, worse, much time. I have a little sketch map somewhere on which I recorded the advancing clearing of the fields and the various additions to the house. It took me three years to reach the creek, not more than two hundred feet away. I crossed it by means of a bridge that I built on four long telephone poles abandoned by the local telephone company. The stone wall protecting us from the roadside, the deck, the pond, the bridge, the clearing of the other side of the creek, the first of our vegetable gardens, the brick of the garden terrace, the screened porch built atop the deck—I recall these years clearly, without having to resort to that sketch map: 1956 (deck), 1957 (wall, pond), 1958 (bridge), 1959 (terrace), 1963 (porch). Much of this I had to do myself (and I am, at best, only moderately capable with my hands) in the summers, when the humid near-Atlantic heat weighed on me like a beached and breathless whale. So often I sensed that this land was hostile and Indian. I am not speaking of the few Indian arrowheads I found when digging or plowing. What I knew was that the land tends to conquer the conqueror. The very soil had a

dark, acrid, hard, sometimes savage bitterness in it.* The southeastern Pennsylvania climate and flora were at times, and in some
instances, subtropical. The weeds and the rank grass sprang and
grew and coiled around my feet hellishly fast. The thickets beyond
the clearing, with their spiky, thorny vines and ferns, were impenetrable: nothing like this in the Old World. So often I knew that I
was an alien working in—and against—an alien land. Yet I had an
abiding affection for this part of Old America and for an Old
American past. So I was pioneering on, in ridiculous small ways.

We led an odd existence. People around us did not know (if they
cared at all) what to make of us, in that ungainly, ochre-colored
house on the roadside, on the edge of overgrown thickets. Yet that
house was like a jewel box from the inside, almost from the beginning. That contrast, from the beginning, gave me a deep kind of
satisfaction, perhaps especially after the hot summers were gone. I
would walk out in the late afternoon. The lights of the automobiles
on the road had died away. From the high, silent fields I could see
the lights of our house. This was a scene from another time. Yet this
was the second half of the twentieth century, close to the ending
of the Modern Age. At least for now, this was my house, my family,
my place in the New World. How often did I take a deep breath
of satisfaction from the contrast of chill and warmth, from that of
the snow-laden sleepy meadows and my knowledge of a fireplace
burning inside, of the acrid smell of ice and then the first scent of
woodsmoke coming from our chimney—after a fallow walk in the
fields with my gun and dog† seeing my house and its lemon-yellow

---

*Around us there had been murders, attempts at murder and dark suicides in
the past. The year before we bought the house a girl from Phoenixville had been
dragged to its abandoned outhouse, where her strangled body was found. The
murder was never solved.

†It must not be thought that I ever led, or aspired to lead, the life of a shootin'
and fishin' squire. Yet at times I have a longing for some of the outdoor climate
in the lives of those rich Canadians described, on occasion, by Robertson
Davies: those fathers taking their sons on their customary hunting trips in cold
gray days along Georgian Bay, with their autumnal Protestant luxuries of the
best guns and best whiskey and best tweeds, walking Anglo-Saxon masters of
a land, with the comfortable securities of their great wood-paneled houses in

windows on a cold morning or the western windows crimson with the fire of the setting sun in the late afternoon. The weeds were now dormant, the thickets were frozen and passive. This land still had to be conquered, ceaselessly, without letting go; but here in Pennsylvania this was not like so many other places in the United States. Unlike much of the American West, this was not a country still waiting to be made into a landscape.

Nor was it cemented over—at least, not yet. Only thirty-five miles from downtown Philadelphia it kept much of its rural character. Our township did not fit into a standard sociological or geographical category. A few years after we had come here the word *exurbanites* became current, invented by a New York journalist, defining people and places that were more than suburban but not rural. Well, we, too, were exurbanites, but only in the literal sense of that word: former city-dwellers.* True, the county and the township were filling up with people from Philadelphia who elected to live here while they worked in the city. The traffic grew, and so did the commerce at the Valley Forge Post Office and the commerce of cocktail parties before Christmas. We had a few fashionable people moving in around us. Many of the newer residents preferred to shop on the Main Line, half an hour away; they also preferred the Valley Forge mailing address. We tried—sometimes, alas, impractically—to depend on the stores of Phoenixville, a mere three

---

Ottawa or Westmount behind and ahead of them. Or for the lives of Old Charlestonians leaving their desks on a mild winter noon and going in their station wagons, for snipe or quail or odd waterfowl in those ever green fields and marshes, and coming back to beautiful wives, grinning cooks and oval dining rooms in the opalescent night of the South. (Once, about fifteen years ago, I was a guest at a week's party on a large estate in South Carolina. I shot two miserable coots.)

*To this I must add that thirty, even twenty years ago, when this part of Chester County was more rural than it is now, many more urban conveniences were available: milk, beer, *The New York Times* on Sunday mornings, groceries on occasion, were delivered to the house (and doctors would come, too, when needed). Now mail is the only thing delivered; I expect that will be gone soon too. Public transportation, including reasonable railroad connections with the cities, has dwindled, too.

miles away, a town made and marked by the broad black cut of the iron company* in the middle of it, a depressed small town already by 1960. There were a few attendant pleasures: the fire of the open-hearth shop spreading an orange glow across the cold and deserted Bridge Street on a winter evening; or the annual open house on the morning of Christmas Eve at the town butcher for the people picking up their turkeys or roasts, with a giant table set up in the middle of the store, heaped with cold meats and sandwich stuff, with shots of whiskey from under the table for those who wanted it—and why not? a heartwarming hour on cold, crispy mornings of the twenty-fourth of December. On another Christmas Eve, a snowy one, my son and I were going to the house of friends, farther out in the country: my wife was in the hospital, she had arranged for us to spend Christmas Eve with these friends. That Christmas, in 1960, it snowed heavily. Three miles from our destination my car got stuck. We clambered up a frozen field to a small house from which I hoped I could telephone our hosts to tell them that we would be a bit late. We were cold, having tried to push the car out of a drift. We knocked on the door. A gnarled old man peeked out and let us into a room that was full of the smell of the houses of the poor: the brown fug of cheap pipe tobacco, wet steam from the kitchen and the faint light on the dial of an ancient radio (none of the gray metallic flicker of television). The woman of the house wiped her hands on her apron and gave my little son a cup of warm soup. The old man came out to help push our car. We spun out of the ditch. It was a beautiful night, with the clean darkness speckled only by the falling snow, the pale light of the small house on the hillside and a solitary star.

Among my hundreds of memories something compels me to

---

*The iron company: the local name for the Phoenix Steel Co., established nearly a hundred and fifty years ago, from which the town got its name in 1849. In 1960 I took my small son to the Reading railroad station (now gone) to see a special excursion train pulled by one of the last giant Reading steam locomotives. We were standing next to a pile of coal. Another boy, perhaps ten years old, picked up one of the lumps of coal and asked his mother what it was. He had not seen coal before. Yet less than fifteen years before this was the matter on which most of Pennsylvania's prosperity and industry rested!

recount an autumn evening in 1962. That was an unhappy time for me, a time when the often undiagnosable pulmonary illness of my wife had befallen her for the fourth or fifth year, in some ways worse than before. She always read the local paper; in it she had run across an advertisement for a kitten in Royersford. We had our dog, but our cat had died some months before. I bundled up my wife and started the car for a few minutes to warm up the heater. We drove out into the darkening evening with my six-year-old son in the back. Royersford, like Phoenixville and Spring City and many other northern Chester County and western Montgomery County towns along the Schuylkill, was something of a forgotten place, inhabited mostly by working people. On Main Street the few pathetic Thanksgiving decorations were strung up between the modern inhuman magnesium light poles, swaying in the damp wind. We found the address: not in a newer "development" but an American-Victorian house on a side street, with its fret-worked hardwood porch, two long oval windows at the main door, like twin cheval glasses whose sparkle had died many years before, and an ungainly old ceiling fixture casting an inadequate light on the parlor. The two old women of the house showed us the kitten. Before entrusting her to us they were vetting us, in their way: would she have a good home? Eventually we were all smiles; they liked us and we liked them.* During the drive home I was filled with an odd sense of contentment. I was thinking of the presences in that dark and ill-lit, simple and unpretentious Victorian house, less of its appurtenances than of the phrases and the sentiments of these two old American women. There was the fact—yes, a fact—that this existed even now, in 1962, in the year of the Cuban Missile Crisis, of Central Intelligence Agencies, Inter-Continental Ballistic Missiles, Students for a Democratic Society and *The New York Review of Books.* I was driving away from that dank old house, where I would not have chosen to live for a day. Yet I was not going from the past to the future, but from one past to another: to one that was our present,

---

*We instantly named the kitten Tillie: a natural. The women sent her a Christmas card.

suffused with the sense of a living past and not with the abstract fear of a future.

The next year—1963—many things brightened my life, including the apparent recovery of my wife. We designed and had built our screened porch, an odd eyrie above the terrace, and the source of many summer pleasures for twenty years. In 1964 we left for ten months in France, where I taught at the University of Toulouse. We returned with thirty-one separate pieces of luggage, including many things we had bought for the house. When we drove homeward from the New York docks I felt something new after we turned off the New Jersey Turnpike to the bridge leading to Pennsylvania: perhaps for the first time after eighteen years in this country I knew that I was coming home.

By that time we had lived in that house for ten years. It had become near-perfect for me. I somehow felt that I had tamed it: that the old house, with its thick, uneven walls, was no longer indifferent or perhaps even hostile: it was becoming used to me. This reference to a reciprocity is not a fancy figure of speech: I am convinced of our participant relationship to everything around us.* So, among

*This post-Cartesian conviction of our human participation in the universe is a main theme of *Historical Consciousness;* but I must now recount an experience—mental and spiritual—that came to me on a December evening in 1963 when my wife and I were driving home from a wedding in Lancaster. She had had too much champagne; she was dozing next to me. I was driving east in the early winter evening, on the south side of a ridge, between sleeping fields, under a benevolent dark and quiet heaven. I do not remember whether that sky was starry or not. What I remember is a sudden mental realization of my conscious participation in the universe; and the knowledge of my gratitude to God for this. This is the knowledge that the mystery *and* the reality of our lives consist in the understanding that we are coming from somewhere and that we are going somewhere, and that between these two mysterious phases God allows us to live and to know that we live while we live. Out of what is darkness to our imperfect minds, for sixty or seventy or eighty years we are living in the light, in the open. This earthly existence is God's greatest gift to us, because during our conscious lives we are not only passive particles of the universe but a knowing and living part of it, through our consciousness among other matters, which allows us to understand our participation in it.

other matters, was my relationship with the acres of my backyard. I had conquered that stony, muddy soil, those bushes and thickets and weeds; they had submitted to me, though still *contre coeur*. My relationship to them, unlike with the house, was that of master and servant because I had to keep imposing my work and will on them, lest they sense my lassitude and break out in an unruly, spiky, savage reconquest. But these were the burdens and duties of a normal human life, breaking through the dumb determinism of things. What worried me was something else: the dangers of a human jungle coming closer, propelled by human beliefs in an inhuman determinism. The cement trucks were coming closer because people believed that Progress was inevitable, that evolution was determined. Again a reversal had occurred. One hundred years ago our ancestors, whether in rural Hungary or in rural Pennsylvania, hoped that the railroad or the telegraph or the stagecoach line would come close to where they were living, the sooner the better. In our time the news that a new highway or a new pipeline or a new shopping mall was coming close put fear and loathing in our minds and hearts. This was not the snobbery of newfangled landowners or of countrified solipsists, with their selfish addiction to exclusiveness. We knew, from experience, that so often Construction had come to mean Destruction: not the development but the constriction of accustomed ways of life. Some of us knew, too, that the democratic pretenses of the planners and the contractors were lies from beginning to end. They claimed that they had to provide housing for people who, like well-to-do people not so long ago, wanted and were now entitled to their houses and land in the suburbs. Yet by the 1960s the very pattern of Development belied this. Less than ten miles to the east of us the construction of a gigantic shopping mall began. In 1960 King of Prussia was a simple crossroads with half a dozen buildings and stores; by 1970 it was a gigantic moonscape with skyscrapers of stores and hotels. We were, as yet, separated from it by the green barrier of Valley Forge Park; but I watched its development angrily. The King of Prussia circus maximus (first a "mall," then a "Plaza," then a "Court," eventually merging in what is allegedly the largest shopping mall in the East or, perhaps, on the globe) had nothing to do with the needs of people. To the contrary: the stores and the highways came first and the people came later. It was not built because of the people: people would come because it had been built. When the department stores and the marts and the space laboratories and the office buildings and the eateries and the theatres and the apartment hotels and the health clubs and the sports arenas and the convention centers had been erected* they attracted tens of thousands of employees from elsewhere in the Philadelphia city and region, for whom the booming realty firms were eager to promote developments and housing.

Driving to work on the dreadful Schuylkill Expressway, by 1968 I saw something that took the planners fifteen more years to recognize: at eight-thirty in the morning there were more people going to work from the city to the suburbs than from the suburbs to the city. So much for theories of Urbanization. The Experts, as usual, were wrong: wrong not only in their purposes but in the very statistical projections of their planning. Halfway to 1984 we had become threatened not by totalitarian dictators but by a totalitarian democracy where people might be helpless before the packaged regulations and dictates of planners, bureaucrats, administrators and speculators. The danger was no longer what conservatives for two hundred years had feared: not the tyranny of the majority but all kinds of accumulating tyrannies perpetrated by "hard" minorities imposing their ways on "soft" majorities.

But the question remained, and remains: who were (and who are) "the people"? Who were the majority? and the minority? And thereby hangs a tale—the not entirely unhappy tale of a small subchapter in my life. It involves my only involvement in politics: in small-scale local politics, affecting my neighbors and me. I was European and reactionary enough to be pessimistic and skeptical— skeptical, rather than cynical—about democratic politics, including local politics, because of their tendency to corruption. And indeed the supervisors of our township (at least two of the three among

*When the first department store (Wanamaker's) was opened in King of Prussia a state senator (later United States Senator) announced that this represented a Victory Over Communism.

them) had declared that Progress ought to be followed and not resisted; that the time for scientific planning in our rural township had come; that this was as desirable as it was inevitable. One evening in 1966 my wife—unlike myself, American-born, with a respect for democracy bred in her bones—came home dejected from the township supervisors' meeting. The handwriting was on the wall. The motion had been made, and carried, to put a proposal for a referendum on the November ballot, to change the name of our township from Schuylkill to Valley Forge Township. It would improve our image, the supervisors said. A public relations man who was often vocal in civic affairs would direct the campaign. It would bring prosperity to the township, tax monies pouring in through Research and Development. My wife and I knew what this meant. It was not only that we were traditionalists (after all, her ancestors were among the first settlers of this township, whose present name dated back to 1826). We knew that this was but the first step toward the absorption of our neighborhood by the maws of the suburban monster, the roaring circus maximus of King of Prussia.

She and I decided to fight against it: and we won. The supervisors and the Republican Party organization (a customary four-to-one majority in the township) had endorsed the name change. The public relations man arranged a big campaign, including an appearance on one of the big Philadelphia television stations, spending thousands of dollars. A few days before the voting I, a foreigner, debated him at the firehouse hall. I think that I was well received by the audience, but what decided the election was something more important. My wife and some of our friends went on the telephone. They called people they knew, asking them to call other people. The reactions of people were amazing. All kinds of people said that they were relieved to hear that there *was* an alternative. They had thought that there was none: that the name change, with all that it involved, was like so many other things—inevitable; but now they knew that it wasn't. We spent less than $100 on our campaign, which, in addition to the telephoning, consisted of sending out a sheet I wrote, in part detailing the history of the township, run off on the mimeograph machine of my college. We got 58 percent of the vote. Late at night the results were in. The phone woke me up. I leaned out of our bedroom window and pulled the rope of the schoolhouse bell, scratching my naked stomach on the sharp edge of the stormwindow frame. I was not running for any office, but next morning I was pleased to receive a congratulatory telegram of concession from the public relations executive, who left the township a few years later. But this was not what mattered. What mattered was that this experience confirmed my still budding trust in democracy—in a rooted and more-or-less authentic democracy. I have come to believe Burke: "The people must never be regarded as incurable."

Since that time we have gone from paper ballots to voting machines and then to computerized voting. Now we have a computer card and a kind of injection needle, called a "voting stylus," with complicated instructions: we must use this awl to stab a hole at certain numbers at certain points of a folding booklet. Moreover, for the first time in nearly two hundred years, the votes are not being counted by the local election judges. The cards are collected and driven to the county seat in a truck, where they are fed into a computer that then spits out the results in a millisecond. Then these are telephoned to the precincts. The people of the township have not been asked to approve this. As in so many fields of life, the middlemen had made the decision: the promoter and the salesmen of these computers, and the county commissioners (who get a hefty salary for administrative and promotional "work," often of little or no value). Their argument is efficiency. Yes, this process reduces the work of tallying the votes, but it is efficiency replacing responsible effort. Yes, in the past the older men and women who served as election judges had to count the paper ballots after the polls closed, sometimes till midnight. Yet there was something not only old-fashioned but honestly democratic about those November or May evenings when these people counted and checked the ballots, drinking coffee, talking and joking, while some of us were waiting for the results outside. And do we have adequate safeguards against the potential mismanagement of computerized sheets, when the tap of a single computer button might destroy, alter or erase these?

Now the tallying of our votes rests on nothing else but on our confidence in distant officials whom most of us do not know, and on our confidence in the indubitable accuracy of complicated machines about which, too, we know nothing.

That experience, in 1966, was the beginning of my small marginal involvement in local politics. I did not know this then. I was not running for any kind of office. But three years later I was asked to become a member of the township's planning commission, a civic duty that I have kept up for the last twenty years, serving as its chairman on occasion. Here my experiences have been mixed. I have not regretted this work. Most of my colleagues have been serious people, with what they saw as the best interests of the township in mind, almost without exception beyond their personal ambitions and private purposes, properly careful of subdivision proposals, no matter how attractively packaged by speculators. We have been able to reject or to postpone projects that would have changed the character of the township irrevocably. What helped us, too, for some time against the prevailing sociologically and politically fashionable tendency of the courts to break down zoning restrictions, was that, contrary to the Experts' projections, the population increase slowed down, whereby the arguments of Population Pressure proved hollow. From 1955 to 1970 the population of the township grew by as much as 40 percent; from 1970 to 1985 by less than 10.

But the bureaucracy of government kept growing without cease. In 1970 we had five employees, including one policeman; ten years later we had eight. In 1970 we had three supervisors and five planning commission members; twelve years later we had five supervisors and six commission members. The bulk of the zoning and subdivision ordinances became three or four times thicker in ten years. Dependent as we have become on consultants, we are even more dependent on the increasing regulations and bureaucratic procedures of the county and the state. Gradually, slowly, our self-government—in other words, what remains of our democratic independence and autonomy—dwindles and in some instances dies, unnoticed and unlamented. Some of these regulations could not be reasonably avoided. Others could have been. In any event, they consist mostly of verbal and numerical definitions. In order to be protected, in order to chart normal progress, Define Everything. One of the basic differences between Anglo-Saxon law and European Roman law was the reluctance of the former to rely on codifications and definitions. By now the legal, administrative and institutional life of the United States is tied up in a thick, matted web of Definitions. "Definitions," Dr. Johnson said, "are tricks for pedants."

My colleagues among the supervisors and the planning commission have been, with one exception, Republicans; and conservatives, not liberals. They professed no liking for Big Government. Yet some of them would accept the burgeoning bureaucratic procedures, with their dependence on outside and impersonal agencies, without thought. Some of them—the only ones with whom I might have had a few disagreements on the board—seemed to enjoy their cooperation and their actual participation with these outside agencies. Oddly (or not so oddly) they were the most orthodox of Republicans. All of this confirmed my conviction of the devolution of this country from a democracy into a bureaucracy of a new and overwhelming nature—of a country that even a generation ago was saddled with less bureaucracy than with what most European states had inherited long before their democratization.

For many reasons beyond the efficacy of our own efforts we have, by and large, prevailed. At least where I live, the landscape has not yet been destroyed or irrevocably transformed. The suburban monster has been crawling closer and closer, but its tentacles were grinding away on the other slopes of the rolling hills. But in the last few years came another change. The ephemeral prosperity of the Reagan era revived the ambitions of all kinds of developers, often beyond their former dreams of avarice. A gradual change affected the membership of our boards, too. Some of the older, principled, conservative and conservationist men retired from these often onerous duties after many years. To some others any questioning of Progress sounds strange and futile. They are unaccustomed to it.

Yet I believe that it is this question—what *is* progress?—that may be the deepest question dividing Americans now, in every field of life. The rethinking of "progress" has become our most important task, in Schuylkill Township as well as everywhere else on the globe, not only for the sake of the protection of our smallish interests but for those of entire human generations to come.

For twelve years I wrote in the small cherrywood-paneled library of my house. Not more than six by eight feet, it held perhaps one thousand books. I had to put up many bookshelves upstairs. Then, in 1967, we built a library wing on our house. Our mortgage was nearly paid off; I simply extended it. My friend Larry Drake was its architect. It was pleasant to plan it, and it turned out to be beautiful. I had a fair amount of noble paneling left; a fine wood carving brought back from a provincial shop in France; we bought two rugs, an Empire desk and a green velvet sofa for it. The library wing was a plain, Pennsylvania–red barn-like structure outside, and octagonal, paneled, 1820-elegant and cozy inside, in accord with my deep-seated inclination for the best period of high-bourgeois interiority: early-Biedermeier, late-Regency, mid-*Charles Dix*, no matter what I call it: in any case, post-Enlightenment and pre-Victorian. A light-washed, glass-walled corridor led to it, paved with black and white diamond tiles, with two antique bas-reliefs plastered into one wall and potted plants along the other: our "orangerie," as my stepson Charles would call it later. This library fulfilled my working needs for another seventeen years. I was proud of it.

But a year after the library was finished darkness came over our house. My wife fell ill again. Eleven years before, after the birth of our son, her recurrent and varied illnesses had begun. The doctors said that she would not have another child; but now, startlingly and unexpectedly, she was pregnant, at the age of forty-two. She bore the child elegantly; until the eighth month she hardly looked pregnant; her pregnancy was normal and easy. On the first night of October 1968, my son and I awoke to a loud crash. My wife had fallen down the staircase. She lay in a tumble at the bottom of it, her head on the marble floor, unconscious and moaning. We carried her to the living-room sofa. There she came to. She remembered nothing. She must have been sleepwalking. It was five in the morning. Our doctor friend rushed over. She had broken a rib but the child was not hurt. Twenty-four days later she gave birth to a little girl. Yet she never recovered completely. There were moments of great happiness with the baby, including a sharp moment that I remember when we drove with the baby to the doctor a week or so after she had come home from the hospital: she looked like a very young mother. But these were only moments. She had a serious bout of post-natal depression. Then she recovered; but she remained very frail and thin. A year later I convinced her that we ought to embark on a comfortable family vacation. I arranged for a villa in Jamaica, with domestic help. A strange node appeared on her neck. We had to cancel the trip. There was a biopsy, and an attendant X-ray of her chest. On July 7, 1970, at two o'clock in the afternoon, my telephone rang. It was our Greek-American doctor. *"Kakós,"* he said. There were two cancerous masses in her lungs. I tried everything. I forced her—after convincing her with great difficulty—to subject herself to drastic and concentrated treatments at Roswell Park Memorial Institute in Buffalo, under the personal guidance of a great and good friend, one of the best cancer specialists in the world. She returned home in early October, racked and emaciated by the radiations. For a fortnight she seemed to recover; she gained weight. Then she declined again. The ambulance people came to take her to the Phoenixville hospital. As she was carried out through the front door she said: "I won't come back to this house again." She didn't.

There was a strange discrepancy in our lives at that time. For one thing, she no longer loved this house. It was too much for her, she used to say; and she did not only mean its upkeep, its cleaning. Yet I thought that I must keep up this house, eventually alone, keeping it together for my family, my two children. This house was no longer unfriendly to me. It was not the house that had grown on me; I had grown on (or, rather, in) the house; I felt that its walls containing me now breathed a mysterious, reserved, silent sympathy. My domestic life was rent, badly cracked; yet my work went on perhaps more feverishly than before. A week before she died, a dark Sunday, my wife consented to have a priest come to her in the hospital. There, in her bed, she was received into the Catholic Church. When this news came to me, on this lonely black Sunday evening, I was seized with a wild, unexpressible joy. Yet I had not been a good Christian husband. I was praying, and hoping madly, that my wife might recover, that she might live. But I also hoped that she would die, that she would be relieved of her suffering. In the last hours of her life I failed her. The doctors and the nurses at the hospital, with exceptional kindness, allowed me to break the hospital rules and come to her at any hour of the day or night. I stayed with her several times, going back and forth between our house and the hospital. At three in the morning I slunk out, tiptoe-ing quietly out of her hospital room. I fled home. I fled from her. Yet I knew that she would have wanted me to stay. The telephone woke me up at seven-thirty. She was doing very badly, the nurse said. I hastened to dress and the phone rang again. She was dead.

That night, before she died, her upper lip had crept up; she looked rabbit-toothed, a skeletal Anglo-Saxon, reminiscent of the hateful caricatures that Nazi cartoonists had drawn of English people during the Second World War. But in death her face, though yellowed, was quiet and lovable, if not altogether happy and serene. This was nineteen years ago; and I am at times painfully stabbed by the knowledge that, with all of my strong memory, I remember fewer and fewer of the details of our eighteen years together. But I shall not forget her.

I shall not forget her. Nor shall I forget that concordance of somber recognitions I saw during the last years of her life. She was in the hospital with the newborn baby when Jacqueline Kennedy had chosen to marry Aristotle Onassis, and she was hardly back home when Richard Nixon was elected president of her country. She was not that much interested in politics; but she was more than disillusioned, she was shocked. I think that she felt somehow that her native country of decency and order was falling apart. Perhaps she thought that there was no longer a place for her kind. Perhaps she lost her will to live. In this she was not alone. So many of her friends, Philadelphia girls of her youth, were overwhelmed around that time by their sense of loneliness in a society whose conventions they still respected but of whose inclinations they were deeply uncertain. Some of them would hope for forgiveness and understanding in a world of whose existence they were unsure but which, in any event, was another world than this. There was a dark side to the Philadelphia moon around that time. I saw some of that darkness in the disturbed eyes of shy and lonely young women, dutiful daughters of old Philadelphia families, bereft of the rigid conventions of their parents because they knew in their bones that they no longer believed in them. Their breeding had given them courage; but what was their courage good for now, when there were so few convictions to hold on to? Their tragedies were neither suburban nor Gothic; if their young lives were not at all like those described with the crudeness of a John O'Hara, they were not like the mock suburban tragediennes of Updike or Cheever either. So many of them were drawn not to the forgetfulness of alcohol or to the destructive passions of adultery but toward death. The years 1968–70 were the ending of Anglo-Saxon America, and of many other things besides. The history of a democracy is difficult to write.

A week or so after my wife's funeral I had errands to do along the main avenue of Chestnut Hill. I passed a small gnarled man, a veritable homunculus, dwarfed by some kind of dreadful illness. I did not recognize him, yet something in his face was familiar. Then I went into a store whose owner my wife had liked and who was stunned by the news of her death; he told me that he was closing his store, moving away. I heard the faint tones of a piano from upstairs, slowly but finely played, Beethoven or Tchaikovsky. What was that? I asked. It was Mr. D., the owner said. He was the Italian owner of a furniture store where we once had a sofa made and where we had some of our furniture repaired: a jolly, bald, masculine figure, with a long-suffering motherly wife. He was very ill now, and he had taken to the piano. He was the dwarf whom I had seen a few minutes before on the street.

* * *

A few weeks after my wife had died my dear old friend Dwight Macdonald came down to visit me. When I opened the front door and he walked in, he said: "This house is empty." I knew that. For years thereafter I was atremble with sadness on dark evenings when I drove homeward from the nearest suburban station: I knew that I was coming home to a house half empty. This sadness was different, deeper and more painful than any other sadness I had known after the death of someone I loved. Yet I was lucky, too. I found a warm-hearted Irish housekeeper who took care of my little girl and my household, bridging the three and a half years between the loss of my first wife and my wedding to the second. I had the garage under the library rebuilt into an apartment for my son and eventually for one of my stepsons. We succeeded in stalling the prospect of a giant development, a Leisure Village across the road, promoted by the owner of that estate, a very rich and eminent Philadelphian whose addiction to social and civic responsibility was not quite sufficient to dampen his aspiration for swift and maximal profit. Fortunately, "swift" was the operative term: he sold it to another, younger millionaire, for a horse farm, for four times the price he had bought it sixteen years before, which was reasonable at the time. In 1973 I was asked to open my house for a tour of historical houses; among the hundred people who came through it were two elderly women who had taught in the house when it had been a school, half a century before. Next year my wife and I were married in the merry month of May, followed by a small reception for our friends and families on the brick terrace that I had built myself in an irregular manner, though not by design. It was a beautiful day.

My charming, pretty wife liked many things in the house. She didn't like it overall. We changed the kitchen, adding a sunny breakfast room. Her children had grown up; my son was away at college and then he moved away, to graduate school in Baltimore. The house, with its five bedrooms, was getting too big for us. It was too close to the road: twice a day the traffic swished by under our bedroom window, since people had discovered our country road for a shortcut. Moreover (something that women will understand) this house was not my wife's house, after all. There were my six overgrown acres behind our house, on the other side of the creek, where I had tried to flush pheasants years before. But I had to convince her first of all. That field was overgrown with brush; it was impenetrable. Less than thirty years before it had been tilled, from Anderson Place. In an alarmingly short time it reverted to wilderness—a very American phenomenon, that. In 1955 there was only one twisted and half-broken large oak at the north end of it. Now all kinds of trees, from saplings to flowering dogwoods and cedars, had seeded themselves; some of them had become eight or ten feet tall. I bought a shoulder-strapped hand-held gasoline-powered brush cutter, with an accessory blade. On a hot June day in 1979, starting early in the morning, I cut a narrow path, moving slowly northward, across the woods and the field. My arms were lacerated by the masses of small thorns; every few minutes I had to stop because my eyes were stinging with sweat; every half hour I had to stumble back to the bridge because I had to fill up the small motor with gasoline. But by the end of the day I had come through. I had reached the northernmost fence, overgrown and matted with a jungly mass of thick vines, stalks and weeds, eight or more feet high. Between them I could glimpse the sheet of still water ahead. My mind was made up. Two days later we drove to my son's wedding in Washington, in high spirits.

This was true pioneering work. I cajoled Stephanie to walk through the path with me. She was surprised by the many flowering trees. Yet she was not sure whether we should build on the lot closest to the water. Her mind was made up when a year later, in August 1981, I spent another exhausting but propitious day: with three young men, including one of my stepsons, with two brush cutters and two chain saws, we broke down the fence and went on to clear a patch to the edge of the water. The prospect was now before us: the water of the Pickering reservoir* stretching out, in

*The reservoir was built in 1928 when Pickering Creek was dammed up. Three hundred yards downstream from our house was the ford where the British army of General Howe crossed in September 1777, pursuing Washington on their

its shallow calmness, for a mile at least. I dragged my wife thereto. Yes, here we should site the new house; and so we did. I subdivided my eight acres, not without difficulty. I had a gravel drive built, with a culvert bridge across the creek, with considerable difficulty. We had the house built, with much difficulty. We designed it ourselves. We had found a picture of a house in England that we liked. In 1983 I contracted with a firm to build it. I was the general contractor and, on occasion, digger of the percolation test holes. The building manager of the firm was breezy and irresponsible; he was fired during the building; one of the plumbing contractors levanted off midway; the library, whose plans had been incomplete, was almost ruined; at my desperate SOS phone call my friend Larry Drake sped over from his house across the water and saved it at the last moment, pulling down and changing most of the beams of the interior framing.

We sold the old house. In August 1984 we moved into the new one. To my surprise I felt little sadness or remorse for leaving the old house behind—perhaps, as my son said, because I did not move far. It is a short walk away; I can still see it every day. There was another living connection through these years. My wife's old father, a lovable Southern gentleman and architect, had come to live with us. His presence—he was in his nineties, but his mind was bright and clear almost till the end—was another bridge of sentiments across something that, in other circumstances, could have been a chasm.

Our new house has good lines. Because of its traditional fenestration and good rooflines some people think that it is an old house; it is a New Old house, others say. It is still unfinished and not quite as cozy as was the old one—not yet. Except for the roar of the furnace in the winter it is full of quietude, standing in stillness fifteen hundred feet from the road; and it looks out on the water. In 1985 the magazine *Philadelphia* printed a feature "The Best Places To Live," with the answers of some people in and around Philadel-

---

way to Philadelphia. This may have been the westernmost point that the British had reached in the Middle Colonies.

phia about where and how they lived. "I live in a comfortable house," I wrote,

> with old furniture from my family; a well-stocked library and an incompletely stocked cellar. When I look out of my window, everything I see—water, forest and the angle of a single house between trees—looks how a certain part of this world looked more than 150 years ago. For more than 30 years this has been a source of mental, physical, aesthetic and patriotic comfort for me. Here my children were brought up, here my first wife died, here I married my second wife, here I do most of my work.
>
> This is not the wilderness, or upstate; we are less than 35 miles from downtown Philadelphia, a city that, with all of its short-comings, I love. Between us—in some places less than six miles from here—the tentacles of the suburban octopus are slouching ahead, pouring ceaseless cement, swarming with a hideous flow of cars and crowds shuffling in shopping malls, clicking computers, wanging videos, hiving in hotels, bombinating in bars, a compound of the mental (and sometimes the physical) climate of California and Siberia. That is Soviet America: the wave of the future as seen and promoted by Ronald Reagan, his friends and followers. I hope it doesn't get here before I'm gone.

That penultimate sentence was omitted by the editors. Less than two months after the publication of that issue Ronald Reagan descended, by helicopter, to new "Silicon Valley" five miles to our south, to congratulate its developers for their patriotic dedication to Hi-Tech Progress.

I dreamed, for many years, of having a farm, perhaps ten or fifteen miles to the west, with an old, whitewashed farmhouse at the tag end of a short driveway between pollarded trees, leading from a quiet country road to a house ample for our needs, with the Chester County smell of ripening apples, old rugs and a slight scent of lemon-oil polish, with a pantry loaded with homemade preserves: a true working farm, with a barn and a porch under the shade of large plane trees on summer evenings, one big weeping willow, and between a small orchard and woods the open view to rolling fields to the west. A small, wide-armed living: the life, of course, of a man rich enough to be comfortable; and able, on occasion, to drive off with his rosy wife in a smart automobile to the Philadelphia Orchestra on an autumn evening, or to the railroad station on a bright morning, en route to Asolo or Bussaco or even New York, leaving house and farm in the care of a good servant or two. I have not achieved that dream and I know now that I never will. I have achieved many other things that I wanted and perhaps not quite deserved: among them are my old American friends, whose affection for me and for my family is a source of inexhaustible comfort and whose company is a source of unexhausted pleasure. I am a writer and scholar and something of a philosopher; and essentially a surviving bourgeois. Twenty-five years ago I found a beautiful parchment of a seventeenth-century sonnet printed by the famous printing and publishing house of Plantin in Antwerp and written by Christophe Plantin, poet, printer and publisher all in one. It is framed on the wall next to me.

LE BONHEUR DE CE MONDE

Avoir une maison commode, propre & belle,
Un jardin tapissé d'espaliers odorans,
Des fruits, d'excellent vin, peu de train, peu d'enfans,
Posséder seul, sans bruit, une femme fidèle.

N'avoir dettes, amour, ni procès, ni querelle,
Ni de partage à faire avecque ses parens,
Se contenter de peu, n'espérer rien des Grands,
Régler tous ses desseins sur un juste modèle.

Vivre avecque franchise & sans ambition,
S'adonner sans scruple à la dévotion,
Domter ses passions, les rendre obéissantes.

Conserver l'esprit libre, & le jugement fort,
Dire son Chapelet en cultivant ses entes,
C'est attendre chez soi bien doucement la mort.*

This was written three hundred years ago. Another century later Dr. Johnson said: "To be happy at home is the end of all human endeavor." Perhaps this is not an eternal truth through the history of mankind; perhaps it belongs only to a now passing age. Still it accords fully with my aspirations and desires, even though I know that these aspirations were not sufficiently inspiring for an aristocratic nobleman or for a bohemian genius during the Modern Age—or for a radical Christian under the apocalyptic prospect of its passing.

*"A comfortable house, beautiful and proper. A garden adorned with sweet-smelling vines. Fruits, good wine, few servants, few children. Alone, without tumult, a faithful wife. Not to have debts, love affairs, lawsuits and quarrels. Nothing to divide with one's relatives. To be content with little, to expect nothing from the great. To govern one's designs along truthful lines. To live honestly and without ambitions. To give oneself without scruple to devotion. To rule one's passions, to make them obedient. To preserve a free mind and judgment strong. To say one's rosary and cultivate one's harvest. To await sweetly and softly the arrival of death."

CHAPTER 9

Confessions of an Original Sinner

J CAN REMEMBER THE origin of most of my books: the congealing, even before the crystallization, of my thoughts leading to the self-imposed task of writing a book about a certain theme. In this instance I can recall nothing. In my mind there is a blooming, buzzing confusion when I try to remember how the idea of this book—and even how the very writing of it—began. I cannot find the beginning of the skein. But there is a thread. That thread is my knowledge of how every kind of writing is, to some extent, and at some depth, autobiographical. So, at least on one level, this book is not so different from my other books. Perhaps it even ties them together—with a thin and fragile thread, to be sure.

The living thoughts of a man who knows that he is living during the end of an age. Perhaps this is the main theme of this book. Of the passing of the Modern Age I am certain. Yet I know, too, that some of its achievements will be more than venerated in retrospect. They will remain with us. Perhaps the most important of these is the interior development of historical consciousness. Five hundred years ago no one knew that the Middle Ages were passing; the very phrase, and the idea, of "Middle Ages" had not existed then. Sixteen hundred years ago people lamented the decline of Rome; but they did not know that they were living through the end of a great epoch that had begun fifteen hundred years before them in the shining Aegean mists. There rang the tremendous voice of St. Augustine.

But he spoke of something immensely larger than I do now: of time, rather than of history; and of the Kingdom of God, rather than of the earthly kingdoms: he, the Original Sinner. I am only an original sinner.

I am a person of the twentieth century, at the end of which I may no longer be among the living. At the beginning of this century a few European thinkers began to recognize that our civilization, too, is mortal. This had not occurred to Gibbon or to Voltaire. I was not aware of that either, until I read Spengler, around the age of seventeen. The *Untergang des Abendlandes* (whose precise English translation is more awesome than "Decline," it means "the Sinking" of the West) had a mixed impression on me. I knew that I was in the presence of a genius (a sense that I would not have ten years later, reading Toynbee). The brutal power of Spengler's imagination appealed to me: his suggestive capacity to make those astonishing connections of all kinds of matters or, rather, of symptoms: in sum, the achievement of a historian of cultures. Yet I found the Germanness of his categories, of his schematic tables, his rapid dedication to systematizing, a kind of German-idealistic determinism, repellent. I did not yet know that, as Nietzsche had said, "building systems is childishness"; but I somehow sensed it.

In any event, this was around 1940. I was in the center of Europe, impressed and affected by the great whirl of the German storm. I knew that what Hitler and National Socialism and all of their admirers and followers wanted and represented was the end of the Modern Age, and its replacement by something that was both very old and very new. I feared and hated Hitler and the Third Reich; but I also knew that they were an elemental force, not only something superficial, and propelled by something more than the fanatical energy of a madman. I have not changed my mind about this, and I wrote about my reactions to it briefly in the first chapter of this book. I loved and admired and longed for the better things of the past, especially of a past whose presence I could still see and hear and smell and sense, physically and mentally: that was how I became a reactionary. Toward the end of the war came the end of our world and the Russian invasion. That flood from the East was barbarian and primitive and anti-Western. The Communists, with their corroded "progressive" ideas, were wholly outdated, too, and not only because they were so abjectly dependent on the Russians. So amidst these disasters my mind was sustained by something that, for me, was an obvious historical and philosophical consolation. The Decline of the West had not come, after all—at least not in the short run, at least not in my lifetime. The West was way ahead of the East: America and Britain and Western Europe were way ahead, better than Russia and, of course, than Communism. The Soviet system was not the future, and it did not work. The future was the West, not the East. I was a reactionary, a Westerner and a bourgeois.

There was more to this. The future was the past. By this I do not mean "my" future alone, that I chose to be a historian. I chose to live in America, I wrote twenty years later, in my Postscript to *Historical Consciousness,* "because in many ways it represented the past, because it was a country where after two world wars many of the liberal decencies of the nineteenth century were still working, where personal freedoms, academic liberties, certain rights to privacy still existed." That many American intellectuals were still sympathetic to Marxism, that much of American thought depended on the categorical nonsense of economic determinism, that most Americans still had an unbroken faith in "Progress" was disturbing; but I thought that this did not matter much in the long run. I could not believe that the future of Western civilization was California.

I could not, and I did not want to. (Whether in this instance the wish was the father of the thought or the thought the father of the wish I cannot tell.) Now I am not so sure. For a long time I thought that the Western European and the English-speaking nations still had most of the makings of a long and prosperous future, for many reasons, the main one being that the appeal of Communism would diminish and disappear—which is what happened. What I did not know in 1947 but what I surely knew a few years later was that the main threat to the Western world no longer came from the Soviet Union but from divers populations of the Third World.

But I am writing about the passing of the Modern Age, not about the eventual passing of the global predominance of the United States; not about the barbarians outside the gates but about threatening presences inside. Sometime during the 1950s I began to recognize that the restoration of the bourgeois, the old-liberal, the conservative practices and standards and virtues would not happen. During my formative years, during the Second World War and for some time thereafter, I loved the West and wanted it to predominate, because it incarnated and represented many of these things. Was not its victory over the Third Reich essentially a restoration and, in many ways, a conservative one? Had not the United States and Britain helped to reinstate the kings and queens and the old governments of the liberated Western and Southern European nations after the war? And had not American democratic capitalism—that is, the granting of credit to the masses—spread many of its beneficial practices afterward? In my professional existence, too, I was not only an exile in America but someone who considered America not a refuge but the great repository and the preserver of many of the best things in Western civilization.

But I saw many disturbing appearances during the Fifties—well before the fake revolutionism of the Sixties. And between 1950 and 1970, the ages of twenty-six and forty-six, I came to recognize that my hopes about the continuation of Western civilization in its still present forms were illusory. My diary, January 12, 1970: "Since the Second World War I have been preaching the virtues of bourgeois civilization. . . . But perhaps I have been wrong in this. It is not only that the crisis of Western civilization has reached a phase in which a restoration is no longer possible; it is . . . that the bourgeois virtues will no longer do. . . ." (I added: "More important: my respect for the bourgeois virtues has not made me a better man. In this respect Berdyaev et al., no matter how wrong about what 'bourgeois' means, were right. One cannot be deeply bourgeois and deeply Christian at the same time. Thomas à Kempis knew it all, though he did not say it in these terms.")

The vast discrepancies between current ideas (and practices) and the belief in the immortality (and the very existence) of the human soul were no longer reparable. The awful thing about this schism—

probably true of all of the great schisms in the history of Christendom—is that it involves a deep, and often hardly visible, breach between Christians and Christians,* rather than between God-believers and convinced atheists. The greatest danger to mankind is represented not by Satan but by the Anti-Christ, the latter a most handsome and respectable virile male figure, parading and receiving the fearful adulation of masses of believers, since he *seems* to be an incarnation of the Good News in this world. During the dissolute and ugly 1960s I knew that whatever harm they were causing, the satanists, the atheists, the sexual fanaticists, the self-flaunting homosexuals, the radical feminists and the "revolutionaries" were not serious; in the long run they would not last. Earlier than that I had recognized the dreadful dangers of an unrestrained and shallow, nationalist and ideological credulity among Americans; and I knew that credulity is something quite different from faith. When I read the words of President Eisenhower in the 1950s: "Our government makes no sense unless it is founded on a deeply felt religious faith—and I don't care what it is"; or the words of Michael Novak, a principal and eloquent spokesman for American Christian democracy and capitalism, in the 1980s: "The American people are, by every test of fact, the most religious on this planet"; or those of Phyllis Schlafly, a heroine of American conservatives and an exemplary public Catholic woman: "God gave America the atom bomb," I hear not the voices of Satan but those of the Anti-Christ†; not expressions of materialism (of which Americans are so often wrongly accused) but of an evil spiritualism running rampant.

*And often between public and private Christians.
†Diary, October 16, 1981, Claremont, California. "I sense the potential presence of the Anti-Christ in California. This in spite of my reading Soloviev on the Anti-Christ and he is not very good, save for a few profundities: about people who are 'of too feeble a mind, too weak a faith, and too wretched a heart'—that is, professed Christians, to whom 'a straightforward, frank, in a word, *honest* opponent and denier of religious truths' is preferable. 'How greatly I am pleased when I see an open enemy of Christianity, in nearly every one of them I am inclined to see a future St. Paul, whilst in some of the zealots of Christianity there seem to be looming Judas, the traitor himself.' How true, how Californian, how Reaganesque."

Christopher Dawson once wrote about "the Cosmocrats of the Dark Aeon":

> There are forces of nature in the strict sense and there are higher forces of spiritual good and evil which we cannot measure. Human life is essentially a warfare against unknown powers—not merely against flesh and blood, which are themselves irrational enough, but against principalities and powers, against the "Cosmocrats of the Dark Aeon," to use St. Paul's strange and disturbing expression, powers which are more than rational and which make use of lower things, things below reason, in order to conquer and rule the world of man.

I was very young when I recognized that the great danger was Hitler, not only because of the terrible efficiency of German armed force but because National Socialism incarnated a half-truth about human nature, and was therefore more dangerous than Communism, which was hardly more than a lie. Now in America the fuglemen of the cosmocrats of the dark aeon were some who called themselves "conservatives"—propagating the promise of mechanical progress, of nuclear power, space stations, laser weapons, "public relations" and "Star Wars"; abandoning human reality, forsaking this earth, projecting human destiny into the dark vast emptiness of "space."* I was horrified by the puerilism and the brutality of the movie *Star Wars.* It fascinated people who were looking for miraculous scenes and powers outside this world; whose imagination was

---

*At the end of *Outgrowing Democracy: A History of the United States in the Twentieth Century* I wrote: "Outside the airport of Orlando, Florida, the road sign has two arrows. One points to Disney World, the other to the Kennedy Space Flight Center. Under the latter arrow are these words: THIS WAY TO REALITY. No: the way to reality lies within us, within and not outside the bounds of our mother earth: within our historical consciousness, which is nothing else but our consciousness, including the inexhaustible wisdom of the past. 'Life itself,' as the Canadian writer Robertson Davies put it, 'in which man moves from confident inexperience through the bitterness of experience, toward the rueful wisdom of self-knowledge'—at the end of the second American century the American task."

satisfied in watching a war between Good and Evil Empires fighting their sensational battles beyond this world: people refusing to grow old, and yet tired of being men and women of this world—this popular film about Cosmocrats. A few years later the prime prince of this world, the President of the United States, demonstrated—by his very words, and by his proposition of a fantastic space armament program—that his puerile imagination, too, was attracted to the realm of "Star Wars." In the *Star Wars* film there was no word of "God"; but there *was* a substitute for it, a "modern" religious word: "The Force." Men shooting out into space battles were blessed with the phrase: "The Force be with you." This (like "The Evil Empire") must have appealed to Ronald Reagan. In one of his speeches he said something like "We are the Force," or "The Force is with us." Make the Universe Safe for Democracy! Cosmocrat of the Dark Aeon!

"God gave America the atom bomb." No: the atom bomb was made in America with the help of Central European refugee scientists whose ideas of morality could not have been more different from those espoused by Mrs. Schlafly. Humility and a knowledge of sinfulness, these essential essences of a Christian belief have now become entirely absent in the pronouncements—and, presumably, in the minds—of American "conservative" Christians. And about the successful technicians of the Age of "Reason."

I have to attempt to say something now: a kind of summation of how the Modern Age is coming to its end.

Four or five hundred years ago, at the beginning of the Modern Age, Western European man broke through the determinism of the cosmos. He discovered the globe, and he invented the movements of the universe. At that beginning he knew that he had not done this entirely by himself. Kepler, for example, saw the hand of God in this. *Vir sapiens dominabit astris,* someone wrote thereafter—"the knowing man will dominate the stars." After the discovery of mechanical laws such as gravity, it was only a question of time before men would translate them into mechanical action. (Eventually they would be able to fly, defying gravity above the earth and later outside the earth and of its gravitational sphere.) By the eighteenth century, men in Western Europe took satisfaction in their powers of reasoning, in the condition that they no longer saw a necessity for a God in their achievements and in their perceptions of themselves. Then came the achievements of steam power, machines, medicine, biological science, etc., surpassing expectations of the past. Materialism and determinism were becoming the modes of thought (the latter even for those German neo-idealists who also thought in terms of "laws"—laws of "spirit" and not only of "matter"). Darwin's "discovery" that there was no essential difference between human beings and other living beings had been predictable at least a century before *The Origin of Species*. (Darwin, that plodding thinker, was predated by Buffon and De La Mettrie—*L'Homme Machine*, 1747.) The history of man was his evolution; evolution was material evolution; mind was a result of matter. Of course much of this was the result of man's increasing mastery of "nature," of things. In the end it came to the reduction of men and women into things, because of the universal acceptance of mechanical causality, because of the incredibly primitive belief that man's knowledge of things must be mechanically applied to man's knowledge of man, there being no other kind of knowledge worth pursuing or thinking about. All of this occurred at a time when liberal opinion was also concerned with the "dignity of man," propagating equality, freedom, democracy, the pursuit of justice and the myth of individualism, across the world. What a paradox! The pursuit of "freedom" at the very time when man has been taught that he is not free at all; he is governed by the dumb determinism of things. The increasingly senile Left in our times, including our leading Liberals and Scientists, would not, even now, liberate their minds from that determinism.

But the last word is not theirs. Some of us have come to recognize the end of the Cartesian-Newtonian universe, with its separation of object from subject, of observer from the observed, of man's mind from the rest of the world. For the first time in four hundred years we are beginning (but only beginning) to rethink the entire meaning of Progress. For the first time we have now an invention, the atom bomb, which most people wish had not been invented. Resigned and convinced as I have become about the passing of the Modern Age and the decline of the West, I remain not without hope. In these times of impersonality and sexual anarchy the oddest people discover that love—true and Christian love, meaning giving without taking—has become practical.* Closer to the surface there are many indications that much of what was good in the Modern Age will be treasured and preserved, and that these matters will serve as sources of inspiration for many people, because of the development of their historical consciousness. This is already very different from the beginning of the Modern Age, when the first modern thinkers of the Renaissance looked back not at the age then passing—which they rejected—but to an imaginary and exaggerated ideal world of Classical Antiquity. We are looking back at a more recent past, with which we are still connected; and at its "romantic" essence, which has become a part of our consciousness. We are beginning to recognize the other paradox: that it is our minds, not our machines, that break through the determinism of the

---

*Diary February 25, 1970, during the mental depression of my first wife: "A good talk with H., who is spiralling down in her depression, late in the evening. It does her some good, this kind of talking. So far as I go, it is very simple: whenever I truly concentrate on her troubles, my preoccupation with my troubles falls away: it becomes a very light burden, at worst a gray cloud behind this *viator eques,* and not an *atra cura.* This confirms my crystallizing conviction that in this world love has become *practical.* And a related thought. Since I believe that we are living through an important phase in the evolution of human consciousness (at least in the Western world, including the increasing intrusion of mind into the structure of material events—and the recognition thereof), the widespread depressions of so many people mean not only that we are spoiled. (To some extent it does.) It also means that, compared to our ancestors even one hundred years ago, our minds, in spite of their evident faults, malfunctions, shortcomings, have *not* become more coarse but more sensitive—indeed, dangerously so. Now in a cultural environment of growing primitivism and savagery this may be a good thing—though only in the long run."

Meanwhile, on another level, about an ephemeral condition (Diary, September 4, 1981): "The love that dares not speak its name is no longer homosexual—it is simple, courtly, old-fashioned love (probably as ridiculous and out of place in a singles' bar as in an old man's unexpected declaration of love to a prostitute)."

cosmos; and that people who are most ignorant of history are those who are most constrained by the past. The more we understand and know the past, the more free we are to depart from its repeatable patterns, to choose our way—the great, the profound difference between free will and determinism, between the reality of human history and the theories of evolution.

Above the visible surfaces I also know that while the end of the human world—which has now become at least a possibility because of the tremendous development of technology—may be much, much closer than Darwin et al. have thought, it is not yet. And that the presence of God now sustains us not so much *through* but *within* our hearts.

Man is born imperfect and stays imperfect. But *not* hopelessly so. Hope is one essence of his faith in a loving and forgiving God. This is how a reactionary can believe in progress—of a certain kind.

So living during the decline of the West—and being much aware of it—is not all that hopeless and terrible.

I have sometimes thought that I would have liked to have been born a century earlier in Hungary, an eldest son of jovial, prosperous, literate gentry, among my father's ancestors: in a northern Hungarian, yellow-stuccoed, Empire-style low country house, among meadows, orchards, forests, a vineyard, in the sight of a small river: free, comfortable, learned, humorous, in good health. This, of course, is all very foolish. "I would have liked to have been born a century earlier" merely means that I *could* have been happy then. "Could," not "would." In this respect I am not a reactionary. Clocks may be turned back—indeed, sometimes they *must* be—but lives cannot.* That man would not have been I. God has given us the gift of our existence, which is inevitably—inevitably, that is, to our limited eyes—also historical: we are here, on this earth, at a

---

*Diary, March 9, 1981: "What would happen if time could go backwards? ... All the pain and terror would be so much worse than the pleasures and joys, even if we would grow younger in the process, that is, not knowing of what was approaching. Also: the end of life, after months of terror, fear and colic pains, is surely worse than almost any other kind of death."

certain time and in a certain place. Had I lived a century earlier I could have been very unhappy. We all have several crosses to bear, and the heaviest of these crosses are, almost always, those that we carve and manufacture for ourselves. I know that "I" would have manufactured my crosses a century earlier: in plain Christian chant, that I would have been an unhappy sinner.

And here I come to the other question: how is it to live in an age of deteriorating Christianity? I am now moving from thoughts to beliefs, from ideas to religion, from credulity to faith. This is a difficult matter to write about and, in some ways, improper. So many people think that they bare their souls when they are only wearing their hearts on their sleeves. The first is as much a figure of speech as is the second. To sew your heart to your sleeve is not only impractical and messy*; it can be cheap and maudlin and often not honest at all.† I must repeat: this is not an autobiography but, rather, an auto-history. I shall attempt to write about this matter historically, not psychologically. Yes, the Christian churches, and the Roman Catholic Church, mine, are in deep trouble. But when were they not? It is a fateful—though sometimes fruitful—error to believe in an ideal past. At the beginning of the Modern Age the Renaissance thinkers made for themselves a wholly idealized picture of Antiquity which was wrong, yet which led to great achievements (consider only the original esthetic impetus of the Renaissance). Before the passing of the Modern Age there arose an idealized picture of the Middle Ages which, again, was fructiferous in many ways (consider only the great romantic writers and artists of the early nineteenth century). But this idealization of the Middle Ages—or even of the Victorian Age—is fairly wrong. When some of the most honest and intelligent men in the twentieth century incline to think (as Orwell had) that a very great, perhaps the greatest, scission occurred one or two centuries ago, when men

---

*Diary, May 22, 1970: "No one has ever written a diary that expresses his most intimate thoughts, because even if he were to do so (Amiel tried that), their proportion to his real existence cannot be reproduced."

†Bernanos, *Diary of a Country Priest:* "Chosen humility can be truly regal, but vanity run to seed is not a pretty sight . . ."

abandoned their belief in the immortality of the soul, I think that they are wrong. The immortality of the soul is a very deep matter of belief. Therefore we cannot really know *how* people believed in it, if they did at all. There are many people—and not only now— who do not know what they believe; and there are many people who do not really believe what they think they believe. I am writing about something more complicated than hypocrisy. The discrepancy between what people think they believe and what they really believe is hardly a matter for the historian to judge. (Nor is it a matter for the psychoanalyst, for that discrepancy is not one between the "conscious" and the "subconscious.") It belongs to God alone. What the historian may see and say is that the words and the actions of believers and of churchmen and of the Church in past centuries were not perfect. Their ambitions, envies, jealousies, their hatreds and passions, their adjustments of their behavior and of their thinking to circumstances were as human as ever—that is, sinful. (I know that I would prefer the company and the conversation of the once Bishop Talleyrand to that of Cardinal Spellman; but I do not know, and certainly will not say, which one was the better man.) That the respect for Christianity and its religious practice was greater in the past than it is now is true; that religion governed many of the acts of men and women is true; that many people knew much of the Bible and the Gospels while they do not know them now is true. That devolution is lamentable, stunning and sad. But true religion is always a matter of quality, not of quantity. There are fewer practicing Christians now. Yet we cannot say that the quality of their beliefs and, consequently, of their lives, is less Christian than those of their forebears. What we should regret is not the private abandonment of categorical beliefs in the immortality of the soul but the public abandonment of the recognition of the existence of the soul itself: a result of "modern" scientific thinking and of education. Yet a widespread belief in the existence of something like the soul continues to crop up, even more than during the proudly positivistic nineteenth century—sometimes even through the misconstrued categories of psychoanalysis.

But there is the near-absence of belief in original sin. Bernanos:

"Il est assurément plus grave, ou du moins beaucoup plus dangereux pour l'homme, de nier le péché originel que de nier Dieu"—"For men it is certainly more grave, or at least much more dangerous, to deny original sin than to deny God." Belief in original sin brought me back, around the age of twenty, to Catholicism in Hungary; and not only because of the inspiration for that recognition that I found among certain Catholic writers such as Bernanos, though these had contributed to it. During the war the behavior of the Church in Europe was only occasionally inspiring. Many of the clergy, laymen, Catholic spokesmen for Catholic organizations, etc., were nationalists first and Catholics second, by which I mean that they were seldom troubled by, or even aware of, contradictions between their religion and their nationalism when such contradictions existed—which may be the main problem of the Church in this century, when the strongest faith binding most people is their nationalism. Yet, after all was said, after all that happened, the record of the Church and that of believing Catholic men and women with deep (and old-fashioned) religious beliefs was often better than that of other people.* During that war, too, I saw how the moral range of human beings was immense—deeper, greater and wider than what the modern, liberal, scientific, deterministic categories were willing and able to see. Men, as Pascal said, were *both* beasts and angels, and not only in extreme situations.

Then I came to live in a country where Original Sin had become unthinkable. (The trouble with the unthinkable is that sometimes it must be thought about.) In 1945 Arthur Schlesinger, Jr.'s *The Age of Jackson* was an intellectual best-seller. I read it soon after I arrived in America. In it I found this sentence: "Men are neither beasts nor angels." There was a world of difference between that gray liberal egalitarianism and Pascal. When I set foot in the United States I was not newly born; I was not a New Man. I was a representative of the doctrine of original sin.

---

*A note for my Hungarian readers (if any): *Olvassák az öreg Moviszter dr. szavait Kosztolányi Édes Annájában.*

* * *

I must now say something about the thoughts of a European Catholic in America. In my Teaching chapter I wrote about the generosity with which a few older American Catholic scholars and the Sisters governing Chestnut Hill College received me soon after my arrival. Few other communities could have treated me with such kindness. In turn, I was not only thankful; I knew that I belonged to them in this country. I am not a joiner, and I have eschewed membership in most academic societies, but I did become a member of the American Catholic Historical Association. Many years later the membership elected me their president for the year 1977. No academic honor meant more to me. Many years before that I attended one of the annual conventions of the American Historical Association, which includes the meetings of its associated societies such as the ACHA. I remember that late December afternoon, as we gathered in one of the smaller convention banquet rooms of an inhuman giant hotel. I sensed the presence of honest friendships, a serious kind of camaraderie; I knew that my place was within that small community of Catholic scholars, rather than in those wide corridors and halls, buzzing with scurrying academics. Early in America I had recognized the truth of Peter Viereck's aphorism, that anti-Catholicism was the anti-Semitism of American (and, I may add, of British) intellectuals. I did not mind this. I was a member of a minority that may have been disdained, but it was not persecuted; and—perhaps unlike other people who are uncomfortably conscious of their minority status—I was not uncomfortable with that. I am a member (if that is the word), too, of St. Mary's Church, on the North Side of Phoenixville; I do not belong to the parish associations, and I do not participate in the standard envelope system.* Yet my relationship to some of the pastors has been

---

*In most American Catholic parishes the parishioners receive numbered envelopes in which they are expected to place their contributions, twice during each Sunday and on Holy Days of Obligation. Until recently many pastors chose to publish the amount contributed by each family each month in the

marked not only by respect but by real friendship.

At the same time there were inclinations of American Catholicism which disconcerted me. In this I differed from Christopher Dawson. Even before he came to occupy (briefly) the Stillman Chair at Harvard in the 1950s he saw himself as one of that band of "illustrious exiles . . . representatives of the higher culture [who] either lived in or looked to America, not only as a refuge, but a foundation where manuscripts would be preserved in the new Dark Ages." He wrote in 1959 that "in the days of Charles Péguy and Belloc and Chesterton my eyes were fixed on Europe and the European tradition. But to-day I have come to feel that it is in this country that the fate of Christendom will be decided. There is a great opportunity in America today that may never be repeated. That is why I am here." American Catholicism, Dawson wrote, is "a sleeping giant—or perhaps it is a giant that has not yet learned to speak." Well, I heard some of those burbling sounds and gurgling voices; and often I did not like what I heard. The problem, and the trouble, with American Catholicism was not that it was unawakened, still backward. To the contrary, it was strenuously trying to be forward: conforming to every day, to popular Americanism, in every way. How often during Mass have I been disconcerted when the priest begins his sermon with a joke, or with a popular and ephemeral jingle from a commercial or with a reference to some current and popular television show. Many Americans, including most Catholic intellectuals, too, thought (and still think) that the Church was too old-fashioned, too reactionary, too authoritarian. True, in some ways the rigidities of the American Catholic Church were survivals from older, perhaps mostly Irish, inclinations and practices. But in many more ways the inclinations and attitudes of many of the clergy were lamentably mundane, in pursuit of their goal to prove that being a regular Catholic was identical with being

---

parish bulletin. I was taken aback by this practice, while at the same time admiring the munificence of simple people, whose regular contributions of money were impressive.

a regular American.* My first wife, a Protestant, was sometimes disillusioned when she met American priests on social occasions, or even at times in our house. Their conversation was not necessarily shallow, but their preferred topics and jokes obviously wished to demonstrate that they were regular fellows, no different from other jocular American males. She had expected a better, perhaps deeper spirituality from them, as indeed had some of my American Protestant friends. Yet she came around early to see that, after everything was said, the Catholic view of human nature was both more spacious and deeper than the Protestant one; and she embraced the Church and the Church embraced her on her hospital bed, one week before she died.

I was impressed by the religiosity of American Catholics, in so many instances. The churches were full every Sunday; the respect of the Catholic population for the liturgy, for the clergy, for the Catholic institutions was unquestioned and solid. But when one of my colleagues, an exemplary Catholic, told me about the envelope system: "It's there for your income tax record," and when a priest, of whom I had inquired about a local weekend retreat house for laymen, said: "It's a good place to make contacts," I was disheartened. In the curriculum of the Catholic colleges as late as the 1950s an often excessive requirement was that of philosophy and religion courses whose contents were often both rigid and shallow, a fatal combination. The doctrines of Original Sin and Free Will were often underemphasized and even unmentioned. Meanwhile, confession and Communion, two of the most intimate sacraments of the Church, were administered and practiced in a way that, to me, was peculiar. During my difficult adolescence I learned how a good

*This American Catholic combination of rigidity and populism was an old one. Msgr. John Tracy Ellis (with whom I had not agreed when, in 1957, in a famous article he called for more Catholic "intellectuals"—not that I had agreed with his anti-intellectual critics) in 1982 recounted (in his *American Bishops*) what Archbishop Curley had said when he succeeded the sensitive, learned and, in some ways, sophisticated Cardinal Gibbons in the see of Baltimore. Curley thought that Gibbons had been infested with "liberalism," and announced at the same time that he himself had "not come to preach to the first families of Baltimore."

confessor could be a blessing. This is a private matter and I shall not describe my confessional habits either in the Old or in the New World. What I must mention is the relationship of confession to Communion. We had been taught that the taking of Communion (that is, according to the Catholic faith, the mysterious—and not merely "symbolic"—consumption of the body of Christ) is a most serious matter; that it must not happen except in a state of grace, that is, after confession, absolution and penance, in a state of mind and soul emptied of sin and filled with the wish and the resolve to resist its temptations. In the United States I was amazed to see masses of people lining up for Communion every Sunday; and I heard the exhortations of the clergy to the faithful to avail themselves of Communion as frequently as they could—or, presumably, wished. Of course it is not for me to make judgments about the state of grace in the souls of my coreligionists. But when I saw, year after year, how one hundred and forty-five (if not more) of the one hundred and fifty graduating senior girls of the college lined up for Communion during the baccalaureate Mass on their graduation day, many of them bleary-eyed after the bacchanalia of the graduation dance, when, for the first time, they had been permitted to stay out for all hours of the night with their fiancés and swains, I think that I might have had at least some reason for my doubts. By now, after Vatican II, the vital holy connection between confession and Communion has become observed even less; and I dare to say that I see in this a loss for the quality of belief.

Sometimes I was saddened to see among my students something that, to me, was their unquestioning belief in the identity of Catholicism and Americanism—indeed, their unquestioning subordination of the former to the latter. One day (in 1957, I think) I asked the students in one of my classes: "Are you an American who happens to be a Catholic, or are you a Catholic who happens to be an American?" They said the former.* But this was what they had

*This was one of the few instances when I asked my students about their faith. The other, ludicrous and memorable, instance was that of my Theological Tunafish Disputation. Until the 1960s the prohibition of meat-eating on Fridays was one of the most rigorously observed tenets among American Catholics.

been taught, of course. In the 1950s the American Catholic press, with few exceptions, propagated an ideological nationalism that was nothing if not extreme. After 1960 some of this ideological nationalism began to fade; yet its essential strain—the fear of being distinct from popular Americanism, from the American mainstream—continued to prevail. Out of this populist Americanism came all kinds of excrescences: a liturgical exhibition in Philadelphia named The Catholic Vistarama; bishops blessing motorcycles, footballs, basketballs; college basketball players crossing themselves before a foul shot; a photograph and a caption in the yearbook of a Catholic college (not ours): "On her way to the semi-final Mary Jane . . . stops at the Chapel, saying a reverent 'Hello' to Jesus." By 1970 I was saddened to see some of the same priests and nuns who had been partisans of Joe McCarthy in the 1950s adopting many of the superficial and silly slogans of "Liberation Theology" and "ecumenicism." In 1910 Péguy said that "it will never be known what acts of cowardice have been motivated by the fear of not looking sufficiently progressive." That was an affliction among the clergy hardly less than among the laity—at times even more so.

The corrosive element in that fear was insecurity. "The family that prays together stays together"—in the 1950s the diocesan paper printed this unexceptionable phrase as a header in every issue; but isn't the converse of that even more true? After my friend Father Smith had died we had an unfortunate pastor for a few years. Soon after he came, the wrought-iron stand with its flickering candles, where one could stop before or after Mass, to pray and light a candle for a suffering relative or friend, disappeared. When I inquired

---

Sometime in the 1950s a company began to produce hot dogs on Fridays that looked and tasted like hot dogs, though they were made of tunafish. I asked my students which, to them, was the proper thing to eat on Fridays (these meat-tasting tunafish hot dogs were being served in the college dining room): to enjoy a frankfurter that was made of tunafish but tasted like beef, or to consume one that contained meat but tasted like tunafish. Most opted for the former. They had been told, after all, that it consisted of non-meat. That was what mattered; that was the scientific reality. It did not occur to them that the purpose of Friday abstinence was the sacrifice of giving up the pleasure of tasting meat for the day.

about this I was told that the reason for its removal was the fire insurance problem. One Christmas Eve I was heartened by the wish of one of my older friends, an Episcopalian, to accompany my daughter and me to midnight Mass. A thin expanse of snow lay on the grounds, and St. Mary's Church glowed at the end of the silent churchyard. We had come early, aware as I was of the crowd of people at midnight Mass; but as we came to the doors a good twenty minutes before midnight, the pastor and his grim lay helpers closed them in our faces. "I have to be careful about the insurance," he announced. "There are too many inside." I thought of an innkeeper two thousand years ago, turning Mary and her child out of the inn because of the policy of the National Insurance Company of Palestine, Inc., Ltd. What my old friend thought I do not know. On another gloomy Sunday this pastor announced that instead of his sermon he would read the financial statement of the parish. (This was one of the few occasions of my life when I walked out of a church demonstrably, during Mass.) On another occasion he announced that his sermon would be short, "so that you may get home before the Phillies' play-off game." On yet another occasion he ran an advertisement in the local newspaper about a Miraculous Medal Novena. "Every Tuesday Evening, 7:30 p.m. Prayers of the Novena, Sermon, Benediction, Veneration of the Relics, Confessions." The last line read: "Devotion To Last Not More Than One Half-Hour."* Yet this priest said repeatedly that he was "an old-

---

*An advertisement in a national magazine in 1957, by a religious order, calling for vocations: "Do You Want To Become A Priest? Duties Are Few . . ." Twenty-eight years later an article in *The New York Times*, March 8, 1985: "Priests Gather to Ponder Their Dwindling Ranks." "Virtually all of the 615 active Roman Catholic priests in Brooklyn and Queens locked up their churches yesterday and gathered to talk about what their Bishop called a major crisis—the rapidly declining number of priests available to serve the 1.3 million Catholics in the diocese." A Jesuit "theologian in-residence" at Georgetown University said to them: "When I'm saying mass, people should be able to say, 'Hey, he's happy. He believes that Jesus is alive and well.' " Another priest: "If there was optional celibacy, more men would be attracted to the priesthood in the United States. . . ." Pondering their dwindling ranks while pandering to the world . . . It did not seem to have occurred to these churchmen either in 1957 or in 1985 that their ranks have been dwindling, too, *because* "duties are few."

fashioned priest and pastor." One Sunday we found postcards in the pews, sent out by the then Archbishop of Philadelphia. "At their November meeting the U.S. Bishops will vote whether to retain the traditional dates and obligations of the Holy Days." The laity was requested to vote—vote!—their *preference.* "Please check one of the following. (A) Retain the Holy Days of Obligation as they are. (B) Transfer the celebration of the Holy Days of Obligation (except Christmas) to the nearest Sunday. (C) Suppress the precept for Mass for Holy Days of Obligation (except Christmas)." I thought that they might have included (D) "Suppress any Holy Day of Obligation when it falls on the day of the Super Bowl." I thought of the absurdity of Christ, or of a saint, taking a popularity poll. I thought that if this was the Democratization of the Church, and the Participation of the Laity, then the hell with it. A few months later, in January 1981, the Philadelphia television news showed a nun in

---

In 1972 Garry Wills wrote a book with the title *Bare Ruined Choirs.* Reviewing (and emphatically criticizing) it in *Triumph* (a now-defunct Catholic publication), I reproduced an advertisement that ran in a box for weeks in the Philadelphia newspapers at that time:

A MESSAGE TO CATHOLICS

Each Saturday at 5:15 p.m. and again at Midnight The Holy Sacrifice of the Mass is celebrated in the Cathedral Church of Camden.

Attendance at either of these Masses satisfies The Sunday obligation to Worship God.

Also, the Cathedral in Camden is comfortably air-conditioned.

We believe people Pray better when they are not bothered by excessive heat.

So why not come over some Saturday? We're just across the Benjamin Franklin Bridge, 2 blocks up Broadway, opposite Lits (whom we've outlasted with less patronage).

IMMACULATE CONCEPTION CATHEDRAL

AMPLE PARKING IN CHURCH YARD.

(That last sentence made me think of Dwight Macdonald's pithy phrase condemning the language of the New [1961] English Bible: "Like finding a parking lot where a great church once stood. . . .")

a convent who was rooting for the Philadelphia Eagles at the Super Bowl. She was sprinkling holy water on the television screen. Now what would Christopher Dawson have said about that?

This is not a history of the Catholic Church in America (a subject that would be easy to write superficially, not very difficult academically but very, very difficult profoundly), wherefore I shall say little about the reforms of the Second Vatican Council. I regretted the extinction of the Latin Mass for many reasons, one of them being the weakening of the supranational universalism of the Church in an age of tribal nationalisms. But what I have found especially lamentable was the inaccurate and often vulgar television-English of the present texts, psalms, readings, Epistles and Gospels (not to speak of the execrable hymns and songs that appeared in the 1960s). Yet I knew that it was not my business to judge the historical—more exactly, the teleological—meaning of that council. Yes, some of its "reforms" surely contributed to the weakening of faith, to the dissolution of convictions and of traditional customs among the hierarchy of the clergy, and to the alarming drop in vocations. The very rapidity of these developments (which have shown no signs of reversal during the "conservative" 1980s in America) showed how brittle the rigidities and the cast-iron-clad practices and beliefs of American Catholics in the 1950s had been. That I understood. What I did not realize for some time was that, no matter what was happening, the kind of Catholicism represented by Pope Pius XII could not prevail for long. When a few years after Vatican II a Catholic intellectual friend, a former seminarian, said that its reforms were like the rearranging of the deck chairs on the *Titanic,* I jumped at him and asked: Where was the iceberg? There was no iceberg. If the ship was floundering (floundering, not foundering) this was because the crew had become itchy. They all wanted to become passengers, preferably First Class, after which every man and woman would be on his or her own. The *Titanic* was only a ship, afloat in virtue of its airless chambers. But the Church was still a house of many mansions. I see that two months later I wrote in my diary:

13 March 1970. Night. I wake up and things become very clear. The dissolution of the modern world has come down to the core of the Church. We (some of us) believed that the Church, and religion, would provide a core of sanity, a source for the restoration of decency and of common sense, at least for believers in the twentieth century (esp. after 1945) with a meaningful inner radiation, a refulgence for the rest of the world. We have been too optimistic—or, rather, superficial. The crisis is such that it *must* involve the Church. Indeed, deeper than most institutions because of the very nature of both Church and of the crisis of civilization. It is yet another version of *corruptio optimi pessima* or, rather, *profundissima.* (Something deep, simple and purified will emerge from it, here and there: but too late for many of us, including myself, and we will have, in any event, a hard time to recognize it, to live with it.) This is all in accord with the will of God, and with a kind of—this is a paradox but true—profoundly human Divine Logic. Had the Church remained largely unaffected by the awful crisis of the modern world, this would have meant: (a) that the crisis was not really that profound, or (b) that the Church would have become ossified, superficially powerful, but only like the ancient monarchies before their fall.

The Church, of course, consists of the inevitable alloy, too, the earthly material of men and women. What the above means is that they can no longer be even partially exempt from our discernment and criticism. When they forfeit our sympathy it is not because they are backward, racked by deep spiritual doubts and pains; it is because they have been, for a long time, shallow and/or superficial. (In this respect the worldly success of someone like John Kennedy was a *corruptio fidelis:* the self-satisfaction that many American Catholics felt and expressed at the time of his Presidency strengthened not but contributed to the weakening of their faith. It used to be widely said that 1960, the election of a Catholic to the Presidency, marked a turning point in the history of the American people. Yet ten years later, who cares whether Kennedy was a Catholic or not? What difference does it make? What difference *did* it make?)

The great Jakob Burckhardt was probably quite right when he wrote that the Christian feelings of sinfulness and humility were feelings of which the ancient world had not been capable. This was a mutation of consciousness more important, and more profound, than the two great changes of the Modern Age: the development of the scientific method and the evolution of historical consciousness. I often feel that we are on the threshold of another great mutation, for all superficial and dreadful evidences to the contrary notwithstanding, sentiments of sinfulness and humility have not disappeared from the Western world. What has happened is that they have come far from being the near-monopoly of Christians. There exist many *animae naturaliter christianae* in this world now— whether they are aware of this or not. Perhaps that does not matter. What matters is that they are part and parcel of the evolving Christianization of the world, which includes the movement of mankind toward the end of the world.

I am a historian: and I also believe that the coming of Christ to this world two thousand years ago was the central event in the history of the entire universe—a historical event, and not merely an article of a historically disembodied belief—and that consequently the entire history of mankind divides into two chapters, the first one from Adam and Eve to the First Coming of Christ and the second until the end of the world, until the Second Coming, when mankind will again be divided between the camps of the Anti-Christ and the minority belonging to Christ. What this means is that believing Christians are *even now* living a destiny comparable to that of the Jews before the First Coming.

So I go to Mass (not on every Sunday, and not on every Holy Day of Obligation) and hear a priest begin his sermon with a slogan from a television commercial or with a television joke. The congregation chuckles with a soft laughter that is respectful as well as genuine. I don't. Is this reaction of mine a measure of intellectual snobbery? I don't think so: what I react against are not the priest's intellectual standards but against the falseness of those phrases. He did not make them. But he employs them. He found it proper and, perhaps, necessary to serve artificial food to his people. This I know. Do I know it because I am an intellectual gourmet? Yes and no. In this instance I think that I am a nutritionist, not a gourmet. But how much does an intellectual nutritionist know about the spiritual quality of people? And is he a better man than other people? That I know I am not.

How often have I drawn inspiration from one of Péguy's statements: "The true revolutionaries of the twentieth century will be the fathers of Christian families." I have preached this statement to my students on occasion. But I have not been a true revolutionary. I have not tried enough. My first wife came into the Church. My daughter-in-law came into the Church. But I married a divorced woman whom I love, and who refused to have her previous marriage annulled by the Church, even though that was canonically-legally possible. My children miss Mass, as I do, on occasion. I love Christmas much more than Easter. I am hopelessly bourgeois.* Or, more accurately, hopefully so—because I trust in the forgiveness of God: I have been a gambler of sorts. The knowledge of God comforts and terrifies me. I don't only "know" that He exists; I sense his presence sometimes. (Pascal said that we understand more than what we know. Or Simone Weil: "Faith is experience that intelligence is enlightened by love.") But the truest of my ties to Him is my thankfulness. I *know* that without Him I would not exist. Yet I love and serve Him less than I love and serve other people in this world. If I were told before an execution squad: "You must deny either your God or your father who is standing here at the window. You will then go free. If not, we will kill you"—I would find it easier to say "There is no God" than to say "This man

---

*I am an admirer of that quintessential English wit and Anglican clergyman, the good and decent and jovial Sydney Smith, who wrote in 1844: "I dine with the rich in London, and physic the poor in the country, passing from the sauces of Dives to the sores of Lazarus. I am, upon the whole, a happy man; have found the world an entertaining world, and am thankful to Providence for the part allotted to me in it." But I know, too, that our situation is too critical for that kind of comfort.

is not my father."* And not only because I know that God may forgive me while I would hurt my father deeply. Yet there is perhaps an answer to such a terrible dilemma, which is that it is not within our power to injure God. We injure God only by injuring others—and by injuring ourselves. Perhaps this answer is an easy way out. But must you love God more than you love anyone else? He does not need our love either. It is we who need His love.

Why do I believe in God? Because such a belief comforts me? Or am I so skeptical of human beings that I do not want to have the universe explained by human reason alone? I believe because I want to believe; and I know that I ought to ask myself why I want to believe. This corresponds with what I think about the evolution of the historian's task. He ought not only to be concerned with *what* people think. More important is the condition of *how* they came to think this or that—within which the question of *why* they prefer to think this or that is implicit. The evolution of these questions corresponds with what I call the increasing mental intrusion into the structure of events—and possibly to the evolution of our religious consciousness. Roughly put, this evolution, to my mind, has gone through the following stages: from the early, unselfconscious and often animistic stage of the question: *What* is God? to *Who* is God? to *Why* should I believe in God? (a question of the eighteenth and nineteenth centuries in Europe, another version of which may have been: What *can* I believe?—at which point the Nietzschean recognition of the "death" of a merely external God occurs) to the question: *Why do I want to believe?* And this is inseparable from another formulation of it: *How do I believe?:* the question honest believers must face in the twentieth century. Within this question the inevitable, and largely salutary, increase of the recognition that religion is a matter of quality, corresponds to a recognition that

*This, of course, is not what the last heathen king of the Frisians was supposed to have said: that while Christianity might be true and all that, he preferred to be in Hell with his ancestors rather than in Heaven with strangers. *That* was funny.

self-knowledge inevitably includes God-knowledge, at least to some extent. It also corresponds to the realization that we experience the world, *and* God, from the inside out as much as from the outside in.

What Nietzsche meant by the death of God was the fading of the presence of an external God. Yet Christ told us that God exists within each human being. God the Father is not a human being. We know that. Yet we must also be honest enough to admit that it is impossible to imagine God without certain human qualities knowable to us. This is due to the limitations of our minds and of our eyes, the other side of the coin being that it is also due to a divine element within us. I am no admirer of Calvin, but I found this quote from his *Institutes:* "Some sense of the Divinity is inscribed in every heart." In this sense Calvin, at the opening of the Modern Age, was a more modern and existentialist thinker than Nietzsche, who saw the passing of it.

Still, it is often easier to talk about God than to talk to God (and to listen to Him). Prayer requires attention, more than will. And we have sunk low enough so that in our world and in our times the dissolution of attention may cause even more troubles than the weakness of will.

How thankful I am for my existence! (at least until I am racked by the pains of old age). Until then, I admit, I fear death less because of the Divine judgment due me—as I wrote earlier, I am a gambler of sorts—than because of the absence of this earthly life. Much of my life proves what my friend, Caryl Johnston, once wrote: "People can do a lot in spite of themselves." I am lucky that I am a historian, not a theologian. "The object of our search should not be the supernatural, but the world," Simone Weil wrote. "The supernatural is light itself: if we make an object of it we lower it." I am lucky to have been born in Hungary, and in 1924. When Kipling wrote, a century ago, that to be born an Englishman is a first prize in God's lottery, was he right? In 1924 in Hungary it surely would have seemed so. Hence probably my mother's Anglophilia, her having me taught English at a very early age, which helped to make me into an English writer of sorts.

But there is more to that. Where and when I was born and brought up, all of these matters, together with my Hungarian temperament (much connected with my native language), made my thinking and my beliefs impervious to the ravages of the theories of Darwin or Marx or Freud. This was not so for many serious and intelligent thinkers who were born in England circa 1885. Perhaps they were more serious and more honest than I am. But intentions must be judged from acts, and ideas from their consequences. The ideas and the lives of the Bloomsburyites, or of the Cambridge Apostles, or of other Liberals became etiolated by a whiteness whose initial clarity and aspiration to a judicious elegance eventually proved to be symptoms of leukemia, of a fatal bloodlessness. How provincial and backward the beliefs—and the sentiments, and the emotions—have come to seem to me, to this Hungarian displaced person who had come from what at the time of their intellectual flourishing was a provincial and backward part of the world. Their and their parents' Protestant and English beliefs were shattered when they found that the Bible, and Athletic Christianity, and even "King and Country" were not literally true. There was an honesty in that shock of recognition, of which I, born in Hungary in 1924, have been spared—perhaps by my superficiality, perhaps by my temperament but surely by my knowledge of Original Sin. Had they only believed in Original Sin!

I dream a lot. I often speculate about dreams, my dreams, interested as I am not only in *what* I dream but *how*. My fragmentary and intermittent diaries record some of my speculations and amazing experiences in that regard, since my dreams often confirm my conviction how, awake or asleep, the great abiding matter in our life is the workings of our conscious mind; that the "subconscious" (unlike the unconscious) properly speaking does not exist; for what else is it than the projection of our conscious mind into something that we cannot know? So have we reached the stage near the end of the Modern Age where we must begin to think about thinking itself.

* * *

Because of the goodness of God I have had a happy unhappy life, which is preferable to an unhappy happy one. One day in May 1963, I remembered and wrote in *Historical Consciousness*, "Driving down the country road not far from our house I experienced a moment of great happiness. It was a glittering cool morning, full of green and gold, dappled with sunlight and the shimmering richness of fresh, wet, leafy trees. A moment later it occurred to me that while in another century someone touched by such a sense of happiness may have felt the need to exclaim his utter thankfulness to God for having created these leaves, these trees, this sunlight, I felt a deep gratitude to Him for having created *me*, that is, my capacity for perceiving and appreciating these trees, these colors, this sunlight; of allowing me to participate in this world, in this universe, in this conscious way."

Not "I am a camera" (Isherwood, 1932: an affectation of modern objectivity). I am a darkroom. In this darkroom of my mind I could develop all kinds of things: wondrous perceptions, moments of happiness; debasing visions, unseemly pools of unhappiness. I hope that some of the purchasers of this book will be misled by its title. Thereafter they will be disappointed. My sins are unoriginal. I am like all the rest of mankind. It is because my sins are unoriginal that I am an original sinner.

1983–89